Children and the state

Studies in Society

Titles include:

Australian Attitudes Kelley and Bean
Australian Unions and Immigrant Workers Nicholaou
Blue, White and Pink Collar Workers in Australia Williams
Bodily Alterations Seymour
Bound to Care Braithwaite
Caring for Australia's Children Brennan and O'Donnell
Children and Families in Australia Burns and Goodnow
Confronting School and Work Dwyer, Wilson and Woock
Custody and Control Asher
Ethnicity, Class and Gender in Australia Bottomly and de Lepervanche
For Freedom and Dignity Metcalfe
The Gender Agenda Evans
Health Care Issues Bates and Linder-Pelz
Industrial Sociology Williams
Medical Dominance Willis
The Migrant Presence Martin
Practice and Belief Black and Glasner
Regulation and Repression Edwards
Religion in Australia Black
Shaping Futures Wilson and Wyn
Social Theory and the Australian City Kilmartin, Thorns and Burke
Surveys in Social Research de Vaus
Technology and the Labour Process Willis
Time of our Lives Donaldson
Volunteers in Welfare Vellekoop-Baldock
Where it Hurts Russell and Schofield
Women, Social Welfare and the State Baldock and Cass
Work, Organisations and Change Aungles and Parker

Studies in Society

Children and the state
Social control and the formation of Australian child welfare

Robert van Krieken

ALLEN & UNWIN

For Rosanna

First published in 1992
Allen & Unwin Pty Ltd
8 Napier Street, North Sydney, NSW 2059 Australia

National Library of Australia
Cataloguing-in-Publication entry:

Van Krieken, Robert.
  Children and the state: social control and the formation of
  Australian child welfare.

  Bibliography.
  Includes index.
  ISBN 1 86373 095 8.

  1. Child welfare—Australia—History. I. Title. (Series: Studies in
  Society (Sydney, N.S.W.)).

362.70994

Set in 10/11pt Times by Adtype Graphics, North Sydney
Printed by Kin Keong Printing Pte Ltd, Singapore

Contents

Abbreviations   vii
Preface   viii
Introduction: the uses of history and theory   1
   The argument   6
   The plan of the book   8

Part I Historical sociology and child welfare

1 Social theory and child welfare: progress, social
     control and beyond   13
   From 'progress' to 'social control'   15
   Social control and its critics   22
2 Power and the state–family nexus   31
   Social control as an organising concept   33
   Social control: the theory and the evidence 35
   Class, culture and power   37

Part II From orphan schools to child welfare

3 Rescuing the rising generation, 1800–1840   45
   The orphan schools   49
   The Evangelical influence   54
   The first generation risen and rescued   56
4 Towards 'good and useful men and women', 1840–1890   61
   Children 'without employment, without direction,
     without instructions'   63

Industrial schools and reformatories   68
The family principle   72
Boarding-out in practice   75
Economic development and political change   79
5   The formation of a system, 1890–1915   84
    State officials' arguments for change: 'the supply
        must be cut off at the source'   85
    The reality of child welfare before and after the
        Children's Courts   91
    Economic reality, ideological change and family life   100
6   The system consolidated, 1915–1940   110
    Bureaucracy, social science and Australian
        historiography   111
    Organisation, control and administration   113
    Jack Lang and Widows' Pensions   115
    Institutionalised violence   118
    Scientific child welfare?   119
    Youth leisure and child welfare in 1940   129
Conclusion: beyond social control   133
    State expansion in context   133
    Interaction and (other) structural constraints   138
    State intervention, family life and justice   142

Bibliography   146
Index   166

Abbreviations

AGPS	Australian Government Publishing Service
AR	Annual Report
CWD	Child Welfare Department
FOS	Female Orphan School
FSI	Female School of Industry
HRA	*Historical Records of Australia*
HRNSW	*Historical Records of New South Wales*
ISG	Industrial School for Girls, Parramatta
JLC	Journal of the Legislative Council
JRAHS	*Journal of the Royal Australian Historical Society*
MFHB	Mittagong Farm Home for Boys
ML	Mitchell Library
MSPCC	Massachussetts Society for the Prevention of Cruelty to Children
NSPCC	National Society for the Prevention of Cruelty to Children (UK)
NSWPD	*New South Wales Parliamentary Debates*
NSWPP	*New South Wales Parliamentary Papers*
PSB	Public Service Board
SCC	State Children's Council (SA)
SCRB	State Children Relief Board (NSW)
StaNSW	State Archives of New South Wales
VPLA	*Votes and Proceedings of the Legislative Assembly*
VPLC	*Votes and Proceedings of the Legislative Council*
VPP	*Victorian Parliamentary Papers*
YACS	Youth and Community Services (NSW Dept of)
YMCA	Young Men's Christian Association
YWCA	Young Women's Christian Association

Preface

Children and the state is aimed at two audiences: firstly, those with a particular interest in childhood and organised attempts to improve upon deficiencies in children's lives. The book provides the historical background to current issues surrounding children and child welfare so that readers might better understand the larger social and political issues at stake. It outlines how the current Australian child welfare system came into being, and what currents of social and political thought came together in its formation. The discussion stops at 1940, not because developments since then are unimportant, but because an adequate treatment of the historical background to contemporary child welfare structures and practices deserves a book of its own, as does the period from 1940 to the present.

Secondly, the book is also directed at those students and practitioners of history and sociology with an interest in power and its expression in the relations between the state and family life. My examination of the formation of Australian child welfare is preceded and permeated by a discussion of the main streams in sociological and historical approaches to the development of state regulation of family life, and by my own argument against the social control perspective which dominates the more theoretically informed analyses. The historical evidence gathered here casts an important light on some central debates in historical sociology, and the book contributes to those general debates through the examination of a particular case study in state formation and expansion.

Hopefully both these interests will overlap in you, the reader, as well as being woven together, however imperfectly, in the pages that follow.

A number of people have provided me with support, encouragement and criticism at various stages of the production of this book. I would like to acknowledge my debt to them, even though I will have only imperfectly responded to their contributions. Throughout the writing of the PhD thesis on which this book is based, Heide Gerstenberger was both a source of stimulating ideas and limitless encouragement, and a shrewd, penetrating and demanding critic. Much of whatever quality my arguments possess are due to her efforts, and I miss our friendship sorely. Henk Michielse first suggested that I remain content with stopping at 1940 and turn the thesis into a historical work, and he also provided invaluable commentary. Michael Pusey was my PhD supervisor, and his help, particularly in directing me through the process of writing a dissertation, made the whole process seem easier than it could have been.

A number of others have also commented on parts of the book at various stages: Alan Davis, Alec Pemberton, Stuart Rees, John Freeland, Michael Horsburgh, Marie Wilkinson, Stephen Garton and Tony Vinson in and around my place of work, Kerreen Reiger in Melbourne, and Abram de Swaan, Rineke van Daalen, Ali de Regt, Heinz Sünker, Nikolas Rose and Linda Gordon in more distant parts. A number of anonymous journal reviewers have also cast their critical eye over the parts of the book which have previously appeared in print; both their criticisms and their encouragement also contributed to the final product. Little of what Ronnie Arnold, Margaret Chapple, Jane Becket, Mischa Slavensky or Colleen Winney have taught me over the years will be recognisable in this book, but there is some curious connection, and if any fraction of the strength, grace and power of their dancing appears in my writing, I will be more than satisfied.

Thanks also to the Archives Authority of New South Wales, the Mitchell Library and Sydney University's Fisher Library for allowing me to make use of and quote from material in their possession; the New South Wales Department of Family and Community Services for allowing me access to restricted material in the State archives, and the State Archives' archivists for helping me find some of it; Cec Foley for assisting me with material on the St Vincent de Paul Society in the Mitchell Library.

On a more personal note, a number of people have had to endure my irritability and my absence, physical as well as mental, during

the production of the book, and I would like to thank them for
their patience.

Much of the material in the book has already appeared in
another form as articles, and I would like to extend my thanks to
the editors and publishers of the journals and books listed below
for permission to publish their rewritten versions as part of this
book:

Chapter 1: 'Social theory and child welfare: beyond social control'
   Theory & Society 15, 3, 1986, pp. 401–29;

Chapter 2: 'The poverty of social control: explaining power in the
   historical sociology of the welfare state' in M. Muetzelfeldt
   (ed.), *Society, State and Politics in Australia* Melbourne: Deakin
   University and Pluto Press, Melbourne, 1991, and *Sociological
   Review* 39, 1, 1991, pp. 1–25;

Chapter 4: 'Towards "Good and Useful Men and Women": the
   state and childhood in Sydney, 1840–1890' *Australian Historical
   Studies* 23, 1989, pp. 405–25;

Chapter 5: 'Children and the state: child welfare in New South
   Wales, 1890–1915' *Labour History* 51, 1986, pp. 33–53;

Chapter 6: 'State bureaucracy and social science: child welfare in
   New South Wales, 1915–1940' *Labour History* 58, 1990,
   pp. 17–35.

Introduction: the uses of history and theory

The welfare of children and youth has been the subject of considerable public debate in recent years. The main concerns have been physical and sexual abuse within the family, youth homelessness and delinquency, and the workings of fostering and adoption arrangements. A striking feature of this debate, however, has been its lack of either a developed sociological or a historical perspective, and its failure to engage with the conceptual issues raised by a considered examination of the history of childhood and child welfare. This is in spite of a considerable academic literature on both these topics, begun with the publication of French historian Philippe Ariès' *Centuries of Childhood* in 1962, and extended with the emergence of a lively literature on the sociology and philosophy of childhood over the last decade (James and Prout 1990; Qvortup 1987; Scarre 1989).

There appears to be a curious division of labour at work, in which sociologists, historians and social policy analysts beaver away at questions to do with childhood and youth in relative isolation from each other. Historians in particular seem to suffer the more extreme seclusion, with most discussions of current issues viewed in terms of developments since the 1960s. At best one can expect an examination of the whole post-World War II period, but the 1920s and 1930s, let alone previous centuries, belong to the shadowy, ancient realms of prehistory.

An avoidance of history and sociological analysis in the popular debates produces a confused and inaccurate understanding of both the issues at stake and the nature of the solutions currently in place

1

and being argued for. The lack of a historical understanding makes it difficult, if not impossible to comprehend accurately the relationship between child welfare issues and the broader social and economic settings within which they are located. It also encourages the tendency to see promising novelty where there is often recycling of old ideas and old recipes, and disables us from perceiving long-term trends. As David Thomson puts it, to neglect history 'means that we often fail to appreciate that the options facing us now are very familiar to those considered, tried and discarded by previous generations which also had to decide how to care for the lonely elderly, the husbandless mother, the parentless child or the unemployed family man' (Thomson 1986: 357).

In any case there is no such thing as analysis without history, and all social theory has covert historical theses embedded within it. Like ethics or politics, history accompanies you whether you like it or not, and to try and ignore it simply means it gets smuggled on board behind your back. Usually the implicit view of the history being advanced in any analysis of contemporary society lies somewhere between two opposing 'master' historical theses: that of *modernisation*, in which civilization is slowly progressing and improving on a barbarous natural state, and that of *anti-modernisation*, in which essential human freedoms and natural characteristics are gradually being overwhelmed by an increasingly ordered and regulatory society, and particularly by the state (Neustadter 1989). Approaches to childhood and the organised responses to supposed deficiencies in children's lives play a central role here, as children are seen as representatives par excellence of the natural order. The position taken on childhood is thus an index to one's orientation towards modernity itself, and especially to the emphasis placed in Western culture on independence and autonomy, to the neglect of the real experience of dependency which characterises a large proportion of most human beings' lives (Zaretsky 1986). For Michel Foucault the inner nature of the 'carceral system' which typifies modern society was best characterised by Mettray, the French juvenile reformatory that served as a model for reform in child welfare institutions throughout Europe, North America and Australia from the 1850s onwards. Mettray was 'the disciplinary form at its most extreme, the model in which are concentrated all the coercive techniques of behaviour', constituting the very centre of 'the formation of the insidious leniencies, unavowable petty cruelties, small acts of cunning, calculated methods, techniques, "sciences" that permit the fabrication of the disciplinary individual' (Foucault 1977: 293, 308).

The main features of the child welfare system we know in Australia today were laid down, in outline at least, in the course of the nineteenth and the first half of the twentieth centuries. The current debates on the desirability and effectiveness of institutional care, the role of the state in relation to problems in family life, the principles which should be applied in fostering and adopting children, and how youth homelessness and delinquency should be responded to, echo the discussions which took place during this period, and much could be learnt from an analytical understanding of how these issues were approached, what was done about them, and what the political, economic and organisational contexts of their appearance and attempted resolution were.

This is not to say that debates such as that on the merits of institutional versus family-like care made their first appearance in the nineteenth century (Michielse 1990). The basic framework of the current welfare system, however, did take shape during the nineteenth and early twentieth centuries—a system combining institutional care (differentiating among different categories of children by age, background, and so on), fostering, adoption, supervision under probation, and financial support of organisations concerned with children and youth based in civil society ('the community'). Each of these elements of the child welfare system appeared separately, in response to different problems, accompanied by different arguments, with changing effects on those elements already in place. With every change the surrounding social, political and economic context played a different role in promoting new attitudes to how child welfare problems should be dealt with, and what the relationship between the state and family life should and could be.

The developments in child welfare since 1940 have certainly been more than simply variations on established themes, and the changes which took place in the 1960s and 1970s, such as the increased funding of community organisations and the increased medicalisation of child abuse, deserve considered and detailed attention. Nonetheless, it is also fair to say that the period up to 1940 was formative, that the basic structure of the Australian child welfare system has changed very little since, and that one can only understand the current operation of child welfare with at least some understanding of how the system came into being.

The notion that we can only adequately understand the society around us historically, with a sense of the processes of change it undergoes, has been central to the practice of sociology from its inception. The classic sociological theorists regarded it as self-evident that contemporary social structures and dynamics could only be understood as the outcome of specific processes of social change. By 1932 Carl Becker was able to argue that approaching things historically was essential to 'the modern mind', and that 'the modern climate of opinion is such that we cannot seemingly understand our world unless we regard it as a going concern'. For Becker a defining feature of modern thought was to believe that 'we cannot properly know things as they are unless we know "how they came to be what they are"' (Becker 1932: 19). However, a tradition has also built up in sociological theory of insisting on the boundaries between social science and history. When C. Wright Mills made his plea for a historical sociology in 1959 (Mills 1959), he was in many senses a lonely voice in the structural–functionalist wilderness, and it is still a matter of argument whether sociological explanations should have at their core an account of historical development.

It is not necessary to enter into these well-rehearsed arguments (see Burke 1980; Knapp 1984; Moore 1958; Skocpol and Tilly 1981) in any detail here, but it is worthwhile reiterating briefly the two main reasons for doing sociology historically. First, and perhaps most compelling, there is what Marx referred to as the 'weight' of history.

> Men make their own history, but they do not make it just as they
> please; they do not make it under circumstances chosen by
> themselves, but under circumstances directly encountered, given and
> transmitted from the past. The tradition of all the dead generations
> weighs like a nightmare on the brain of the living (Marx 1979: 103).

Any current development occurs under the constraints of its previous history, often apparently irrationally, and the history of any object of sociological analysis is as significant a causal element in its present development as more immediate considerations such as structural constraints or internal dynamics.

Second, an adequate understanding of the structure of social life in fact depends on grasping its dynamics, the manner in which it is changing, as well as its current form and structural context. Any statement on the current condition of, say, the family or the welfare state, has embedded in it notions of what it was like before and what it is becoming. As Philip Abrams asks rhetorically, 'try asking serious questions about the contemporary world and see if you can do without historical answers' (Abrams 1982: 1). To undertake sociology ahistorically can only be done by denying the dynamic character of social relations and by overlooking the fact that social change occurs at all. History, like anthropology, offers a comparative perspective essential to sociological understanding and explanation. This is reflected in the fact that much social theory, certainly classic European sociology, concerns precisely the history of society, the transitions from one stage or type of society to another. Similarly the social theory dealing with my more specific topic, childhood and child welfare, concerns itself largely with their history in order to explain their current forms.

It will have become clear by now from the emphasis placed on 'explanation' and 'understanding' that the kind of historical sociology I will be undertaking will not limit itself to narrative, to identifying 'what happened' in child welfare, although there is some role for simply unearthing new data and evidence. In the first place there is no such thing as purely atheoretical history, which simply presents historical data as it really is, just as there is no such thing as atheoretical sociological data, given that one's conceptual framework determines how one selects what is worth reporting, not to mention how it is reported. Even a supposedly pure narration of the succession of events in history presumes that the events selected are the ones which will be the most informative. There is, in other words, more than one way to approach historical evidence, and its writing is not conceptually innocent. Instead of simply telling the story of child welfare in Australia, a central concern in the pages that follow will be to explain its key turning points and the role that it played in broader processes of change. Although this is probably made obvious by my overarching engagement with previous attempts to explain and analyse child welfare, it is worth emphasising in relation to some of the existing Australian historical work, which tends to leave its narrative structure relatively unencumbered by theory or explanation, having either preceded or chosen to overlook precisely those explanatory ventures.

This book offers both a guide through the theoretical issues for those new to the area and, for those more familiar with it, an argument about how the historical sociology of state intervention and childhood is best analysed. A central problem in much of the Australian literature on child welfare history is a narrowness of focus, which could be called a certain 'welfare-centredness'. Organised attempts to improve childhood should be analysed in their overall context, and their history in intimate relation to the history of the state in general, particularly that of education and the law. The police and courts were a major source of the institutions' inmates, both in their administration of the legislation covering children and in terms of the imprisonment of their parents. The Orphan Schools combined the function of child welfare asylum, school and prison; only gradually did the institutions dealing with children become more differentiated, and they still bear the marks of their common ancestry (Melossi and Pavarini 1981). The welfare of children was seen from many quarters as being enhanced through (re)education, and in practice this 'education' contained a good measure of penal discipline, often to the exclusion of anything else; schooling and child welfare were often alternative strategies for dealing with similar problems. To discuss child welfare thus requires at least making some reference to the history of the education and judicial systems, and it would be a mistake to see welfare and its history as somehow separate and discrete.

The development of child welfare was also closely related to that of the social and economic life into which state agencies were intervening. In other words, the 'problems' which state intervention was meant to overcome were thrown up not by the children themselves, nor, as many of the contemporary accounts would have it, by their parents, but by the particular situations of working-class families, especially those with no male breadwinner, situations which were conditioned by the general question of social order and discipline in and outside the workplace. The actual operation of child welfare was to a large extent conditioned by the form that the labour market took and the demands placed on the labour force. It was thus very much oriented towards the production of 'good and useful citizens', in the sense of disciplined and obedient workers in the case of boys, and hard-working and deferential housewives and domestic servants in the case of girls.

In dealing with these questions the book will thus be 'telling the story' of child welfare in some senses, but in a way which differs from the approach of most Australian historians of welfare, being also concerned to explain the developments which took place in terms of the broader social, political and economic context, as well as engaging with current debates in history and sociology about the relationship between the state and family life.

The argument

In particular, I will be focusing on the prevailing sociological explanations of state expansion and its effect on family life, particularly those which approach the relationship between state agencies and family life in terms of social control and the imposition of middle-class values, beliefs and patterns of behaviour onto working-class men, women and children.

The arguments which arise out of a confrontation between the sociological theory and the historical evidence are, first, that the concept of 'social control' (and all the related concepts) has only very limited explanatory power, and serves more to obscure than to illuminate the mechanisms and processes underlying the oper-

ation of power, social order and social change. The immediate
experience working-class men and women had of their material
and social environment explains as much if not more about the
forms that their behaviour, culture and political action took than
the regulatory activity of the state. Much of this theoretical terrain
is covered in the history of working-class radicalism and respectability (Calhoun 1982; Gray 1977; McCalman 1982); the social
historical debate on social control (Thompson 1981) and the literature on institutions, crime and the law (e.g. Cohen and Scull 1983),
but without much specific reference to either child welfare in
particular or the welfare state in general. It was often poverty
itself, for example, which drove many parents and their children to
an industrial school or child welfare agency, and it is in fact
difficult to maintain that the norms and values embodied in the
work of child welfare institutions and agencies were particularly
'bourgeois'. The majority of working-class men and women had
their own very good reasons to be committed to sobriety, cleanliness, punctuality, orderly behaviour, regular hours, personal
hygiene and so on, without having to be coerced into that commitment by middle-class reformers, and I will explore what those
reasons might be throughout the book.

The second, related argument is that much of the historical
sociology of welfare has exaggerated the role that state action has
actually played in the constitution of a particular social order,
certainly as far as child welfare is concerned. Rather than position-
ing state agencies at the centre of our analysis and explanations, we
should see them as one set of influences among many, and as much
more firmly enmeshed with the civil society they were said to be
regulating. The boundaries between the state and civil society—
the family and the community—have been drawn far too rigidly
and clearly. In fact the boundaries are more often quite blurred;
the state is not a thing which thinks and acts, and the relationship
between state agencies and family life is often characterised by
osmosis and complex alliances and compromises. If we are to
understand properly the workings of power in society and the role
that the state plays in the constitution of social order, instead of
relying on a dominance and control model, one has to examine
much more precisely how those alliances, dependencies and compromises operate, and that will be a central theme running through
my discussion. Although this is a basic point in the more sophisticated discussions of power, authority and domination (Hegel 1976;
Simmel 1971; Sennett 1981; Benjamin 1988; Rose 1990), only
Gerstenberger (1985) has raised it in relation to the sociology of
welfare.

One of the clearest illustrations of this argument is the counter-example where the social control approach *does* accurately account for the operation of child welfare: Aboriginal families and the removal of their children. Prior to the early 1900s Aboriginal children were dealt with under the same legislation as white children, and although there were separate institutions established, generally one sees a similar pattern of a combination of different causes for Aboriginal children coming under state control.

However, from the late nineteenth century a variety of Aborigines Protection Acts were passed which gave separate authority to Aborigines Protection Boards to 'care' for Aboriginal children, and this legislation was used to simply remove as many Aboriginal children as possible from their parents' care without their consent and often through deceit. It made little difference what the family situation really was or how the children were cared for, because being Aboriginal was in itself reason to regard children as 'neglected'. Even on the rare occasions when officials did not regard Aboriginal culture with contempt and fear, the emphasis on marriage and having fixed housing and employment in definitions of 'neglect' was inherently biased towards seeing all Aboriginal family life as neglectful.

The powers granted to state Aboriginal agencies were first limited to cover illegitimate children, but by the 1930s they had been extended to include virtually all Aboriginal children and youth. It may be possible to regard as exaggerated Anna Haebich's characterisation of the Western Australian government's treatment of Aborigines as an exercise in biological and social engineering, an attempt at a eugenicist 'final solution' to the half-caste problem, but I have yet to come across such an argument (Haebich 1988: 351). Certainly the impact on Aboriginal family life and culture over the years has been devastating (Read 1983), and state policy in this area does in fact fit the model of one dominant group regulating and in fact transforming forever the everyday experience of another, almost entirely against their will.

The plan of the book

Part I sets the conceptual stage for the discussion of the formation of Australian child welfare. Chapter 1 begins with an outline and discussion of the main approaches to the history of child welfare and the state regulation of family life. They range from accounts of welfare history as progressive liberal reform driven by ever-kindlier humanitarianism to the more widely held ones which see the state's relationship to the family in less sanguine terms as revolving around a developing social control and regulation of the behaviour of all family members to conform to a particular bourgeois ideal. It then examines the main theoretical critiques of this view of the state and the problems of historical interpretation that it raises.

In Chapter 2 the 'social control' approach to social welfare is shown to be part of a broader tendency in social thought towards a more critical view of the state, and to be based on more fundamental sociological issues such as our understanding of the relationship between the state and civil society, the nature of power, and the role of culture in relations of power. I outline the model of power which is built into the social control approach, explain its flaws and examine alternative understandings of power and control which more usefully explain both stability and change in the welfare state.

Part II examines the historical development of Australian child welfare, divided up into four major periods; in each of these periods one can identify a different kind of relationship between the state and family life. Chapter 3 outlines the role played by children in colonial Australia and the official response to apparently neglected and destitute children. It explains the ways in which child welfare was understood and dealt with during the convict period, its basis in a longer historical tradition of 'rescuing the rising generation' as a means of shaping society, and its reliance on the importation of existing British institutional models, as well as their adaptation to the Australian context.

Chapter 4 covers the period 1840–1890, in which one can see a clear tendency towards a state social policy of helping produce 'good and useful men and women', informed to a large extent by debates and examples from Britain, Western Europe and North America. A major focus of the chapter will be an examination of how developments within working-class culture and politics laid a central part of the foundations for these first steps towards expanding state intervention.

This expansion of state activity becomes most evident in the period covered by Chapter 5, 1890–1915. In this chapter I will examine the first beginnings of a rationalisation of child welfare, the reformers who supported it, the ways in which new ideas about child welfare were translated into practice, in the form of the Children's Court and probation, and the relationships between these changes and broader social and political changes in Australia. This chapter will also discuss the formation of the Aborigines Protection Boards and their role in literally deconstructing Aboriginal family life by the removal of Aboriginal children for placement with white families, the part of Australian welfare history which best fits with the social control approach.

Chapter 6 examines the development of a more scientific approach to child welfare, the reliance on psychological and psychiatric ideas to explain both how problems emerge among children and youth and how they should be resolved. It discusses how this attempt at a scientific approach to child welfare was actually translated into practice and how its impact was stronger at the level of ideas and terminology than in effecting real changes in the experiences of children in the child welfare system. The development of community-based youth organisations was also an important characteristic of this period, indicating a shift from a state-centred approach to one more broadly based in civil society.

The conclusion outlines the implications of this particular historical study for a sociological understanding of social control, child welfare and the role of the state in contemporary Australian society, as well as for an accurate understanding of current child welfare issues, such as the role of the state in relation to problems in family life and the alternatives to institutional care. The focus will be on the need for a more structural examination of the changing nature of everyday family experiences and their intersection with changing state agendas, policies and practices.

Part I

Historical sociology and child welfare

1 Social theory and child welfare: progress, social control and beyond

The historical development of child welfare, like that of social welfare in general, has come to be explained in a variety of ways. It is possible, however, to distinguish two basic types of explanation, even if the work of any given writer usually contains elements of both: those posed in terms of 'structure' and in terms of 'agency'. In the first approach child welfare institutions and agencies are explained as being necessarily and functionally tied to needs. The question of whether another response was possible is not asked, nor why similar conditions at other points in time and in other countries were responded to differently. One classic exponent of this type of explanation was Karl Polanyi, who argued as follows:

> To allow the market mechanism to be the sole director of the fate of human beings and their natural environment . . . would result in the devolution of society . . . no society could stand the effects of such a system of crude fictions even for the shortest stretch of time unless its human and natural substance as well as its business organisation was protected against the ravages of this satanic mill (Polanyi 1944: 73).

In this approach, something simply 'had' to be done to protect the social fabric against the ravages of a capitalist economy, industrialisation, urbanisation, or simply modern times: the choice of terminology depends on the writer's theoretical framework, but the underlying logic is the same.

A kind of double structural functionalism operates: social conditions like urbanisation, industrialisation and the development of capitalism are seen as automatically producing social problems

13

like 'neglected' children, which in turn automatically produced a response like orphan asylums and schools (Humphries 1981: 9). This explanatory logic is inherent in any failure to refer to alternative possibilities, and in a heavy reliance on concepts like 'need' or 'necessity'. It appears in arguments such as the one that 'social conditions' were one of the 'forces' leading to an increased political interest in child welfare in nineteenth-century Sydney (Dickey 1968: 138), or the assertion that the development of orphan asylums 'reflected ... the special needs of families in transition' (Downs and Sherraden 1983: 272).

It is a seductive explanatory logic, one which we all use to some extent, and it is both difficult and easy to dispense with functionalism in history and sociology. The difficulty in bringing about its demise arises precisely because of the explanatory power it appears to possess. There is a good deal of sense to using this kind of reasoning, as one central aim of social science is to identify the structural constraints on human action, and the social and economic context of phenomena like child welfare clearly lies at the heart of their development. Jon Elster has pinpointed nicely why we will probably have to argue against functionalist social science for some time yet:

> The attraction stems, I believe, from the implicit assumption that all
> social and psychological phenomena must have a meaning, i.e. that
> there must be some sense, perspective in which they are beneficial
> for someone or something; and that furthermore these beneficial
> effects are what explain the phenomenon in question. This mode of
> thought is wholly foreign to the idea that there may be elements of
> sound and fury in social life, unintended and accidental
> consequences that have no meaning whatsoever. Even when the tale
> appears to be told by an idiot, it is assumed that there exists a code
> that, when found, will enable us to decipher the real meaning (Elster
> 1983: 55–6).

It is therefore not surprising that many of the sociological accounts of social welfare adopt a functionalist orientation. Even if the term function is not used, a telltale sign is the widespread reliance on some notion of 'necessary development' (Titmuss 1976). Many of the Marxist analysts of the state and social welfare in particular have found it difficult to resist the temptations of functionalism, largely because of a reluctance to explore properly the complex connections between economic relations and the realm of politics and culture (O'Connor 1973: 150).

At the same time, the notion of functional necessity is also quite easy to dismantle (Goode 1973: 64–94). The point is that the compulsion of structure is often not nearly as powerful as we imagine it to be, and the mere existence of needs or problems does not guarantee that anything will be done about them. In fact, 'it is social reform not social passivity which needs explanation because the latter is far more typical of the human condition' (Roach 1978: 22), and very little 'had' to be done at all, especially in relation to poverty. Little had been done for centuries of European history, and most of the world's population currently lives in poverty with little apparent compulsion towards its alleviation.

One can point to examples of similar situations producing quite different outcomes, or one can demonstrate the inability of functionalist accounts to explain why different outcomes that would have had the same effect did not eventuate. In fact it is logically incoherent to explain anything about society in terms of the effects it subsequently has, and the functions that are meant to be served (such as 'the survival of capitalism') are often so elastic and explain so much that they end up explaining nothing. It is very difficult to show that anything at all was necessary in history, given that there is usually a range of possible outcomes to any sequence of events. The most we can do is show that they were probable to some extent (McCullagh 1984: 205), and the least, that they were made possible.

Although sociology clearly concerns itself with the compulsion of structures and material conditions, structural compulsion 'sets the stage' for human action, and an adequate social theory relies on a notion of human *agency* acting on that stage. The relationship between structure and agency is a dialectical one which cannot be 'resolved', theoretically or practically, so I will not be attempting to disentangle coercion from consent in the constitution of human action (Dawe 1979). The point is more to explain and understand how given social and economic contexts have been responded to with particular political strategies. Few writers will now hold to a purely structuralist position, with most adding to their discussion of socioeconomic developments some kind of 'agency' explanation which refers to the political choices of action made by individuals, groups, governments, corporations, and so on, where the world is populated by historical subjects as well as structural forces.

From 'progress' to 'social control'

Up until about the late 1960s the orthodoxy in the social history of child welfare was to explain the relation between children and the state in terms of an increased humanitarianism, a flowering of concern for unfortunate children, a gradual progression from the barbarism of pre- and early industrialisation to the humane and responsible practices of the modern welfare state. This humanitarianism was attributed either to a general subject like 'society' or 'the community', or to specific warm-hearted and hard-working individuals, reformers like Mary Carpenter, Dr Barnardo and the Hill sisters in Britain; Charles Brace in New York; and Catherine Spence, Mrs Jefferis, Henry Parkes, Arthur Renwick and Charles Mackellar in Australia. The explanatory logic was that of 'progress' in the attitudes of church leaders, government officials and administrators, politicians, and 'the community' towards the poor and the underprivileged, and is often referred to as the 'Whig' view of history (Gettleman 1974: 150–57).

This understanding of the development of the welfare state came under strong attack with the explosion of critical social science literature in the 1970s, which gradually made it rather difficult to hold to such an innocent view of the history of state intervention. This 'revisionist' social theory, as it came to be known, was part of a general shift in attitude towards state intervention, a more critical approach to the relation between the state and relations of power in 'capitalist patriarchal society'. Other theoretical traditions were also drawn on, but a lot of the conceptual impetus came from a desire to apply both feminism and Marxism to areas other than production and the workplace, to include the state, social reproduction, culture, ideology and all the social practices occurring beyond the sphere of production.

For child welfare the turning point was Anthony Platt's *The Child Savers*, in which he 'exposed' the reformers by examining in detail what they actually said about their own work (Platt 1969), to reveal that benevolence and humanitarian concern did not appear to be their central sources of motivation. They spoke mostly in political–economic terms of producing better-disciplined workers; preventing and combating delinquency and crime; cutting off the supply of paupers; producing industrious and self-reliant citizens, thus halting the drain on the state imposed by the poor; of danger to property, the dangerous classes, and so on. Rather than altruism, Platt saw child-saving as the result of a number of other factors:

a a middle-class desire to control the dangerous and perishing classes,

b a push from middle-class professionals working in the area to improve their status and the scope of their work, as well as opening up new fields, and

c the desire of middle-class women to widen their sphere of influence.

Platt's book was both useful and long overdue; anyone who could seriously argue that the establishment of reformatories, industrial schools, the juvenile court, probation and fostering were simply or even largely the result of a flowering compassion and benevolence had done their homework badly, if at all. The 'progress' or 'Whig' view of history constituted more a projection of presuppositions backwards through history than a careful examination of the evidence, and Platt's book performed an inestimable service in telling the story with far more precision and detail than was usual, certainly in relation to the Children's Court and probation.

The second edition of *The Child Savers* (1977) told a slightly different story, in the new introduction and conclusion at least, and the differences with the first edition are instructive. By then the critical criminologists were in full flight, and Platt consequently indicated a certain dissatisfaction with the theoretical rigour of the first edition. Instead of simply exposing the claims made about the juvenile court as being exaggerated and inaccurate, and instead of examining the political motivation of the various actors in the piece, Platt wanted instead to make more use of a structural explanation and analyse the origins of the juvenile court in political economic terms.

Platt made much bolder claims about the overall significance of the child-saving movement, which he now explained as 'part of a much larger movement to readjust institutions to conform to the requirements of the emerging systems of corporate capitalism' (Platt 1977: xix). The child-saving movement, claimed Platt, 'would not have been capable of achieving significant reforms without the financial and political support of the most powerful and wealthy sectors of society' (Platt 1977: xxii), citing evidence of the financial support given to agencies like the New York Children's Aid Society, various Catholic Orphanages, and so on. Platt reiterated the point of the first edition that 'the child-saving movement was not a humanistic enterprise on behalf of the working class against the established order'; and added:

> On the contrary, its impetus came primarily from the middle and upper classes who were instrumental in devising new forms of social control to protect their power and privilege. The child-saving movement was not an isolated phenomenon but rather reflected massive change in the mode of production, from laissez-faire to monopoly capitalism, and in strategies of social control, from inefficient repression to welfare state benevolence (Platt 1977: xx).

Platt thus explained the changes in child welfare around the turn of the century in terms of the middle and upper classes developing new forms of social control in a changing socioeconomic context, defined as the emergence of monopoly capitalism.

The Child Savers ushered in a new orthodoxy in the analysis of child welfare, although with various streams to it. Basically it can be called the 'social control' perspective; elsewhere it is referred to as the 'revisionist' approach to history and sociology (Cohen and Scull 1983: 1–14). The concept of social control itself was first popularised by Ross and the early American sociologists (Ross 1901; Thomas and Znaniecki 1927; Mead 1925), and there are a variety of ways it can be utilised. However, in this more recent literature the purposes and effects of child welfare, like a broad range of social reforms from education to sanitation, are seen as guaranteeing the stability of the class structure of capitalism, controlling the unruly elements among the working class, and generally maintaining social order.

The subject of this controlling process can, as in the 'progress' approach, either be 'society' in general, or more specific groups like 'the middle class' or 'the ruling class', and its object is generally something like 'the working class'. Part of the problem here is the looseness of terminology and the lack of specificity. Given that the social control paradigm is employed in a variety of ways, it is useful to distinguish some of its main exponents in order to more clearly identify what they all have in common.

Platt's work deals specifically with child welfare, but the arguments are similar throughout the literature dealing with the state and family life. One of the strongest and most influential statements of the social control position comes from Christopher Lasch in *Haven in a Heartless World*, his widely cited book on the family (Lasch 1977). Describing developments like the juvenile court as part of the 'socialization of reproduction', Lasch is uncompromising in his view that child welfare constitutes the assertion of social control by capitalist-inspired, middle-class social pathologists like social workers, psychologists, teachers, doctors and so on, over the working-class family. In his words:

> During the first stage of the industrial revolution, capitalists took production out of the household and collectivized it, under their own supervision, in the factory. Then they proceeded to appropriate the workers' skills and technical knowledge, by means of 'scientific management', and to bring these skills together under managerial direction. Finally, they extended their control over the worker's private life as well, as doctors, psychiatrists, teachers, child guidance experts, officers of the juvenile courts, and other specialists began to supervise child-rearing, formerly the business of the family (Lasch 1977: xx–xxi).

For Lasch the family had been undermined and taken over by the professional experts, with its socialising functions transferred to outside agencies like the school, the juvenile court, and the child guidance clinic. The juvenile court 'best exemplified the connections between therapeutic conceptions of society, the rise of social

pathology as a profession, and the appropriation of familial functions by agencies of socialized reproduction' (p. 15). The attempts
of child welfare workers to substitute parental with state authority
clearly overrode the wishes of the 'anguished parents'; Lasch
quotes one as follows: 'When my son is so ruthlessly torn away
from me, it gives me much pain' (p. 16). Just as industrialisation
had stripped workers of control over their labour, so too social
work and child welfare made people 'unable to provide for their
own needs without the supervision of trained experts' (p. 19).

Lasch sees the role of the social pathologists in the development
of working-class family life as instrumental and decisive. Bourgeois
domesticity did not simply evolve among working-class families:
'It was imposed on society by the forces of organised virtue, led by
feminists, temperance advocates, educational reformers, liberal
ministers, penologists, doctors and bureaucrats' (p. 169). In the
1920s and 1930s all this was merely accentuated with the help of
the greater sophistication of 'science'. Psychoanalysis and social
science served largely to reinforce the power of the experts even
more, and the picture Lasch paints of the contemporary American
family is a rather pathetic one of aimless and powerless parents at
the mercy of both their children and the army of social pathologists at their door.

There are both similarities and differences between Lasch's view
of the relation between the state and family life and that of another
influential writer in the field, Jacques Donzelot (1979a). Like
Lasch, Donzelot sees the family as having been 'colonised' and
'policed' by outside agencies. Prior to the French Revolution of
1789 'there was a continuity between public power and familial
power' (p. xx), but thereafter there was a 'transition from a government of families to a government through the family' (p. 92), so
that, in general, the sphere of family life came to be 'overshad-
owed' by what Donzelot calls the sphere of 'the social'. Donzelot
writes in terms of the family being subjected to a 'tutelary complex', especially among poor families, where:

> ... the neutralization of patriarchal authority would permit a
> procedure of tutelage to be established, joining sanitary and
> educative objectives with methods of economic and social
> surveillance. This procedure involved the reduction of family
> autonomy, a reduction that was facilitated by the appearance, in the
> closing years of the nineteenth century, of a whole series of bridges
> and connections between Public Assistance, juvenile law, medicine,
> and psychiatry (p. 89).

The family had become 'a sphere of direct intervention, a mission-
ary field', as a result of 'the gigantic hygienic and moral campaign

inaugurated among the poorer classes at the end of the nineteenth century' (pp. 89–90).

Following Michel Foucault, Donzelot rejects the notion of an agent of power, particularly that of a capitalist class or bourgeois state dominating power relations in society, and is less inclined than Lasch to identify particular groups as the instigators of these moral campaigns. In relation to the notion of the bourgeoisie exerting social control over the working class, for example, Donzelot says:

> If today's family were simply an agent of transmitting bourgeois power and consequently entirely under the control of the 'bourgeois' state, why would individuals, and particularly those who are not members of the ruling classes, invest so much in family life? To assert that this is the result of an ideological impregnation comes down to saying, in less delicate language, that these individuals are imbeciles, and amounts to a not too skilful masking of an interpretative weakness (p. 52).

Donzelot prefers instead to write in the passive form, so that the family was 'policed', 'colonised' and 'transformed' without specifying the subject of these processes. However, this serves only to avoid the problem of agency, for the implication remains that the agents of these disciplinary processes were the middle-class organisers of charities, teachers, social workers, doctors, bureaucrats and so on, as in Lasch's account.

There are points where Donzelot appears to go beyond the social control approach, when he refers to the alliance between professionals and women, who he said 'were the main point of support for all the actions that were directed toward a reformulation of family life' (p. xxii), because the general effect of the transformation of family life was to increase their overall status and power in relation to their husbands and children. He also mentions that there was a 'tactical collusion' between working-class families and the state, although for different reasons:

> What troubled families was adulterine children, rebellious adolescents, women of ill-repute—everything that might be prejudicial to their honour, reputation, or standing. By contrast, what worried the state was the squandering of vital forces, the unused or useless individuals. So, between these two types of objectives there was indeed a temporary convergence on the principle of the concentration on the family's undesirable members (p. 26).

Nevertheless, this kind of explanation is an exception, and its effect is to build a contradiction into his analysis, leaving the nature of the relationship between collusion and tutelage opaque. The overall tone is still that of the family as an object: of surveillance, penetration, supervision, policing, and so on, and his assessment of the shift from the family and the community to the state and 'the social' is a negative one.

Later, Donzelot speaks of 'the monstrous state', 'paralysing society and destroying sociality' (Donzelot 1979b: 75), and Donzelot has also described *The Policing of Families* as partly 'an indictment of the whole movement towards normalisation and manipulation of the family', describing the contemporary family, in terms very similar to Lasch's, as 'no longer capable of having its own autonomy, of making its own decisions'. Donzelot does not wish for a return to the classical family, but he does see its 'normalisation and manipulation' as having destroyed a social fabric which needs replacement (Donzelot and de Swaan 1984: 10).

These arguments might not be of any interest at all if it were not for the fact that they are central works in the area and have exerted, and continue to exert, a significant influence on most recent analyses of child welfare. It is difficult to find a writer who does not either avoid the issues altogether, thus running the risk of lapsing into the 'progress' approach by default (Rooke and Schnell 1982: 157–79), or adopt the social control approach, even if only through the use of typical social control language such as 'policing', 'management' and 'regulation'.

A recent book on juvenile justice, for example, begins by describing the juvenile justice system as 'an element in a steady expansion of state control over the working-class young' (Harris and Webb 1987: 1). Social welfare and the welfare state are perceived as reinforcing 'the prevailing ideologies of individualism, family life and the work ethic', and social workers as 'exercising a variety of forms of social control on behalf of the state—social, psychological, moral, ideological, and material—in the process of regulating access to welfare services and benefits' (p. 220).

Through social policy, we are often told, 'the state manages the politics of life to shape the social to accord with the tasks and exigencies faced by the state' (Hewitt 1983: 67). A widely read and acclaimed history of working-class life in Melbourne describes compulsory education as a vehicle for the state and organised religion 'to invade the privacy and integrity of the working-class family' and as an agency for 'the imposition of middle-class culture on the working class' which 'policed the shaping of future citizens' (McCalman 1984: 71). Donzelot's impact is evident when the welfare state and the helping professions are described as making decisions for working-class people ill-equipped against 'the modern policing of the family' (p. 75).

All of these authors go on to provide valuable discussions of their particular topics, in fact McCalman's study provides much of the evidence against the underlying logic of a social control analysis, but what is at issue here is that they feel compelled to adhere to some form of social control thesis. The state and the bourgeoisie are presented as the dominant actors, and child welfare as a means of regulating, policing, controlling and penetrating working-class families, largely to facilitate adherence to a bourgeois family lifestyle, with the assumption that such a lifestyle was an alien and usually unwelcome intrusion of working-class family life.

Social control and its critics

While it is clear enough that control of a sort was and still is a central and ever-present concern of child welfare—institutions like reformatories could hardly be seen in any other way—a flurry of problems arises when one looks closely at how one should conceptualise the subject and object of social control, as well as its overall purpose and effects.

The first problem with analysing child welfare in terms of the imposition of social control is that the evidence for this view is almost invariably the words of the reformers and welfare bureaucrats themselves. The usual procedure is to bundle together the most colourful and strident quotations one can find about the evils of the lower classes and how this or that institution or piece of legislation will civilise and regulate them, and this is presented as conclusive proof that child welfare was clearly part of a process of social control.

Either one accepts that the object of analysis is solely the intentions and objectives of child welfare reformers and administrators, making it a piece of intellectual history alone, or there are claims being made about the effects of child welfare and the real lives of historical men, women and children with little or no effort being made to actually investigate them. It is entirely possible, for example, that every child welfare institution ever established failed miserably in the stated intention of controlling working-class children, that they only incarcerated a minute proportion of them and even those they did get hold of did not substantially change their behaviour. It is self-evident that the arguments for reform would be posed in this way; the political context of attempting to loosen the state's purse strings virtually made it essential that the arguments be presented in terms of the overall political–economic benefits to the state, and to concentrate only on the 'view from above' makes it difficult to ever ascertain what the reformers 'really' believed (Goode 1968: xii).

It is also never made clear how significant a role child welfare agencies played in the overall maintenance of social stability. The fact that only about 0.5 per cent of the population under 21 in New South Wales was ever under the supervision of child welfare bodies (van Krieken 1985) suggests that the role of child welfare was a relatively marginal one. If there was any social control going on, most of it was probably happening elsewhere, in the work of the police, schools and in the discipline of necessity imposed in the workplace. As Gareth Stedman Jones puts it in relation to attempts to explain middle-class interest in working-class leisure, 'The greatest "social control"—if one wants to use the word— available to capitalism is the wage relationship itself—the fact that in order to live and reproduce the worker must perpetually resell his or her labour power' (Jones 1977: 169).

If one operates with a welfare-centred view of the world it becomes difficult to see that the problems child welfare was said to be addressing—poverty, crime and delinquency, working-class morals—were in fact being dealt with, probably far more effectively, in these other areas.

There is also the implication that poor children were somehow less controlled before the appearance of child welfare asylums, the Children's Court and so on, with a rather romantic view being taken of whatever period preceded any given social control theorist's frame of reference. The problem is that the behaviour of children has always been controlled in one form or another; for those who are poor, the life of the streets itself has a form of control embedded in it as ruthless and uncompromising as any other. To argue that child welfare imposes a previously absent social control on poor children one would have to demonstrate the relative freedom of their lives before it developed, and it is clearly difficult to sustain such an argument. In other words, rather than child welfare suddenly imposing class control, it seems to make more sense to see it as constituting a change in the form of working-class socialisation—then the debate might be focused on how that change should be assessed.

Another assumption in the social control approach is that child welfare imposed values and habits which should be seen as middle- or ruling-class, itself a problematic enough category. However, if one looks closely at a statement like the following—'The fundamental purpose of the reformatory was to incarcerate the children of the dissolute poor and inculcate in them habits thought appropriate for the respectable working class, such as obedience, discipline, honesty, cleanliness and sobriety' (Humphries 1981:

324)—and asks *who* thought these habits appropriate, the immediately apparent problem is that there was a division between the
respectable and non-respectable working class (Lawson 1972;
Kumar 1983; McCalman 1984), and that many workers themselves valued most of these habits.

Artisans and skilled workers had for centuries attempted to distinguish themselves from the casual labouring poor, even if, in
fact, they were poor themselves, and the boarding-out of children
was premised on that distinction. It was only respectable working-
class families that children were boarded-out to—feelings of moral
hostility towards the 'lower orders' were not confined to the bourgeoisie. As McCalman puts it in her study of the Melbourne
suburb of Richmond, 'class distinctions aside, the great and most
significant divide in Richmond life was between the respectable
and the rough' (McCalman 1984), and the respectable working
class often 'had little sympathy for the dirty, the unchaste and the
drunken—these were self-disciplines that cost nothing' (p. 24).
One could query the extent of respectability among the working
class in the period before 1880, but given its long history in Britain
and Europe, one can reason that respectability built up gradually
from the convict days, and it was certainly valued by immigrants
to Australia.

The visiting English economist, William Stanley Jevons, divided
Sydney's population into three 'ranks' in his 1858 social survey:
the first included 'all who may be termed gentlemen and ladies,
including mercantile men, clerks, and other chief employees, professional men, chief shopkeepers, independent gentlemen, etc.' The
second consisted of 'most mechanics or skilled artisans, shopkeepers, shopmen, etc.' It was primarily from the third class of
'labourers and the indefinable lower orders' that the problem of
destitute and neglected children was supposed to come. Jevons did
not specify the proportion of the population in each rank, but the
important thing is that the second rank of 'a respectable tradesman
and mechanic class' existed at all, and its political significance
would have outweighed its numbers (Jevons 1929).

Not that having some sort of faith in certain values was automatically translated into corresponding behaviour, nor can one assume
that when identical words were used people meant the same things
by them. There was considerable working-class scepticism and
resistance towards middle-class moralising (see James 1969), and
one has to 'distinguish between the "respectable working men" of
middle-class ideology and the radical working men who wished to
be respected on terms of genuine independence' (Tholfsen
1976:18). But even working-class criticism of the middle class, as
well as working-class militancy itself 'assumed forms which were

congruent with a culture that pre-supposed middle-class pre-eminence' (Tholfsen 1976: 12). As Tholfsen argues, the working and middle classes did not constitute 'two discrete value systems, each socially determined, one of which was achieving domination over the other. Rather, there was a clash between divergent versions of common values, along with extensive overlapping, as well as areas of unresolvable incompatibility' (p. 16).

For example, both the liberal bourgeoisie and the respectable working class were committed to the education and moral improvement of the working class, but for different reasons. Moral improvement was seen by the liberal bourgeoisie as a means of keeping the lower orders in their place, but for sections of the labour movement, at least, it was potentially a means of improving the working class's material condition. As Simon says of England,

> The leaders of the new unions of skilled workers ... in general ... held that workers and employers must work together to develop production and trade in the face of competition from other nations; that cooperation between masters and men, rather than independent working class action, were the best means to prosperity and the securing of a just society (Simon 1960: 351).

Working-class resistance to compulsory schooling was based on specific problems like the loss of their children's income and resentment at the intrusiveness of truancy inspectors rather than an objection to the general idea of education as 'bourgeois'.

While child welfare institutions were designed to impose a discipline and morality which suited the bourgeoisie, the general principle that discipline and morality might be improved among a lot of working-class children was not in itself antithetical to working-class interests. For example, the Colonial Secretary and later Premier of New South Wales, Henry Parkes, believed that discipline and control within the working class of its disorderly elements was a means of social advancement, in fact a means precisely of undermining bourgeois power. The training and discipline which industrial schools could develop in poor working-class children could better equip them to deal with the world around them, by developing their skills and capacities and taking on what had hitherto been 'bourgeois' qualities themselves. Without that they 'would ... be lost to themselves, lost to their parents, and lost to their country' (*Sydney Morning Herald* 13 July 1854).

As Hobsbawm has remarked, the 'line between personal and collective improvement, between imitating the middle class and, as it were, defeating it with its own weapons, was extremely thin for the 19th century worker' (Hobsbawm 1975: 226–7). The source of conflict was not that the working class rejected the notion that they should be 'good and useful men and women', but that their assessment of what that meant differed from that of the middle class. It was this coincidence of aims, for different reasons, which was ultimately to overcome the conservative resistance to expanding state involvement, leading to more comprehensive state intervention into the lives of the working class, beginning with their children.

Child welfare agencies were concerned with the construction of a certain kind of worker and a certain kind of family life, and on both these questions, particularly in the latter half of the nineteenth century, it is difficult to identify a clear working-class/middle-class opposition. On the question of industriousness, a favourite in demonstrating 'class control', Parkes expressed well the philosophy of work and achievement which came to dominate working-class organisations such as trade unions, and friendly and cooperative societies. Rather than being imposed from above by the middle class, it came to be central to the assertion of working-class worth, integrity, dignity and independence in the face of middle-class condescension:

> No one need be ashamed of being a working-man. It is the
> non-working man that needs to be ashamed. If there is an unworthy
> object in the world it is the non-working man—the man who rises
> late and consumes the day heedlessly and unprofitably to himself,
> and who lays his head on his pillow at night without the reflection
> of having performed a single act or done a useful thing to lull him
> to sleep. I am one of those who think that hard work is necessary to
> give happiness. Some may inherit great wealth, but they cannot be
> truly happy without hard work (Parkes 1896: 214).

Similarly in relation to sexual behaviour, it would be misleading to argue that the morality and values embedded in the dealings of child welfare agencies with working-class girls were simply 'middle-class'. Sexual responsibility, as Judith Walkowitz points out, 'became the hallmark of the labour aristocrat, anxious to distance himself from the "bestiality" of the casual labouring poor' (Walkowitz 1980: 152).

Social control theorists rely heavily on the middle-class reformers' own views and arguments about the purpose and effects of child welfare, at the expense of examining the independent development of working-class culture. This produces a view of the world in which working-class men, women and children are the passive objects of control, in which certain values, attitudes and habits are imposed on them by the middle class, the state, social pathologists, and so on. It is self-evident that the more powerful in society would see themselves as dominating and controlling everyone else in every sense, but that does not mean that they were in fact doing that with any success, nor does it tell us what the supposedly controlled thought about it all. The 'fateful error', as the Tillys put it, 'is to take the lives and words of the dominant classes to describe the everyday experiences of the population as a whole' (Tilly and Tilly 1980: 259–60).

The historical evidence that is available suggests that one should not view the relationship between parents and children as a naturally close one, with only organised interventions ever separating them. The abandonment of children provided 'the primary means that ancient and medieval families had for regulating family size and shape' (Boswell 1984: 12), with children often improving on the position in life they would have had within their natal families. Children thus had a very fluid role in premodern European families, a fluidity which later reformers were to try and regulate, rather than create *ex nihilo* as the social control arguments imply.

Rather than being the passive objects of control, nineteenth century working-class men and women generally came to use the police, the courts, reformatories and the child welfare system for their own purposes (Philips 1977: 127–9). During the 1860s and 1870s, requests by parents to have their children sent to reformatories by the London Police Courts 'became so frequent that magistrates tried to discourage the practice by charging parents up to five shillings a week for the child's maintenance' (Davis 1984: 332). While working-class families resisted legal intervention when it was invoked by someone else, at other times they were also willing to take the initiative in using the courts and the law themselves.

Michael Katz has also emphasised that the image of working-class degradation, helplessness and passivity presented by the promoters of institutions, should be treated with caution. He points out that 'parents themselves provided the largest source of commitments to reform schools' (Katz 1978: 14). This is borne out by Barbara Brenzel's study of the State Industrial School for Girls in Lancaster, Massachussetts, in which she finds that 'more than half of the girls were sent to Lancaster on complaints made by their own families, which almost always meant their parents', with the proportion going as high as 77.8 per cent in 1880; the most common charge was 'stubbornness' (Brenzel 1983: 119).

This sort of evidence does a great deal of damage to the social control approach: As Brenzel puts it, 'Dickensian images of the heartless State hauling off weeping, protesting children from their humble, helpless parents stir our emotions but are historically inaccurate' (p. 122). Ironically, Donzelot comes up with similar evidence, but neglects to pursue its implications for his overall orientation (Donzelot 1979a: 25). Rather than their children being herded into the institutions to be re-socialised by bourgeois social workers, a number of working-class families made use of them to educate their 'stubborn' offspring or as somewhere for them to stay during periods of crisis.

The bourgeois commentators' view of the lower orders as holding to a completely different set of values—such as dishonesty, idleness, sexual promiscuity and so on—and thus needing reformation, was simply wrong. In England, Europe and the USA, working-class radicals asserted this repeatedly (Tholfsen 1976: 243–67; Thane 1984), and for Australia the evidence suggests that even the supposedly 'bestial' labouring poor held to values not very distant from those of the middle class, but of course their respectability was only rarely recognised by outsiders, including other workers (Mayne 1982: 117). Working-class men and women were gradually changing their way of life, even if attempting to resist bourgeois domination of that process and have it occur on their own terms (Jones 1974). Although interventions of the bourgeoisie played a crucial role in shaping the direction taken by that change in working-class culture, so too did the active participation of the workers themselves. It is a mistake to underestimate the development of a family-centred morality and work ethic which cut across class boundaries, and to reduce it to a process of control and domination of one class by another (Zaretsky 1982: 203; de Regt 1982: 142).

If we move to the 1920s and 1930s, a similar picture emerges. One study of the case records of a child guidance clinic between 1925 and 1945 found that the rhetoric of reconstructing morally decaying families which surrounded child guidance and family social work often had little to do with the reality of the client–social worker relationship (Horn 1984). Social workers often 'reinforced the authority of parents', and 'often became embroiled in internal family conflicts in which they supported the mother as a way to establish a working alliance with her, while the mother "used" the social worker to pursue her own agenda or strategy for her family' (Horn 1984: 26, 33).

The increasing provision of state income support during the twentieth century also had the overall effect of rendering families more independent of child welfare agencies. Even if one grants that there was greater supervision and surveillance of working-class families, that went alongside a lower incidence of removal of children from their families to be either institutionalised or fostered. In the case of the US mothers' pension program, there was a trade-off: the program did authorise bureaucrats and social workers to supervise the behaviour of mothers, but at the same time, 'in contrast to earlier methods of caring for dependent children, income support for widows did allow thousands of families to remain intact' (Vandepol 1982: 232).

In her study of the rationalisation of domestic life in Australia, Kerreen Reiger makes the point that while women were largely the object of 'the ideology of the rational home and family', they were 'not just the unwitting dupes of a male ruling-class programme'. In many of the issues women took the initiative, and in relation to the question of how women responded to the professional and expert involvement in family life, Reiger argues that 'there is considerable evidence that they were active participants, either accepting, rejecting or modifying the experts' decrees', depending on what sort of sense the advice made of their own particular circumstances (Reiger 1985: 215–27).

It is true that the operation of child welfare reflected its location in a class structure, especially in that by definition only working-class children came under its control. But the strength of the ideology of the family and work lying at the heart of child welfare was precisely that there was a muddled sort of consensus on its desirability, a coincidence and overlapping of values and attitudes which was part of the overall political developments of the period, in which an uneasy alliance developed between sections of the labour movement and the liberal bourgeoisie.

The steadily employed wanted desperately not to be poor, and this desire, when confronted by an unyielding economic reality, often turned to the signs and symbols of not being poor, translating into a desire to not appear poor, to be respectable, to be different. As Heide Gerstenberger puts it for the introduction of social insurance in Germany, the interventions of the state in the area of social welfare 'did not destroy "solidarity among the working class" ... what it did was organise the desire to be different' (p. 83). Once certain cultural forms, of family life, leisure, and so on, take root among working-class men and women, it is surely problematic to continue to describe them as 'bourgeois'. If we grant the working class any independence of thought and action at all, if we are to avoid all the mistakes of the concept 'false consciousness', the social control approach is a misleading one.

The ideological hegemony around the family and work which developed in the second half of the nineteenth century was, as the word 'hegemony' should imply, part of a relation of alliance and compromise, although an asymmetrical one, between the working class and the bourgeoisie. If there was any villain in the piece it would have to be respectability itself, the development of a certain family ideal and everything that accompanied that, such as the impoverishment of women's work. This gives us no clearly identifiable villains or solitary targets of criticism. The reality was and is more complex than that, and our understanding will only improve once we go beyond hunting down villains, and, above all, go beyond 'social control'. This is, however, easier said than done, as the roots of the social control approach reach much deeper into the form and structure of contemporary social theory than the concept itself. The next chapter will explore in more depth the fundamental conceptual issues which need to be addressed if we are to go beyond 'social control'.

2 Power and the state–family nexus

There have been extensive critiques of social control as an explanatory concept (Higgins (1980: 1–23), Thompson (1981), Ignatieff (1983) and Gordon (1986)) resulting in an apparent rejection of a 'crude' understanding of social control, with Stan Cohen describing it as 'something of a Mickey Mouse concept' (Cohen 1985: 2). Despite these critiques, however, it continues to display remarkable resilience. It remains commonplace in historical sociological analyses of social welfare and social policy to work with an explanatory logic which relies heavily on a social control paradigm of the relationship between the state and its subjects. The concept 'social control', rather than being simply a Disneyland relic of our sociological childhood, is an example of what Merton has called 'the Phoenix phenomenon' (Merton 1984: 1092), namely the continued resilience of concepts and theories despite their repeated 'falsification', although for different reasons than the ones Merton examines.

The more critical view of the state which emerged in the 1960s and 1970s is anchored in a broader-ranging argument in political and social theory, that the liberal distinction between the state and civil society has been breaking down since the advent of parliamentary democracy. Jean Cohen and Andrew Arato (1989) have recently pointed out that as diverse a range of writers as Carl Schmitt (1985), Niklas Luhmann (1982), Michel Foucault (1977, 1979a) and Jürgen Habermas (1984, 1987, 1989), albeit from quite different perspectives and in very different ways, all question the continuing viability of the notion of state and civil society as separate spheres of interaction. Cohen and Arato highlight the argument contained in Schmitt's critique of parliamentary democracy, that one of the consequences of increasing democratic pressure on the state to respond to an ever-larger range of constitutive interests has been to increase the degree of state intervention into society to such an extent that the distinction no longer applies, and we should now be speaking of a *Sozialstaat* (Cohen and Arato 1989: 486–7). Luhmann argues from another standpoint that the tripartite division of society into state, economy and civil society does not make sense of modern social systems, and that they are in fact differentiated along quite different lines, as interaction, organisation and societal systems.

Michel Foucault, on the other hand, reasoned that the similarity of the logic structuring social interaction in the different spheres of society, the logic of disciplinary power, has produced a dense web of interrelated power networks which undermine the meaning of the distinction between state and civil society. The latter, for Foucault, has become yet another arena for the operation of disciplinary power relations, which construct a self-disciplined, individualised subjectivity, rather than being a sphere of life in any way autonomous from the state (Foucault 1977: 486–91). Similarly Habermas, put very crudely, sees civil society as having been eroded by the welfare state, through processes such as juridification and bureaucratisation, leading him eventually to argue for the reinvigoration of the public sphere and an alternative modernisation of civil society, in opposition to the internal colonisation of the lifeworld (Habermas 1987: 332–73).

There are a number of ways in which this background understanding of a fusion between state and civil society continues to be translated into a more or less submerged social control paradigm in the historical sociology of welfare, despite the sophistication of the theoretical debates around power, agency, structure, and constraint (see Burns 1986; Clegg 1989; Crow 1989; Lloyd 1989; Wrong 1979). Even when there is some scepticism about the cruder social control arguments, a dark vision of an ever-expanding network of surveillance, domination and control still haunts much of contemporary social theory (Cohen 1985). In the historical sociology of the family and the welfare state, in particular, the social control approach appears to retain the status of a central myth. Like all myths it organises our perception and understanding in a very particular and, I will argue, misleading way, producing an understanding of power which disables us from grasping either the bases of social stability or the sources of social change.

Social control as an organising concept

There are significant differences between various writers on the historical sociology of welfare in their understandings of the operation of power, and it is clearly impossible to identify a coherent 'social control paradigm' that a unified body of theorists all share. There is, for example, a world of difference between an orthodox Marxist approach, one inspired by the work of Antonio Gramsci (Gramsci 1971), and the approach to power and discipline which emerges from Michel Foucault and those influenced by his work. Even within the work of one writer there may be contradictions in their approach to social control. Nonetheless, it is possible to identify a set of explanatory principles which are widespread throughout the literature on the historical sociology of the welfare state, and most commentators will rely on at least one of these principles.

The first is the idea that the state generally, and social welfare in particular, are the primary, if not the only *locus* of power and social control and, conversely, that the welfare state's *impact* on civil society is primarily that of social control. Second, even when the state is no longer seen as the centre of power and power is conceptualised in terms that go beyond domination and repression, there still remains a persistent tendency to see most individuals, but particularly the 'powerless' as the *objects* of management, administration and intervention, their actions, beliefs, behaviour and thoughts policed, administered, regulated and colonised by teachers, social workers, doctors and psychiatrists (Kittrie 1971; Castel, Castel and Lovell 1982: 320).

The contribution that the objects of social control and social regulation make to the process as individual or collective subjects is most often regarded as *resistance* (Levy 1977; Barbalet 1985). Resistance to control and domination—the opposition of the working class, women, children and youth to the attempts of the state and welfare professionals to regulate their lives—is what introduces the primary element of fluidity and human agency as opposed to the iron requirements of structure. This was how the arguments of both action sociologists and the Foucault of *Discipline and Punish* were incorporated, as an antidote to the functionalist tendencies of structuralist radical sociology, to acknowledge that systems of domination and regulation do not work perfectly, that people are capable of opposing techniques of social control and refusing to acquiesce to its demands.

On occasion one also encounters arguments (see Patton 1989: 270–1; Miller 1987; Miller and Rose 1988; Melossi 1990: 174–80) which make use of Foucault's later work on 'government', where he emphasised that power organises and promotes particular aspects of individual freedom (1979a: 14). A power relationship, unlike a relationship of violence, is based on a two-way relationship, so 'that "the other" (the one over whom power is exercised) be thoroughly recognised and maintained to the very end as a person who acts'; power 'incites, it seduces, it makes easier or more difficult', it is always 'a way of acting upon an acting subject or acting subjects by virtue of their acting or being capable of action' (Foucault 1982: 220). However, ultimately there is still an assumption that individual actions and capacities have been organis*ed* rather than having any independent organis*ing* effect of their own. Foucault still spoke of his project in terms of a concern with how 'human beings are *made* subjects' (Foucault 1982: 208). He put the active constitution of the self by acting subjects into the specific category of 'technologies of the self', leaving 'technologies of power' defined as those which 'determine the conduct of individuals and submit them to certain ends or domination, an objectivising of the subject' (Foucault 1988: 18).

The general spirit of this literature is well-illustrated by the rather lovely and telling example chosen by Dario Melossi to close his recent study of theories of social control:

> There is, in the Museum of Anthropology in Mexico City, a statuette of a man carrying on his back an idol, in human form. Because the man is so bent under the weight of the idol, his face is hardly discernible. One can see little more than the beaming face of the idol and the hunched body of the man who is carrying it. The power of the idol lies entirely with the man, but he does not know it. He thinks it is an honor to carry such an important and powerful idol (Melossi 1990: 185).

The important characteristic of this illustration is that while the man carrying the idol is said to constitute the power of the idol, he is also regarded as being unaware of that power, and thus ultimately at the mercy of the idol, its *object*, because of that lack of knowledge.

As we saw in Chapter 1, these arguments and theoretical perspectives have a somewhat problematic relationship to the historical evidence on the development of social welfare, which can frequently be read, in a very different way, to tell a story where the character of the relationship between the controlled and controllers, between people and idols, goes beyond resistance to include not just acceptance, but positive encouragement, and not simply an organised or governed encouragement. Such an account would view the impetus for the expansion of state intervention into civil society as including the active desire among the controlled for a more active state, for an expanding welfare bureaucracy. Such an expansion of state intervention might be said to have diminished rather than increased their subjection to control and domination. Social historians (Fox 1976; Muraskin 1976; Thompson 1981; Cohen and Scull 1983; McGovern 1986) have been arguing along these lines for some time now, and it is perhaps one of the main sources of the irritation historians feel towards sociologists, but their arguments have failed to penetrate very deeply into the historical sociology of the welfare state.

Social control: the theory and the evidence

It is possible to deny the consensual view of functionalist sociology, in which most of us simply became socialised to accept the dominant social norms, leaving only deviance and abnormality outside those norms, without having to argue that there is no value consensus at all, or that it must have been put in place through a process of state-controlled social engineering. Ideological consensus is maintained by processes other than state intervention, whether it be through welfare, the law, or the education system.

The media's construction of our perceptions and self-perceptions of need and desire can be regarded as perhaps the most central feature of social control in contemporary capitalism (Mathieson 1987), and institutional forms of social control are often based on informal, pre-institutional social control, such as the media and the social formation and organisation of 'individual and collective everyday knowledge' (Abele and Stein-Hilbers 1978: 173).

State power depends to a large extent on the intermediary institutions and organisations which structure everyday life, especially the workplace, and Stuart Henry emphasises the relative autonomy of this sphere of 'private justice' (1983). If one examines the relationship between the state and the economy, it quickly becomes clear that 'the institutional networks affecting state action extend well into society, in such a way as to expose the state again to societal influences', so that the state should be regarded as 'a network of institutions, deeply embedded within a constellation of ancillary institutions' (Hall 1986: 17).

One can see evidence of the embeddedness of state agencies in the surrounding social context when one examines the ways in which working-class families responded to various forms of state intervention. There was, for example, active working-class involvement at a grassroots level in the expansion of state education, and the opposition to it was of a very specific and limited nature. Parents resisted education where their child's labour was seen as

essential for the family's economic survival, and not as a princi-
pled opposition to the whole idea of state-controlled education of
their offspring (Wimshurst 1981; Kaestle 1983: 69). As one writer
has said of the history of education in the USA:

> Struggles for playgrounds, free breakfasts, social centers, and other
> welfare reforms as well as for fair community representation on the
> school board were an integral part of larger community activism by
> working-class, socialist, and neighbourhood interests hostile to
> business rule and centralised decision-making . . . . school innovation
> and reform were produced by interaction, resistance, adaptation, and
> accommodation, with the power of capital clearly in a dominant
> though never unchallenged position. Liberals, Socialists, and business
> efficiency advocates all agreed that schools would be important social
> institutions in the twentieth century, and for that reason many of the
> period's most radical thinkers understood that public schools like
> other political institutions were contested ground (Reese 1986: 239).

Although there was sometimes apathy, resentment or hostility
towards compulsory schooling, when one considers the extent to
which it intruded into the lives of children and their parents, 'the
ease with which public education entered social life stands out as
truly remarkable', and the popular acceptance of public education
'reflected popular acceptance of the ideology of democratic capitalism' (Katz 1976: 400–1).

The counter-argument to this 'embeddedness thesis' is that there
were clearly coercive aspects to the involvement of welfare professionals in family life, as Greta Jones emphasises in her argument
against Jacques Donzelot's account of welfare clients operating in
alliance with social work experts (Donzelot 1979a: xxii). Jones sees
no ambiguity at all, arguing that experts were not invited into
family life, but invited themselves, sometimes forcing their way
into the home. Rather than any kind of alliance or complicity,
Jones points to evidence of 'a subterranean revolt among families
at the intrusion of the expert in which women took part equally
with men' (Jones 1986: 37–8). In any case, as Lasch points out, for
Donzelot, too, women clients were always the subordinate partner
in the alliance (Lasch 1980: 29).

However, this is only part of the story. There were also times
when state intervention was invited, even if the hosts disliked the
ultimate outcome. In cases of family violence, for example, Linda
Gordon has found that clients frequently initiated intervention;
even when the stakes were as high as losing one's children, most
complaints came from parents or relatives mobilising their own
standards of child-rearing (Gordon 1986: 469). A favourite indi-
cator of working-class fear of state intervention has been the fact
that the Massachussetts Society for the Prevention of Cruelty to

Children became known as 'the Cruelty', (Katz 1986: 109), but this did not prevent parents, relatives and neighbours from contacting the organisation. As much as 60 per cent of the complaints to the MSPCC in its first ten years came from family members, requests for help which 'came not only from victims but also from mothers distressed that they were not able to raise their children according to their own standards of good parenting' (Gordon 1986: 472).

Gordon also argues that the process of intervention into family life by state agencies must be seen as precisely that: a *process* with ambiguous outcomes, and one in which clients actively participated, often having a significant impact on the final outcome (Gordon 1988: 289–99). Once one recalls that families are not homogenous units, that they consist of power relations with weaker and stronger members, it becomes easier to see that the impact of state intervention into family life was frequently to modify those power relations, 'usually in the interest of the weaker family members' (Gordon 1986: 472; see also Lewis 1986).

Class, culture and power

Behind the problem of the centrality of state intervention and the interpretation of historical evidence lies another, perhaps more basic and difficult one of how we should conceptualise the relations between:

a class, gender and race divisions,

b the market definition of desire and need, and

c culture, the arena of everyday life, morality, behavioural norms, family ideology and relationships. By culture I mean basically what Raymond Williams means by it: institutions, manners, habits of thought, intentions, way of life (Williams 1960: 327).

The point at issue is whether we should agree that there are fundamental and clearly identifiable oppositions between working-class and bourgeois culture, between men and women's attitudes to family life, and so on, within which the state and social welfare play a significant, formative role.

The perception of the formation of culture which informs the social control paradigm in historical sociological studies of social welfare owes much to Marx's famous remarks on ideology, that the ideas of the ruling class are always the ruling ideas, that the class controlling material production also controls ideological production, so that generally 'the ideas of those who lack the means of mental production are subject to it' (Marx and Engels 1976: 59). In this formulation working-class culture is doomed to be over-shadowed by the ruling class and the state, and at best confined to opposition and resistance. If there is any agreement between bour-geois and working-class culture, it occurs because the working class have been socialised, coerced, or gently persuaded into it.

One Australian commentator provides a good example of this style of reasoning when he speaks of an 'artificial' working-class culture 'filtering though' to working-class family life. He argues that 'many of the working class parents and/or their children were won over, and were happy to absorb the artificial working class culture (tuned to upper class values and interests) pervaded by the schools, the churches and in the popular literature of the latter years of the nineteenth century'. Schools then became 'instruments of upper class hegemony', cunningly creating ideological divisions in an otherwise unified working class (Bessant 1987: 20).

Within this logic, in which the world is divided into the domi-nating and the dominated, the only possibility for a genuine working-class culture lies in the revolutionary subject and a social-ist revolution which overthrows capitalism's basic relations of dominance. Even in the more sophisticated Marxist analyses of ideology influenced by the work of Antonio Gramsci, his concept of hegemony slips and slides from the original meaning of a *coa-lescence* of different ways of life into a single one, to the notion of a dominant ideology imposed on the working class. This is most clearly manifested in the persistent use of terms like 'bourgeois hegemony' or 'middle-class values'. This logic also persists in the literature which argues against Marxism's primary focus on class, to also examine gender and race, for the basic assumption of the ideological and cultural powerlessness of the controlled remains essentially the same.

However, Marx also made some other, equally famous remarks on the formation of consciousness which provide a different under-standing of the culture of the dominated. Consciousness, he argued, 'can never be anything than conscious existence, and the existence of men is their actual life process'. His materialist start-ing point is that consciousness be taken as 'the real living individ-uals themselves, and consciousness is considered solely as *their* consciousness' (Marx and Engels 1976: 37). Gramsci's understand-ing of hegemony included the winning of the consent of the dom-inated, and this often involves their quite active participation in the construction of the 'dominant' ideology.

Richard Gray has argued for England that hegemony should not be seen as a 're-moulding' of the respectable strata of the working class in the bourgeois image, as whatever integration took place was 'a two-edged affair', in the sense that the aristocracy and the middle-class also had to alter their norms and behaviour in response to a moral critique which cut across class boundaries (Gray 1977: 87–8). The particular form taken by features of everyday life such as family and work morality are thus never simply 'bourgeois' or 'middle-class', their concepts shaped as much by working-class as by bourgeois experience, politics and culture. In throwing out the 'bathwater' of functionalist socialisation models, it is important to avoid abandoning the 'baby' that connects social control to a wider context of social organisation, a connection which 'is mediated as much by the consciousness, desires and goals of those who are to be controlled as the interests and agendas of the controllers' (Spitzer 1987: 57).

The historical critiques of theories of social control suggest that it is essential to develop a sensitivity to the ways in which particular patterns of family life and social interaction have developed in relation to a given economic and cultural environment, independently of, as well as in response to, state action and attempts at social and psychological regulation (Sieder 1986 is an excellent example). The kind of explanatory logic which responds to this requirement is not one based on concepts like control, regulation, repression, domination or administration, but one of asymmetrical negotiations, alliances and compromises occurring within structured fields of power relations (de Swaan 1988: 248; Rose 1987: 71–3; Miller and Rose 1988). One cannot properly realise the notion that power is not a thing which some people, groups or institutions possess (but is rather a social relationship) without also jettisoning the zero-sum logic which lies at the heart of notions not just of social control, but also of policing, regulation and colonisation, and perhaps ultimately the very notion of the dissolution of the distinctions between state and civil society. Those who are disadvantaged in a power relation continue to act and have agency. Even domination is a process of interaction, as Georg Simmel argued in 1908:

> Within a relationship of subordination, the exclusion of all
> spontaneity whatever is actually rarer than is suggested by such
> widely used popular expressions as 'coercion', 'having no choice',
> 'absolute necessity', etc. Even in the most oppressive and cruel cases
> of subordination there is still a considerable measure of personal
> freedom ... Interaction ... exists even in those cases of
> superordination and subordination ... where according to popular
> notions the 'coercion' by one party deprives the other of every
> spontaneity, and therefore of every real 'effect' of contribution to the
> process of interaction (Simmel 1971: 97–8).

Unless the agency of the powerless (less powerful?) is treated as autonomous to some extent, even and *especially* when it consolidates rather than resists existing power relations, we have returned to the logic of dominated/without power versus dominant/with power. Thus we are unable to explain coherently the persistence of social order generally, and in particular the role that state action played, or did not play, in the constitution of society.

The problem has been neatly captured by Bruno Latour in his distinction between a 'diffusion' and a 'translation' model of power. In the diffusion model, essentially that underlying the social control paradigm, a person or group is endowed with power, which enables them to diffuse their will—in the form of what Latour calls a 'token', orders, claims or artefacts—throughout the surrounding social space, which is regarded as a medium with greater or lesser resistance, such as poor conviction, inertia, opposing interests, and so on. The occurrence of a phenomenon is explained in terms of the power of those who possess it, with the objects of that power only acting to either transmit it (through obedience) or to resist it. Latour's argument against this model is that the 'medium' of this transmission of power—the individuals upon which it acts—are not a medium at all, but constitute the very stuff of the action taking place. They are all doing something essential for the existence and maintenance of power, and they all 'shape it according to their different projects'. As he puts it:

> 'Power' is always the illusion people get when they are obeyed; thinking in terms of the diffusion model, they imagine that others behave because of the master's clout without ever suspecting the many different reasons others have for obeying and doing something else; more exactly, people who are 'obeyed' discover what their power is really made of when they start to lose it. They realise, but too late, that it was 'made of the wills of all the others' (Latour 1986: 268–9).

In this sense power is not the cause of collective action, but its consequence, or simply an aspect of it, and the causes must be sought in something more complex, namely the collision and combination of a constellation of projects and strategies, even if unequally resourced and practically effective.

In order to take seriously the problems associated with 'social control' as an organising sociological concept, we need to do more than heap scorn on it and make some more fundamental changes to our conceptual apparatuses. The problems lie not simply in the term itself, but in a particular orientation towards the state, state intervention, and civil society, and they demand, first, a much more complex understanding of ideology, culture and social change, one which does not see the state or the professional middle class as the centre of power or the focal point of all processes of stability and change.

Over recent years, in their anxiety to 'bring the state back in', many writers (e.g. Evans, Rueschemeyer and Skocpol 1985; Staples 1990), many writers seem to have developed a peculiar amnesia about the fact that the social world does not revolve around the state. Even for those who agree that it doesn't at a *theoretical* level there is no guarantee against the Phoenix-like persistence of the social control paradigm in the substance of their analyses. Lenin would probably not have agreed, Stalin certainly not, but we can do worse than take more seriously than we have Marx's argument that 'only political superstition believes at the present time that civil life must be held together by the State, when in reality the State is upheld by civil life' (Marx 1975: 121). But this is only an opening requirement, for it is possible to 'de-centre' the operation of power while still seeing the majority of the population as the objects of power, with their primary contribution being resistance.

The second, more difficult implication of the problems with the social control paradigm is that the closer one looks at the operation of power, the clearer it becomes that we need to include not only the desires and aspirations of everyday subjects, but also the possible *realisation* of those aspirations. State agencies and policies are themselves produced and constantly re-produced within a framework of broader social structures and processes, within a complex constellation of human actions, desires, efforts and projects, and we are ill-equipped to understand either the stability of existing social relationships or how and why they might change while we remain attached to a view of human beings as the *objects*, whether passive, resistant or seduced, of control, social engineering, management and discipline.

In approaching the social history of child welfare, then, we need to work with a different conceptual framework from one which posits a straightforward relation of dominance between the state and the family. We have to ask a more complex set of questions which the social control theorists have tended to neglect, such as: what were the responses towards state intervention of, firstly, the families who were affected by child welfare agencies and, secondly, other working-class families not so affected? What was the active role that they played?

An adequate understanding of child welfare has to identify how the current practices compared with previous ones, and where the political support for changes in child welfare legislation and arrangements came from (as well as the political opposition). It is important to analyse how the impact of child welfare fitted within other social developments, like compulsory schooling, changes in the labour market, state income maintenance, changes in working conditions, in the political relationship between the labour movement and the bourgeoisie, in working-class culture.

We need to know whether child welfare institutions and agencies ever failed to meet the expectations of their creators, going off in completely different directions and having quite unintended consequences, and whether the operation and development of child welfare was the product of internal bureaucratic and organisational politics which might have had only a distant relationship to broader political and economic structures and developments. Substantive answers to questions like these are far more likely than a social control approach to provide an accurate picture not just of child welfare, but also of the actual fabric of state action and its relationship to working-class family life, and these are the questions I will be posing as I discuss the historical developments of Australian child welfare in the following section.

Part II

From orphan schools to child welfare

3 Rescuing the rising generation, 1800–1840

The history of Australian child welfare begins in the simplest sense in 1795, the year that Philip King opened a Female Orphan School on Norfolk Island. The roots, however, do go back further: ideologies and institutional forms were transported along with convicts, soldiers and settlers, so that the earlier history of child welfare in England and Europe forms the background to the Australian story. The Christian Church has always made special arrangements for children apparently orphaned, deserted or destitute. Orphan asylums and infant nurseries were established early in the Church's history, and children were boarded-out (fostering is the current term). Monasteries also provided for the education of 'orphan and neglected children', and St Basil (330–379) advised:

> . . . that poor children of every age should be received; that they should be trained to a life of virtue and religion; that the history and maxims of the Scriptures should be taught to them; that a director, at once mild and firm, humane and prudent, should watch over their habits and form them to a moral rectitude; and finally that, while still remaining under the care and supervision of their protectors, they should frequent the shops of workmen skilful in those mechanic arts and professions for which they showed an aptness (Wines 1968: 70–1).

These aims are similar to those of a nineteenth-century industrial or reformatory school although, as in those later institutions, it is likely that simply maintaining discipline took precedence over education.

By the sixteenth century it had become common practice for local authorities to apprentice poor children out to other families, up to the age of twenty-four for boys, and eighteen for girls, or until they married. The English Act of 1536 authorised every parish 'to take healthy idle begging children between the ages of five and fourteen and apprentice them to masters in husbandry or other crafts (Pinchbeck and Hewitt 1969: 95). This sort of transfer of children from unapproved to approved families was also in operation in eighteenth-century North America, where the apprenticeship system 'contracted children—and not only orphans or the very poor—between families, with the new family being made responsible for education and upbringing' (Zaretsky 1982: 197). Boarding-out was thus a common means of dealing with orphaned and impoverished children.

Around the sixteenth century, however, there was a significant increase in vagabondage and begging, for a variety of reasons including the effects of war and famine driving peasants to the towns to beg for food. The towns 'soon had to protect themselves against these regular invasions, which were not purely by beggars from the surrounding areas, but by positive armies of the poor, sometimes from very far afield' (Braudel 1973: 40). The problem for town authorities was 'to place the poor in a position where they could do no harm', and it was this self-protective response on the part of town burghers which produced a shift towards the confinement of the poor into a variety of institutions: asylums, prisons, workhouses, orphanages, all with the original intention of teaching their inmates the virtues of hard work:

> These institutions, part houses of correction, part locations for centralized handcraft production, had as their goal to separate all those groups of society supposed to be the most inclined towards laziness and disorder, especially beggars and vagabonds, to discipline them with a strict regime of work and moral instruction, to turn them into a docile and profitable labour force (Lis and Soly 1979: 117).

Whether children were confined or put to work often depended on the value of their labour, something determined by local economic conditions. In 1775 English children were put out to nurse until they were four, and then they either returned to the workhouse to pick oakum, tease horsehair or spin, or 'if their labour was worth 6d a day to a master, they were apprenticed' (Cleverley 1971: 88).

At the same time there was also an important ideological transformation taking place. Paralleling the increasing secular, economic power that the bourgeoisie was gaining over the world around them, more and more philosophers and theologians were arguing that one could also effect some sort of transformation of the social world, perhaps resolving phenomena such as vagabondage and poverty, rather than simply accepting it as God's will.

Johannes Vives (1492–1540), a Dutch-Spanish Humanist, was one of the earliest writers on the topic of educating the children of the poor as a means of solving the problems of crime, prostitution and vagabondage (Michielse 1990). He argued that only an institutionalised education and training could break the cycle of the reproduction of begging and criminality from one generation to the next (Sauer 1979: 12). Vives drew up a proposal for how this could operate most economically and effectively, which was given to the citizens of the Flemish city of Ypres, as well as influencing English thought on the subject (Pinchbeck and Hewitt 1969: 91–2). However, Ypres also made some fundamental changes to Vives' scheme, and the effects of those changes merely reinforced Vives' arguments for the institutional solution.

Instead of building asylums, they extended their boarding-out system. Poor children living in criminal or vagabond families were, like orphaned and deserted children, to be placed with foster families who would receive a payment; older children were apprenticed. However, in the economic conditions of the sixteenth century, the boarding-out system was faced with a fundamental problem. The families of the bourgeoisie and the aristocracy rarely took children in, whereas poor families, and all of the lower classes were poor, were not really in a position to raise other children in the desired manner.

> The Ypres attempt to place children neglected by their parents in poor foster families quickly turned out to be a 'complete disaster'. Despite the high boarding-out payments, the children frequently learnt nothing other than 'thieving and begging'. In particular these families shamefully neglected the religious education so essential for the internalisation of the work ethic (Sauer 1979: 13, my translation).

Boarding-out was seen by the authorities as a particularly ineffective solution, and more and more orphan asylums, schools and reformatories like the English Bridewells were consequently built throughout England and Western Europe.

The education of the children of the poor remained a contentious issue from then on, being seen by religious reformers, such as Vives and John Wesley, state officials and sections of the bourgeoisie as an essential means of ultimately controlling crime and delinquency. In fact economic conditions were a more significant factor, and in the midst of the abject poverty of the lower classes, their children continued to pose a constant problem for upright

and respectable citizens. One such respectable English citizen complained as follows in 1678:

> Let any man that hath occasion to either walk through the outparts
> of the city (where mostly our poor people inhabit), tell but what he
> hath seen of the rudeness of young children, who, for want of better
> education and employment, shall sometimes be found by whole
> companies at play, where they shall wrangle and cheat one another,
> and upon the least provocation swear and fight for a farthing
> (Pinchbeck and Hewitt 1969: 104).

The failure of institutional solutions led the English to some drastic alternatives. In 1619 the city of London raised money to ship
100 children from Bridewell to Virginia, and by 1627 'it was
claimed that 1400 or 1500 children had been sent to Virginia'
(Pinchbeck and Hewitt 1969: 107). In the eighteenth century the
Act of 1703 provided for pressing destitute boys into naval service
as apprentices, which was of course very useful during the naval
wars of the eighteenth century and the Napoleonic Wars. The Act
of 1717 also provided for the penal transportation of 15–18 year
olds to North America. These attempts at dealing with the consequences of widespread poverty were of course no more successful
than their predecessors, and there was still more than enough
scope for religious reformers and educators to lament the immorality of the lower orders and argue about how the children of the
poor ought to be raised.

   The long and complex process of transformation of family life
which the development of child welfare was part of had both an
ideological and a *political-economic* dimension to it. In ideological
terms children became the specific object of greatly increased
organised attention at the time that religious reformers—usually,
but not always Protestant—embarked on a program of planned
social transformation, from around the fifteenth century (Aries
1973). Much of the increasing attention being paid to the education and rearing of children can be attributed to the struggles over
the religious allegiance of the rising generation (Sommerville 1982:
97).

   For Puritans in particular, their profound dissatisfaction with
prevailing morals and beliefs led them to reject existing forms of
socialisation and argue for the separation of children from their
immediate environment into schools and asylums, which would
form the basis for a broader change in religious and moral beliefs.
But education was not solely a Protestant concern: in this period
of profound ideological and political turmoil and conflict, the long-
term strategy adopted by reformers of all persuasions, whether to
establish Protestantism, rationalise society or simply to improve

lower-class morals and behaviours, was to gain the hearts and minds of children, and this concern with the rising generation has been a central element of any strategy of social transformation (or consolidation) ever since.

While schooling and education would not affect the majority of the population until well into the nineteenth century, one area where educational philosophies would find practical application was child welfare. Orphanages, asylums and reformatories operated on a scale that allowed for reliance either on philanthropy or on the limited financial resources the state would provide, so they offered more immediate opportunities for productive effort than did the more distant and ambitious goal of universal schooling.

The treatment of the children of the lower classes in the period up to 1800 had two essential characteristics. First, there were three basic means of dealing with orphaned, destitute and delinquent children: transportation to the colonies (the most drastic, and specific to England), boarding-out, and placement in some form of institution, usually an asylum or orphanage. Second, little changed and everything failed. Delinquency and crime did not disappear, children and youth were constantly seen by respectable citizens as disrupting social order, failing to conform to Christian principles and badly in need of education and moral improvement. One underlying reason for this was the persistent poverty of the lower classes, and little headway towards integrating their children into the social order would be made until that changed and the foundations were laid for a universal school system, towards the end of the nineteenth century. This was the general background to the Australian story, which begins with complaints from clerics about the morally abandoned state of the new colony.

The orphan schools

Shortly after King had established a small orphan school for girls on Norfolk Island, in 1796, the Reverend Richard Johnson claimed that he could have filled an orphanage with the totally neglected children in and around Sydney, (*HRA* Series III, 3: 184) and the Reverend Samuel Marsden also mentioned the numbers of children ' . . . totally relinquished and cast upon the Government for support and protection' (Cleverley 1971: 90). In a similar vein, the British Secretary of State drew Governor Hunter's attention to the fact that more than three-quarters of the women and children in the colony were being supported by the government (Shaw 1974: 25), and one of Governor King's main tasks when he took office in 1800 was to do something about that.

The problem was that what the British wanted, a self-supporting penal colony, was a contradiction in terms, and meant turning New South Wales into something other than a penal administration. The principle which the British government and the colony's administrators hoped would take root was announced by Phillip at the landing at Farm Cove: 'the industrious sh'd not labour for the idle; if they did not work they sh'd not eat', (*HRNSW* 2:393). But this is a principle notoriously difficult to establish through penal discipline alone. For hard work and self-supporting social reproduction to take place, there usually needs to be other processes at work. Some of the colony's founders realised this, hoping that the experience of the chain-gang would be a means rather than an end for male convicts, ultimately transforming them into sturdy workers who would marry, have children, form settlements, engage in agriculture and acquire a little property (Daniels 1977: 163). In the context of this overall aim, the action Governor King took in relation to children was to set up a female orphan school, which he saw as 'the only means of obtaining any reform among the inhabitants of which this colony is composed' (*HRA* Series III, 3:13).

The term 'orphan' was used loosely to refer to any destitute child (Bridges 1973: 8), and in the social conditions prevailing in the colony at the beginning of the nineteenth century, there were quite a number of them. Marriage implies some sort of settling down, which people rudely and unwillingly uprooted from their homeland are usually reluctant to engage in, so many of the children born in the colony were illegitimate. This was accompanied by a marked reluctance on the part of sailor, soldier and convict fathers to support their offspring. The pay of a soldier in Governor Hunter's day was insufficient to cover a legitimate, let alone an illegitimate child, and free settlers and emancipists were quick to disown parental responsibility when the mother was a convict.

Governor Hunter thus later told the Select Committee on Transportation (1812) that 'a considerable number of children were born without knowing who was their father' (Gandevia 1978: 56). The primary form of employment available to their mothers was domestic service, which usually made it impossible to care for children: hence 'the poverty and destitution of lower class women and their inability to provide proper care for their children', which the elite defined as 'neglect' or sometimes 'abandonment' (Daniels and Murnane 1980: 66). However, the social problem we observe being generated here was not simply the result of the dominance of a ruling elite or ruling class. Also at work was a particular kind of family ideology, which the men and probably a number of women of the lower classes also adhered to, in which men were to be attracted to contributing to child care through marriage and the commitment that implies, while women simply were responsible for children.

What we observe in this period is the beginning of 'the great Australian male habit of wife desertion' (Daniels 1977: xiii), and it was the women and children who were left in need of support. In the absence of a commitment by many fathers to stable union, or some other means of dealing with child care, the continuing dominance of this family ideal meant that the colony's organisation of economic and social life was incapable of dealing properly with the problem of social reproduction, leaving the burden on women and producing a social problem when they were no longer able to bear it.

A number of children were thus being left more or less to fend for themselves, but this in itself does not explain why an orphan school was established. It is certainly an inadequate explanation to argue in terms of a need which was simply and mechanically met. Things could have simply stayed as they were, or other solutions could have been sought. Before the Male Orphan School was opened in 1819, King made use of a boarding-out system. Full rations of provisions were given to destitute children to induce people to take care of them (Ramsland 1986: 2), and the convict boys who arrived in the colony were 'put apprentices to the boatbuilder or carpenters, and several made themselves very useful' (*HRA* Series III, 4:81–2).

Pauper children had been sent to work this way for centuries. Although exploitation of child labour had existed previously in Western Europe, 'it took on greater proportions than ever in the seventeenth century' (Lis and Soly 1979: 112), and in England 'there was a drastic increase in the intensity of exploitation of child labour between 1780 and 1840' (Thompson 1982: 366). The Dutch Benevolent Society, as another example, shipped pauper children off to agricultural colonies between 1822 and 1868 (Roeland 1980: 26). The approach which was widespread in Britain and Western Europe was simply to set children to work, down the mines, in textile mills, at home, in the fields. At least two other factors need to be taken into account to explain the establishment of an orphan school.

First, as well as putting children to work alongside adults, there was also a second tradition of institutionalising children. King, for example, had been most impressed by an orphan school he observed *en route* to Port Jackson, describing it as an 'infinite service to the common people' (*HRA* Series III, 2:517–18). There were thus two precedents to inform colonial administrators in relation to children: first, simply leave things as they were, assuming that the discipline imposed by the necessities of survival, apprenticeship and convict assignment would impart an appropriate work discipline, supplemented perhaps by a rudimentary boarding-out system. Second, establish institutions in which the children of the lower orders were deliberately and consciously taught how to be useful and productive—the 'Vives solution'. In practice it was easy enough to do both, catering for different 'markets', so to speak, depending on the particular situation of different categories of children, producing two systems operating 'in tandem' (Kadushin 1976: 17).

Apart from the example set by already existing orphan schools, Marsden and King were finally attracted to a similar venture by a second consideration. The problem was that the convicts were proving very difficult to discipline. They refused to marry and settle down, and persisted in being disorderly, so that a number of influential colonists were of the opinion that they were beyond rehabilitation (Cleverley 1971: 8). The solution sought by the despairing Richard Johnson was that of educators from Vives to Locke: *education* as a means of transforming children into morally respectable adults. In 1794 he reiterated the principle which was to be the most powerful argument for the establishment of both schools and orphanages: 'If any Hopes are to be formed of any Reformation being effected in this colony, I believe it must begin amongst those of the rising generation' (cited in Cleverley 1971: 10).

In the face of a continuing lack of cooperation by the convict population, the 'rising generation' idea attracted possibly more support among the authorities than it might have back in Britain. It was echoed by Marsden: ' ... the only prospect of a minister's usefulness is in the rising generation' (cited in Cleverley 1971: 10); in a slightly different form by King: he 'perceived the absolute necessity of something being attempted to withdraw them from the vicious examples of their abandoned parents', (*HRA* Series III, 2:525); and from London by Lord Castlereagh:

> In a Settlement, where the irregular and immoral habits of the
> Parents are likely to leave their children in a state peculiarly exposed
> to suffer from similar vices, you will feel the peculiar necessity that
> the Government should intervene on behalf of the rising generation
> and by the exertion of authority as well as encouragement, endeavour
> to educate them in religious as well as industrious habits (*HRA*
> Series III, 6:18–19).

In order to construct a society of good workers and good Christian families, then, the colonial elite saw it as essential that the existing 'vicious' family relationships be broken up, with the children, in Elizabeth Paterson's words, 'to be entirely secluded from the other people and brought up in the habits of religion and industry' (Cleverley 1971: 91). The perceived lack of suitability of the majority of the colony's population as parents precluded boarding the children out to other families. It was not until much later in the century that there was enough of a respectable working class to make this a viable option. All in all, an orphanage seemed the obvious thing to do. As John Cleverley put it, 'faith in its social efficacy stifled discussion of viable alternatives and it became its own justification' (Cleverley 1971: 91).

On leaving Norfolk Island and the small girls' orphan school he had already opened in 1795, King thus moved quickly, after taking office in Sydney, to establish a girls' orphan school there—girls because it was female children who were seen as sexually vulnerable and as most essential for the construction of Christian domesticity in the colony. A house was purchased and a committee formed to manage the orphan school's affairs. The committee consisted of Johnson and Marsden, colonial surgeons William Balmain and John Harris, and Anna King and Elizabeth Paterson.

However, the ambitious plan to rescue all the colony's 958 children 'from future misery to be expected from the horrible example that they hourly witness from their parents' (Marsden, cited in Cleverley 1971: 92) did not work out quite as expected. Only 31 girls were registered when the Female Orphan School opened its doors in August 1801, and only 217 girls passed through over the next 20 years (Cleverley 1971: 92). The legal power to coerce children into institutions like this did not develop until the 1850s, leaving only the coercion of necessity. There turned out to be people in the colony taking care of 'neglected' girls who 'were not tempted by the thought of them learning needlework, spinning, reading, writing, straw-hat manufacturing and singing, when they were worth their keep at home as shepherdesses or house-helps' (Cleverley 1971:92). Parents also seemed to make use of the Orphan School to care for their children during a temporary crisis, and the committee was to complain about the admission of this type of case.

There was also talk of boys living in 'idleness and vice', but lack of funds delayed the new building at Parramatta until 1819, when the girls were moved there and the Male Orphan School opened in the Sydney building. Both orphan schools were financed from a variety of taxes, levies and fines as well as private donations. Although the committee consisted of 'private' citizens acting in an honorary capacity, the government appointed the committee, so the orphan schools 'set a pattern of joint government and private control of charitable institutions which ... dominated institutions concerned with social welfare throughout the nineteenth century' (Gandevia 1978: 57).

The overall impact of the orphan schools on the colony's children appears not to have been very dramatic, and 'there is no evidence that they fared any worse than the rest of the native-born' (Burns and Goodnow 1979: 26). But the schools did turn out to be much more expensive and difficult to manage than expected. They went through a number of administrative storms and, together with an abortive attempt at a farm, ended up costing roughly £1500 a year, which undermined any eagerness to engage in similar projects.

The committee did not do its work very efficiently, often consisting of people 'with no direct interest in the institutions who arouse themselves to vote only when they wished to carry some partisan motion' (Cleverley 1971: 99), again setting a pattern in non-government welfare which has persisted to the present day. By 1826 the orphan schools had been taken over by the Church of England and in 1827 another institution, the Female School of Industry, opened its doors. To understand this re-alignment, we need to examine some of the changes which occurred in the colony as a whole.

The Evangelical influence

The land beyond the Blue Mountains was gradually being settled from 1820. Together with an increase in population from around 6000 to 39 000 in the 25 years from 1801 to 1826, this fuelled the colony's economic growth. Expansion in the pastoral industry produced a high demand for male labour (Connell and Irving 1980: 42), and there was always a shortage of girls and women as domestic servants and wives. But what was founded in 1826 was a Female School of Industry—given that the labour shortage applied to both males and females, we have to look further afield to explain this particular focus on girls and young women.

In England the Evangelical movement had grown in influence and was busy promoting its particular brand of middle-class Protestantism, with its emphasis on hard work and sexual purity. They attacked the moral laxity of aristocrat and worker alike, and 'soon acquired colonial agents' (Connell and Irving 1980: 65) in the 1820s, headed by the Protestant clergy. They received a boost in 1825 with the arrival of Governor Ralph Darling and, more specifically, Eliza Darling, who was very much a part of the Evangelical movement in England. Together with similarly inclined wives and clergy, military officers, magistrates, surgeons and merchant traders, she sparked off a revival in colonial philanthropy. Around 1826 'there seems to have been a wave of enthusiasm and inspiration in welfare work in New South Wales' (Peyser 1939: 121). Again, precedent played a role—Eliza Darling wanted to set up a Female School of Industry (FSI) like the one in her hometown Cheltenham, and did precisely that in 1826, heading 'the first institution conducted entirely by women in Australia'. A second school also operated at Parramatta between 1829 and 1835 (Windschuttle 1980b: 3).

The aim of the FSI was twofold: to rescue destitute girls and to train them as domestic servants. The latter aspect certainly played a major role in its ability to attract funds. Subscribers were given preference for graduates of the school; the 'servant problem' 'provided a powerful stimulus to subscribers and, in the school's early years, it was flush with donors' (Windschuttle 1980b: 12). However, for reasons which are not entirely clear, it was a dismal failure in this respect—up to 1831 there were nearly 400 subscribers but only 7 servants produced. In contrast the Female Orphan School (FOS) fared much better, sending out 71 girls between 1825 and 1829, so only those interested in FSI's rescue function continued subscribing after the departure of the Darlings in 1831.

The FSI only ever dealt with a small number of girls—never more than 45 in any one year compared to the FOS's annual average of 120 (Govan 1951: 89). Why was rescuing such a small number of girls so important to those who kept pouring money and time into the FSI? Their evangelical concern with religious and sexual purity, especially and primarily among women, seems to have been sufficient to motivate them to try and generate as much of it as they could within an easily captured audience. Charity was also one of the few avenues of activity open to middle-class women, and thus a central part of their 'ever-widening sphere' (Grodden 1982; Windschuttle 1980a).

The demand for domestic servants helped the original foundation of the FSI, and although that rationale lost a lot of its force once the FSI was established, like most organisations it became its own justification. A remaining question is why the same energy was not put into the FOS, an already existing enterprise with similar aims, but factionalism probably had a lot to do with that: very likely, its turbulent and sometimes rather sordid history deterred evangelicals like Eliza Darling, leading them to prefer a fresh start. Faction fighting probably also had something to do with the change which took place in the Orphan Schools, when they were handed over to the Church of England, with the arrival of Archdeacon Scott. The transfer was effected in an Act of Parliament in

1826, which also dealt with the regulation of children placed in apprenticeship.

During this period other, less visible forms of child welfare were also undertaken. For example, the Benevolent Society, founded in 1813 with its Asylum built in 1820, often included children in its work, in varying numbers and usually accompanying their mothers. The young children of convict women in the Female Factory at Parramatta also spent some time there before being released with their mothers or, more likely, moved on to the Orphan School or the School of Industry, or some form of apprenticeship. Juvenile offenders transported from Britain were also held in the 'Carters' Barracks' near the Benevolent Asylum, where 'by frequent application of the birch, they were taught a trade then released on a tied apprenticeship system' (Cannon 1975: 59; Earnshaw 1979: 82–97). By 1831 nearly 1000 juvenile convicts had passed through this system. Between 1815 and 1829 there was also the Native Institution for Aboriginal Children in Sydney, which was 'in effect a third orphan school' (Bridges 1973: 8). There were thus a variety of fates for destitute children, with luck probably having a lot to do with where one ended up and how one survived.

In Van Diemen's Land an Orphan School was established by Arthur in 1828. Largely modelled on Sydney's Orphan Schools, it followed similar moral urgings from clergy such as Archdeacon Scott. They admitted similar categories of children, and were similarly grimly penal in nature. A large number of convict boys were also sent to Van Diemen's Land in the early 1800s, and the local authorities regarded them as too difficult to house in large numbers within existing accommodation. Australia's first reformatory was thus built at Point Puer on the Tasman Peninsula in 1834, housing up to 800 boys in 1842 (Brown 1972: 25, 60). From that point onwards fewer boys were being sent out as convicts, going either directly into apprenticeship and employment or into a probation system, and when the numbers dropped to 162, Point Puer was closed in 1849, and the cessation of transportation finally took any boys' reformatory off the agenda until the 1860s.

The first generation risen and rescued

Set as they were within a context of fear and loathing of the lower orders, the intentions and practices of the people running the colonial child welfare institutions produced a form of child welfare that was difficult to distinguish from punishment and imprisonment. Like all charity since the sixteenth century, protection was intended to be combined with reform and education, the point of which was largely to produce good workers and wives who knew their station in life within basically exploitative working relations. According to the regulations of 1818, the girls in the Female Orphan School, for example, were:

> ... to be educated only in view to their present Condition of Life, and future Destination, namely as the wives or Servants of Common Settlers, Mechanics, and labouring people. They are therefore only to be taught to read and write, so as to be able to read and understand the Holy Scriptures; but they are to be well-instructed in common Needle-work; in making up their own clothes; in washing of Clothes and Linens; in Spinning and Carding; the Management of a Dairy; in Banking, Cooking, and all Species of Household work. They are also to be worked, occasionally, in the Garden and Field, as a Useful and Wholesome exercise, as well as with the view to fit them for Wives of Farmers (cited in Govan 1951: 74).

All this was done within a context of coercion and regimentation. The history of the Sydney orphan schools has been described as 'a saga of the raising of walls and fences, of the fitting and turning of locks, of the patrolling of domestic constables and ultimately of the segregation of the morally unclean from the rest' (Bridges 1973: 567–8), and Hobart's orphan school was no different (Brown 1972: 32). The discipline at the Female School of Industry was more lenient, but here too the primary concern was the imposition of a regimented routine and socialisation through instilling a sense of constant moral guilt, an evangelical conviction of one's essential sinfulness (Windschuttle 1982: 25).

We should also note that the institutions were limited to children under twelve, were closely linked to the apprenticeship system and thus operated as a channel into the labour market. One of the actual effects of the orphan schools, the Female School of Industry and the Carters' Barracks was to prepare children for work, thus ensuring that the money spent on their welfare had an outcome beneficial to the overall concern of keeping the population working. This also helped attract funds: the award of apprentices 'served as a tangible reward for persons associated with the management of orphan affairs' (Bridges 1973: 662). This 'work-preparation' aspect remained a feature of child welfare institutions throughout the nineteenth century (Horsburgh 1980: 33–54).

The theory of socialisation and deviance behind these activities was that the supposedly immoral example set by parents was likely to produce deviant behaviour in their children, and that the only way to change the behaviour of the lower orders was to separate children from their 'vicious and abandoned' parents said to be neglecting their upbringing. It was basically a 'culture of poverty' theory. Despite the fact that only a minority of children were actually separated by school or orphanages from their 'vicious' parents, the first generation of native-born Australians was later described as 'in defiance of all expectations, a self-respecting, moral, law-abiding, industrious and surprisingly sober group of people' (McNab and Ward 1962: 289). In 1823 Commissioner Bigge wrote that the native-born 'neither inherit the vices nor the feelings of their parents', and even John Dunmore Lang wrote in 1834:

> I am happy, indeed, to be able to state, as a result of ten years' extensive observation in the colony, that drunkenness is by no means a vice to which the colonial youth of either sex are at all addicted. Reared in the very midst of scenes of drunkenness of the most revolting description and of daily occurrences, they are almost uniformly temperate (McNab and Ward 1962: 291).

Lang himself held to the non-explanation that the native-born were simply 'naturally and constitutionally indisposed to intemperance', which no doubt had a lot to do with his hostility towards Irish convicts. Totally contrary to the 'rescuing the rising generation' idea, he explained the virtue of the native-born 'on the principle that disgust at the scenes they have been accustomed to witness from the infancy has produced a general disinclination to indulgence of that particular description in the youth of the colony' (McNab and Ward 1962: 305).

This latter theory also appeared in the *Edinburgh Review* of 1828, with the author drawing on the writings of leading colonists like Wentworth: 'The character of their parents, by the miseries of which they must see it unproductive, and the ill-treatment which doubtless if often brings upon themselves, operates as a beacon, rather than as an example.'

This is, of course, merely banal when one realises that all that was being said was that people do not like being miserable, but it was worth saying (and still is) given the inclination of respectable commentators to seriously believe that people willingly live in misery and poverty.

In any case, whether the behaviour of children and youth is explained in terms of the viciousness of their parents contaminating or repelling them, both lines of argument rest on the assumption that convict and emancipist parents were in fact 'vicious'. Clergymen were the most persistent critics of colonial morality, and for them 'denunciations of vice were an occupational obligation' (Sturma 1983: 4). It seems more probable that 'convict parents were neither as vicious nor as unconcerned about their children's welfare as is commonly supposed' (p. 78), and that both the view of emancipist parents as vicious and their children's supposed rejection of their values were part of a political concern to compare ex-convicts unfavourably with free settlers.

More important as a determining factor than the supposed degeneracy of the lower orders seem to have been the overall social and economic conditions in which children were raised. The very conditions of life in Australia, particularly the almost constant labour shortage, had a lot to do with the first generation's 'good' behaviour. London children, denied employment opportunities, simply followed in their parents' criminal footsteps, while in Australia 'manifold opportunities to earn an honest living—and a very good one by contemporary standards—existed' (McNab and Ward 1962: 292). Girls were snapped up as domestic servants and wives, and boys were sent out to work at an early age—twelve at the latest. Labour shortages do not by definition go together with industriousness and temperance—the New South Wales Colonial Secretary, Henry Parkes, argued precisely the reverse in the 1850s—but given the unskilled nature of the work and the fairly uncomplicated, not to mention coercive, character of the labour market, it was relatively easy to channel most children into work of some sort. Generally the children of both the urban working class and agricultural labourers throughout Australia 'had little option but to accept the responsibility of work alongside adults as soon as they were able' (Garrick 1988: 26).

As tools of social policy (and 'rescuing the rising generation' was an early and crude form of social policy), it is difficult to attach very much significance to the orphan schools and the Female School of Industry in themselves. Far more important than their moralising eduction was what happened to all the other children in the colony and the apprenticeship system they were fed into. There were roads, houses and bridges to be built, fields to be cleared and tilled, flocks of sheep to be minded—all mostly within a coercive system of state labour assignment. Once past the age of twelve it made little difference whether one was a juvenile convict assigned to work, was put to work by one's family, or was an orphan apprentice, going one's own way still meant getting on the wrong side of the law (Bridges 1973: 629–30). Both inside and outside the institutions, there was little difference in the treatment of children 'in need of care' and those being punished for offences.

The origins of child welfare in Australia have been described as 'one step in an ambitious movement to destroy the cultural values of disorder, irreverence and promiscuity, and replace them with those of discipline, obedience and submission' (Windschuttle 1982: 27). That was certainly how the philanthropic bourgeoisie saw their work, but it nonetheless turned out to be a rather small step. The penal atmosphere of the orphan schools prevailed throughout colonial Australia, so only the Female School of Industry could claim to have had a unique impact on its girls, with its combination of relative material well-being and moral improvement, and the numbers it dealt with were small.

Although it is correct to argue that the overt intention of those running the institutions was to keep the lower orders under control, one also needs to add that they played a relatively minor role. It was more the character of the labour market itself, with its sexual divisions, ample work available and effective mechanisms for coercing people into it, which operated to impose the cultural values of discipline, obedience and submission, and the orphan schools and the FSI were largely ancillary to that. As Connell and Irving put it in relation to attempts at moral reform in general, 'the state's first ideological efforts paid few dividends' (Connell and Irving 1980: 62), and it is difficult to escape the conclusion that the overall social effect of the institutions was mainly to tidy the colony by getting destitute children off the streets.

This particular kind of labour market had a limited future, though. As the numbers of free settlers and emancipists grew, so did their opposition to the competition posed by convict labour. This, together with moral abhorrence on the part of liberals and evangelicals in Britain and Australia, led to the cessation of transportation, in fits and starts, between 1840 and the 1850s. During the next 50 years New South Wales and Victoria were to experience enormous and continuing economic expansion, growth in the size of their urban centres, the introduction of representative government, an increasingly powerful labour movement, and the growth of a popular press, all of which produced new problems and issues, new political actors to deal with them, and a new generation of child welfare practices and ideas. The 'rising generation' was to remain a stunted child for some time yet, but it nonetheless formed the nucleus of the more complex system of child welfare established in the second half of the nineteenth century.

4 Towards 'good and useful men and women', 1840–1890

> ... as a matter of political economy, it would be better to spend a few pounds extra per annum in creating good and useful men and women, who will add to the national credit and prosperity, than to train up more cheaply useless members of the community who would eventually ... either relapse into pauperdom or come back upon the state in a still more objectionable form. (Renwick, State Children Relief Board Annual Report (SCRB AR), 1883: 873).

In the second half of the nineteenth century Australia shared with Western Europe, Britain, and North America a tendency towards greater state involvement in the regulation of childhood, through the establishment of universal schooling, reformatories, industrial schools and boarding-out systems. By 1890 one can perceive more clearly a pattern of social policy in the state's dealings with children. The questions which this chapter will address include why the state became so actively involved in attempting to regulate childhood in this period, what social impact these attempts had, and how they related to more general social and economic changes.

An overall coherence among the different institutions and agencies arose in this period, and it is important to go some way beyond the existing historical literature to develop a broader view of the ways in which the relation between the state and childhood changed. One could point to the increasing influence of the middle class in creating areas of employment and intervention for themselves (Platt 1977; Mackinlay 1973; Walker 1979), and this was certainly one element in the process of state expansion, but there was more to it than that. There was also a fundamental change in class relations in the nineteenth century, in which political and economic equality became a real possibility, irrespective of how accurate the popular perception of this possibility was. The ideological concern among reformers and officials to improve the morals and behaviour of the lower classes had been around for some time, and that remained unchanged, but the effects of nineteenth-century economic and political developments added some new ingredients that would produce the potent mixture we now know as 'state expansion'.

The flesh-and-blood character who appears in the extensive literature on the asylum and social welfare in the nineteenth century is the 'middle-class reformer'. Anthony Platt concentrated on the later reform of the juvenile court, but he argued generally that the impetus for the whole child-saving movement 'came primarily from the middle and upper classes who were instrumental in devising new forms of social control to protect their power and privilege' (1977). This is a view which resonates with more specific historical studies such as Christine Stansell's of New York, where she argues that moral reformers 'sought to impose on the poor conceptions of childhood and motherhood drawn from their own ideas of domesticity', in large part by constructing a particular perception of urban geography in which the streets became a place of danger, unfit for children (Stansell 1982: 312; see also Bellingham 1983). In relation to education Richard Johnson also argues that 'the early Victorian obsession with the education of the poor is best understood as a concern about authority', a concern which constituted 'an enormously ambitious attempt to determine, through the capture of educational means, the patterns of thought, sentiment and behaviour of the working class' (Johnson 1970: 119).

However, as Johnson goes on to say, this conclusion in itself does not tell us very much. The difficulty here is the focus on the stated intentions and aims of moral entrepreneurs, at the expense of an examination of how the products of their enterprise actually operated. Like Donzelot's 'policed family', the objects of all this activity also remain oddly silent and passive. The assumption is that all impetus for change came from middle-class moral entrepreneurs, that the role of working-class men, women and children was always to oppose their efforts, and that the only position working-class families ever took up was that of 'resistance' (Sydney Labour History Group 1982: 11; Bessant 1987: 11). Together with a discussion of the impact of the changed ideas, policies and practices of bureaucrats and moral entrepreneurs, this chapter will examine the role played by changes in the material and political conditions of working-class life itself in the rise of a state social policy of regulating childhood.

Children 'without employment, without direction, without instructions'

Disorderliness and its policing resurfaced as public issues in the 1840s and 1850s throughout Australia, partly in association with the social turbulence of the gold rush. Two widely publicised murder cases in Sydney, for example, sparked off press indignation about a 'crime wave' in 1844, and contemporary reports remarked on a general rowdiness in the colony, with occasional riots and groups of exuberant male youths like the Cabbage Tree Hat Mob tormenting more respectable members of society (Sturma 1983; King 1956; Grabosky 1977: 18, 70). This rowdiness extended to the workplace, causing concern among employers about the orderliness and discipline of the lower classes.

One of the more significant general changes which occurred in work patterns during this period was similar to what E.P. Thompson has analysed as the transition from pre-industrial to industrial forms of labour process and work discipline, and the appearance of the work rhythm of the factory (Thompson 1967). The problems of discipline before 1840 were those of a convict colony, but after the 1850s the men and women entering the workforce were bringing with them old habits, values and patterns of behaviour. These patterns conflicted with what the new breed of entrepreneurs expected of both themselves and their employees, raising discipline, industriousness, social integration and order as 'social problems'.

The merchants, traders and entrepreneurs building their fortunes understood that their success depended not only on their own temperance, industry and strength of character, but also on that of their employees, and in this respect the problems of Australian entrepreneurs were no different from those of their counterparts in the US (Faler 1974: 376). Henry Parkes, later to become Colonial Secretary in New South Wales, had considerable difficulties with his employees on his newspaper, the *Empire*, prosecuting a number of strikers for conspiracy in 1853. He blamed the shortage of labour, high wages and intemperance for the 'haughty and discourteous bearing of workmen' (cited in Martin 1977: 359). Much of this haughtiness stemmed from a taste for drink, so widespread that in moral terms Sydney and Melbourne were presented in the popular press as falling apart at the seams: 'Drunkenness and blasphemy meet us with their idiot stare at every corner of our streets' (*Empire* 4 February 1854).

There were a number of things that could be done in response to this supposed moral laxity, including improving the organisation, efficiency and size of the police force, controlling the sale of liquor, undertaking temperance work and philanthropic visiting (Mayne 1983: 567). A more long-term strategy, however, was to 'rescue the rising generation'. The *Empire* provided the formulation of how poverty and vice should be dealt with 'scientifically'. The urban poor simply did not work hard enough, and were morally resistant to change, so the only hope lay in the rising generation:

> ... it seems to us that if any just principles can be laid down towards reducing public charity to a practical science, it is this, that the earlier in life that pauperism is laid hold of, the shorter time at any stage of life it is allowed, until it is yoked into some productive occupation, the greater will be the benefit to the State in the saving of expense on the one side, and in the gain of industry on the other (*Empire* 1 April 1854).

This argument agreed with the views of Sydney's conservative gentlemen: two years earlier the *Sydney Morning Herald* had carried the announcement of the need for a Society for the Relief of Destitute Children and an asylum which 'drew support from the respectable in the community in a way unequalled by any other charitable institution in this period' (Dickey 1968: 140).

The arguments around the regulation of childhood and youth were both to be continued and in some sense redirected in the 1850s and 1860s, with a variety of government reports on the character of Australian social life reporting a state of disorder among children and youth. In Sydney the Select Committee on the Condition of the Working Classes of the Metropolis, chaired by Henry Parkes, dealt with a range of issues in its report, published in 1860: unemployment, the level of wages, housing and juvenile delinquency, all of which were held to be interrelated. Unemployment was high, wages were low, housing 'deplorably bad', exacerbated by 'the general system of overcrowding which has been induced by high rents', and the streets were 'infested by a large number of vagrant children'.

The Report from the Select Committee echoed the claims of the accounts which had appeared in the *Sydney Morning Herald* and the *Empire*, in the 1850s, of boys apparently doing as they pleased with little parental supervision and control; 'morally destitute' children were described as 'floating about the streets and lanes like fish in a pond' (Select Committee on the Condition of the Working Classes 1859/60: 1271, 1312). In Hobart there were reports of 'wandering and discarded children ... known by the characteristic appellation of "The City Arabs"—sleeping in out-houses, sheds, pig-sties, under bridges' (*Mercury* 30 March 1858). In Melbourne 'youthful Bedouins' were said to be wandering around in a state of 'nomadic wildness' (*Argus* 5 May 1857).

In relation to boys, the Sydney Report argued that there was in fact very little real destitution and homelessness. Inspector Harrison declared, 'I have made diligent inquiry for male vagrants among the youth of the city, and I can confidently say, there are not fifty houseless boys in Sydney', and in his summing-up Parkes said that, 'it may be doubted that there are many entirely destitute of home and kindred'. The problem was more their moral condition: 'the evidence abundantly shews that a large class exist to whom the possession of parents is of no value in giving direction to their lives, and who are growing up to be an incumbrance and a curse to society' (Select Committee on the Condition of the Working Classes 1859/60: 1456, 1272).

The situation was less clear with respect to girls. The evidence tended to be limited to colourful accounts of particular cases of 'young' girls soliciting as prostitutes or living with older prostitutes, and probably the only observer with a comprehensive overview of the situation, Inspector McLerie, was uneasy about committing himself until he had accumulated more data. In any case it was clearly difficult to determine the age of the girls concerned; they usually claimed to be older than Inspector Harrison's assessments. Overall the picture drawn was not one of children being cast out on the streets by either their parents' poverty or their heartlessness and neglect, but more one of a perceived lack of instruction and control of working-class children.

There were a number of important qualifications to this dissection of colonial morals, the attack was not undiscriminating. Some of the Sydney witnesses saw the real problem as lying with the poor quality of working-class housing:

> We cannot be surprised if a mother, engaged in her ordinary
> domestic occupations, and cooped up in a closed room with half a
> dozen noisy children, is glad to be for a period relieved of their
> presence; or, if the children are delighted to escape from their
> prison, to breathe the comparatively fresh air of the street, and to
> play with their young neighbours (p. 1353).

If the quality of housing could be improved, concluded Parkes, 'one effect of it would be a decrease of the juvenile destitution found in the streets'.

Parkes also took care to distinguish between the 'abandoned classes' and the 'labouring masses'. There was indeed a 'region of depravity and moral death', and the Committee felt obliged to report it, but it was a region with boundaries. Parkes reckoned that there were no more than 1000 destitute children of 'the most abandoned classes', and pointed out that the Committee's witnesses had painted a picture of the majority of the working classes possessing 'a high character for honesty, intelligence and sobriety' (p. 1272). Others would not make such fine distinctions, but for Parkes and the Select Committee, if there was a problem it lay with only a small proportion of the working classes; only a minority exerted insufficient parental control, with most being quite respectable and raising their children accordingly.

In general the concern seems to have been that a number of children were not kept under adequate supervision, for a variety of reasons ranging from parental disinterest to unemployment and difficult living conditions. These children, said one witness, 'grow up untaught in all that is necessary to make them good citizens, and become learned in vice' (p. 1353). The material environment of urban Australia, especially post-goldrush Melbourne and Sydney, seems to have created space for children to escape being socialised as the authorities wanted, and that was an evil 'pregnant with the most dangerous consequences to society' (p. 1274). According to the Melbourne Sheriff in May 1854, instead of being 'educated by the country' and becoming useful citizens, they were in danger of becoming ' a disgrace and a curse to society and an encumbrance to the State' (cited in Bignell 1973).

The use of words such as 'teaching', 'learning' and 'education' is significant here, for the problem was to a large extent part of the general question of the education and socialisation of children, raised in another form in arguments for a universal and compulsory school system (Wimshurst 1981; Mitchell and Sherington 1985). The universalism underlying the notion of the state representing 'the general interest' extended to the realm of morality, so that it too was turned into a universal affair.

Christopher Lasch has commented on the impact of egalitarianism here, arguing that a concern with equality seemed to become associated in the late nineteenth century with 'a heightened awareness of deviancy and of social differences of all kinds, and with a growing uneasiness in the face of those differences'. Egalitarian theory and practices insisted on the rights of everyone to citizenship, but this insistence was coupled to another, 'that all citizens live by the same rules of character and conduct' (Lasch 1973: 17). If it is true that white Australian working women and men held to an egalitarian ethic, then this other side of egalitarianism might not have positively encouraged 'a heightened awareness of deviancy' (Lasch 1973:16), but it certainly would have failed to provide very much resistance to the logic behind a police force capable of taking one into custody for using obscene language.

There was also the question of differentiation within the criminal justice system; if one set out from the Lockean principle that children were psychologically or, in the terms of the day, morally different from adults, and the police were taking children into custody and charging them in any substantial numbers, it followed logically that one should provide separate facilities for them. Magistrates tended to discharge children brought before them because there was no separate provision for them, and the cure of incarcerating them together with hardened adults likely to further educate them in the ways of vice seemed worse than the disease. Those responsible for policing the cities shared the 'rising generation' idea that the reform of children could only be undertaken properly in isolation from more corrupt adults, and the argument for juvenile reformatories was merely the expression of this idea in an administrative form for the criminal justice and prison system.

Whereas in the early 1850s the police and magistracy might have been able to look upon the problem of dispensing with young offenders as one they could more or less live with, the simple demographic fact of a rapidly growing population, especially in Sydney and Melbourne, was making such a position less and less tenable. It conjured up visions not of a couple of dozen larrikins roaming the streets, but of several hundred, and the popular press made much of this vision. The solution was most often seen to be education.

Rusden argued before a Geelong meeting in 1849 that 'where there is a large amount of money devoted to education, less is required in the repression of crime' (cited in Austin 1958: 129), and later Henry Parkes declared in New South Wales that 'To prevent crime we must enlighten the people. Better have schoolmasters than gaolers; better schools than gaols' (Parkes 1896: 216). Together with the more general concern with 'improving' the working class, leading towards a universal education system, this consideration was to provide at least part of the impetus towards an increased state involvement in the regulation of childhood.

Not all the activity around child welfare was state-based. The Ragged Schools, for example, were a non-government response to the issues identified by the 1860 report. Modelled on the English Ragged Schools movement, they were set up by a group of Anglican clergy and evangelical laity, the central figure being Edward Joy, a Sydney merchant (Ramsland 1982: 223). The first Ragged School was established in Sussex Street, Sydney, in 1860, with others following later, and they continued into the 1920s. The aims of the movement were no different from those of the orphan schools and the larger institutions like the Randwick Asylum, but its methods were.

For the first time it was argued that children could be 'saved' without physically removing them from their parents—in fact parents were seen as part of the reforming process. Ragged School workers like Miss Danne visited the children at home and 'advised' their parents, in the belief that the family as a whole should be the object of attention rather than the child alone (Ramsland 1982: 227). This was thus a more optimistic view of working-class culture: in need of reformation perhaps, but at least reformable, rather than something to be smashed to pieces. In this sense the Ragged Schools were the forerunners of a number of current child welfare practices, such as family casework and community-based youth work. They also anticipated a number of other ways of dealing with the children of the poor which were introduced on a larger scale later, boarding some children out and hoping to establish small family-style cottage homes in the country.

Industrial schools and reformatories

In 1866 the New South Wales Select Committee on the Unemployed reported that at least 3000 men were unemployed, and said that the evidence it had collected showed:

> ... that distress to an appalling extent—to an extent never before experienced in this city—does exist; that many able-bodied men, with wives and families dependent on them, are unable to obtain employment or the means of supporting their families; and that this state of things is not confined to the ordinary or unskilled labourer, but that a larger number of mechanics and artisans are in the same condition of extreme distress (Select Committee on the Unemployed 1866: 621).

These economic conditions were producing stresses on the maintenance of family life, whatever its form, for which charitable agencies like the Randwick Asylum, the orphan schools and the Ragged Schools were simply unable to compensate. In general the opinion which came to dominate among the authorities, with little coherent opposition, was that the upbringing of at least some working-class children and youth had become a problem which could only be remedied by state intervention of some sort.

By the early 1860s, then, the political foundations for some sort of state involvement in child welfare institutions had been well and truly laid. It was no longer a question of persuading anyone of the validity of the idea of government-run industrial schools, but more of how it was to be executed. The relevant legislation was passed in

South Australia, Victoria, New South Wales and Tasmania in the 1860s, providing industrial schools for children under sixteen found 'wandering', and reformatories for those convicted of an offence, although the actual pattern of institutions provided varied from state to state.

In Hobart the government only provided the capital finances for industrial schools and reformatories, assuming that non-government agencies would establish and staff them (Brown 1972: 137). Sydney, Melbourne and Brisbane, on the other hand, established government-run industrial schools and reformatories. The pattern was an industrial school and reformatory for girls, and nautical school ships for boys—the *Vernon* in Sydney, the *Sir Harry Smith* in Melbourne, the *Proserpine* in Brisbane, and the *Fitzjames* somewhat later (1880) in Adelaide (Shorten 1976: 24).

In South Australia Emily Clarke and Catherine Spence had been waging a campaign promoting boarding-out, with effect, and the legislation passed there in 1867 provided for both industrial schools and boarding-out, although it took until 1873 for the boarding-out scheme to start working with real effect (Dickey 1986: 53–8). The industrial schools were essentially a state-run version of the orphan schools and the Randwick Asylum, with one important difference: the legislation extended the powers of the police to force children into institutional care by giving them new categories with which to charge them. One of the more common charges was vagrancy. (Public Charities Commission, 2nd Report, *VPLA* 1873/74, 6)

The histories of these various institutions have already been examined in detail by others (Williamson 1982; Dickey 1968, 1979; Horsburgh 1976), but some aspects are worth re-emphasising. First, although the industrial schools were intended for poor, homeless and vagrant boys and girls, to a large extent they became part of the criminal justice system, operating more as reformatories. Local magistrates often regarded them as places for punishment, as did their inmates, given that they were deprived of their liberty. The maintenance of discipline remained the central concern for their superintendents (Dickey 1979: 49–50). There were also continuing demands from magistrates, police and others for increased differentiation: industrial schools alone were seen as insufficient because no real distinction could be made between 'delinquent' and 'destitute and neglected' children.

The picture drawn in the newspapers of the day was one of heartless parental neglect. In 1865, for example, *Sydney Punch* (21 January) carried an article on 'The Little Boys in the Streets', speculating on the fate of 'the many ragged youngsters' with 'no occupation, no school to go to, no home to take refuge in, no friends to look after them'. In 1881 Sydney's *Daily Telegraph* (1 August) told of youngsters forced to earn money selling matches, 'the little fellows being afraid to go home unless they have obtained a certain sum, for fear of a beating'. Child labour of this sort made an important contribution to many families' finances, especially where the father was absent or casually employed (O'Brien 1987: 172–82), but we should nonetheless view this sort of presentation of generalised working-class neglect and cruelty with scepticism.

A major issue since the early days of the orphan schools had been the conflict between the desire of parents to have their children returned to them and the authorities' reluctance to do so. Years later, Arthur Renwick was to complain that 'no matter how degraded a woman may be, she seems as a rule to have some kind of affection for her offspring, and this natural sentiment is a source of infinite trouble and perplexity to the Board and its officers' (Horsburgh 1977a: 26; SCRB AR 1885: 544). Mothers often made attempts to recover custody of their children, and the admission documents of Dr Barnardo's homes in England, in contrast to the usual picture of neglect and abuse among poor families, 'show strong family affection and family cohesion among the labouring poor, reveal parents more respectable than suspect and record more admissions on economic than on moral grounds' (Parr 1980: 63; Radi 1979: 126).

According to the *Vernon* Entrance Books, roughly 25 per cent of the admissions to the *Vernon* were recorded as occurring with the consent of the parent or relative (StaNSW 8/1740–46). The Entrance Books' definition of 'consent' should be approached with caution, but they do indicate that not all the *Vernon*'s inmates had been herded on board by the police against the family's wishes. Often a boy was admitted because of the (lone) parent's impoverished circumstances, and the absence of the informal family support which kept other children in similar circumstances out of the institutions. Jane Knowles, for example, told the Court in 1868 that her husband was at sea and that her son was,

> ... in the habit of leaving home to go to school in the morning and
> of remaining away eight or nine days at a time; she is not aware
> what company he keeps, but believes that he sleeps on wharves and
> on Hyde Park; she has no control over him, and considers that it
> would be for his benefit that he should be sent on board the Vernon;
> she is willing to pay 4s. a week for his maintenance (StaNSW
> 8/1741).

Cases were also reported in the press where parents rejected responsibility for their offspring, even though their financial situation appeared stable. The father of fifteen-year-old Thomas

Wright told the Central Police Court that his son kept bad company and that he had no control over him.

> The boy, in reply, said that he was never out late but when he was at the theatre, when, rather than disturb the family, he slept where he might, but that he kept no company. He begged his father, with tears, to forgive him this once, to give him another trial, and he would not stay out any more. His father would not listen to his request, and the magistrates ordered the boy to be sent on board the Vernon (*Sydney Morning Herald* 20 January 1870).

To give a completely different example, Aboriginal missions had been established in Western Australia since 1849. They received Aboriginal children under the provision of the WA 1874 Industrial Schools Act, and most of the children going to the missions 'were sent in by their parents, in the same way that white children were sent to boarding school, or were orphans voluntarily surrendered to the care of the missions' (Haebich 1988: 67). An important aspect of how the institutions operated was thus the significance of poverty itself and a sense among some parents that their children would be somehow better off in the care of the state.

The girls' industrial schools and reformatories operated in quite a different way from those which the boys entered. Girls generally entered them for reasons connected with their morality and sexual behaviour rather than petty crime. Honora Williams, aged fifteen, was brought to Sydney Central Police Court by her mother in 1870 because 'she left home this day fortnight, since which she has kept company with girls of bad character' (*Sydney Morning Herald* 8 November 1870). Given the ideological construction of women as bearers of society's domestic virtue, the girls' moral behaviour and the threat it posed to respectability was examined more closely than that of boys. This moral dimension seems to be what led to 'fallen' girls being seen as more 'difficult', and to the treatment of girls being more repressive and punitive. The girls' industrial schools were a regime of stone walls, bashings, solitary confinement, bread and water diets, straitjackets and various other forms of ill-treatment.

This was quite a different situation from that on board nautical ships like the *Vernon*, where there was some trade training as well as better staff (Williamson 1982: 377–80). Whereas the *Vernon* came to be regarded with some civic pride, particularly while Frederick Neitenstein was Superintendent, Sydney's Industrial School for Girls was located first in a former military barracks and then in the ex-convict stone barracks on Cockatoo Island. It was given incompetent and brutal administrators, and the girls protested repeatedly by rioting.

Many of the institutions, particularly the Randwick Asylum in Sydney, Magill Reformatory and Industrial School in Adelaide, and the Queen's Asylum (formerly the King's Orphan School), were relatively large, housing up to 800 children at the peak of their usage in the 1870s. Their sheer size was to play an important part in the change in perception of how effectively they could produce good and useful citizens.

The family principle

In 1855 the Governor-General of New South Wales criticised the 'utter inefficiency' of the orphan schools 'to produce any good effect upon the children maintained in them' (Orphan Schools at Parramatta 1855: 1007). As time went by and news about the workings of the different institutions filtered out, various liberal intellectuals who may have supported their original establishment began to doubt their legitimacy. In their critique of the asylum, or 'the barracks', they made use of an ideological dichotomy between what can be called the 'family principle' and institutional care (Sauer 1979). Institutions had a predictable efficiency, better health conditions, and were more easily controlled by the authorities, but they were also mechanical, anonymous, de-individualising, and undermined self-reliance. If care for destitute children took place in ordered family or family-like settings, it would encourage individuality and be more humane; however it was also harder to police and more difficult to prevent neglect and abuse.

Ferdinand de Metz had established his agricultural colony for children in Mettray, France, in 1840, and both his arguments and the example of his 'cottage home' system played an important symbolic role in debates on child welfare throughout the Continent (Dahl 1985; Dekker 1985), in the US (Kett 1977: 131–2), Britain (Driver 1990), and Australia (Jaggs 1986: 33). Two leading proponents of his arguments against large-scale institutions were Florence Hill (1868) and Mary Carpenter (1851; Ramsland 1980), who were generously quoted as authorities in the various commissions of inquiry set up around Australia to examine the operation of child welfare. The point made by the 1873–74 New South Wales Public Charities Royal Commission was simply that the existing children's institutions were not doing what they were meant to do: produce self-reliant individuals who would go on to be hardworking, industrious and morally virtuous citizens, forming cohesive families of their own. This was said to be a feature of any large-scale institution, any asylum which of necessity treated its inmates as anonymous parts of a collectivity rather than as separate individuals. Girls especially were said to suffer from the lack of domesticity. Hill was quoted by the Royal Commission as saying that asylums 'must . . . have a hardening effect upon their characters, destructive to the purest and noblest of womanly feelings'.

The reformers argued that if one wanted to produce respectable individuals and families, children had to be raised within respectable families, or at least family-like settings, and certainly removed from previous associations. Asylums had little reforming value because 'the farther the life of these young people differs from that of the work-a-day world, the more difficult will they find it to accommodate themselves to its demands when they go forth and earn their living' (Public Charities Commission 1873/74: 40–42), nor were children removed from 'unhealthy' contact with their like-minded peers. Note here the medical analogy; like epidemics and plagues, vice and crime were contagious moral diseases best treated with isolation and quarantine. If their bearers were confined together in one place, they would only spread the more quickly and effectively.

The Royal Commissioners' sources for this family principle argument included the work of Johann Wichern and his Rauhe Haus in Hamburg, founded in 1883, as well as de Metz's agricultural colony in Mettray, although the whole French system of agricultural colonies for children was, in fact, under heavy attack by 1870, 'for the same abuses and shortcomings perceived in the adult penitentiary system: poor security, mismanagement, high recidivism and homosexual activity among inmates' (O'Brien 1982: 137). They also drew on the writings of Mary Carpenter, the Hill sisters, their cousin Emily Clark and Catherine Spence.

The family principle arguments were translated into boarding-out schemes in South Australia, Victoria and Tasmania in 1872–73, and in New South Wales illegally in 1879, and legally in 1881. Throughout Australia the authorities were thoroughly convinced by the critique of 'the barracks', and ended up boarding children out to respectable working-class families, who would be given some financial assistance towards their support. The argument for de-institutionalisation was a complex mixture of political economy, child development theory and administrative commonsense; it would be cheaper and would better reform the children.

The explanations Australian historians have offered of the development of boarding-out are not, however, very persuasive. One commentator, for example, sees 'the community of New South Wales' as having changed 'its' attitude to child welfare (Dickey 1979: 57), when in fact we have very little evidence on what 'the community' thought, whether they supported or opposed the idea, or whether they had any opinion at all. Most of the activity involved was undertaken by a philanthropic elite, with the only 'community' participation being that of families who took in children. There was an opposing argument put by the critics of boarding-out, who argued that children were taken in more for the slight financial assistance involved and the provision of an extra pair of hands than an increased inclination in the community 'to protect children from the excesses of poverty, violence, disease and crime' (Dickey 1979: 57).

A clue to a more precise explanation of boarding-out can be found in the opposition to the legislation in New South Wales, which reveals something important about the social and economic conditions of the day that at least made the development of boarding-out possible, and could be said to have constituted its social foundation. Those who opposed the Bill were arguing that there was not a sufficient stock of respectable working-class families to take in children, that in most cases they would be mistreated and in effect be worse off than they would have been in an institution; they would become 'hewers of wood and drawers of water': '. . . the likelihood is against having a majority of the poorer classes who will be fit to stand in the relation of parents, or who will think of the children as they would their own. They are more likely to regard them as little machines by which money may be made' (NSWPD 1881, 5: 976).

The critics of boarding-out were drawing on a long tradition of such arguments. Similar points about failed attempts at boarding-out in England and Western Europe had been made since the sixteenth century (Sauer 1979: 10–63), and it led Marsden and Johnson to argue for the original establishment of orphan schools. However, the dominant opinion in parliament was that 'there were many people of great respectability and high moral character, and well to do, who would be glad to take these children and act towards them as foster parents' (NSWPD 1881, 5: 977). They had to be working-class families, or else the children would feel uncomfortable above their station in life. The question was thus whether it was possible to distinguish between the 'vicious' families the children came from and the respectable working-class families they were to be placed in.

Before the 1870s it would have been difficult to respond to this question in the affirmative, given the absence of a liberal bourgeoisie and the kind of modest and precarious material advancement which made respectability increasingly possible among the working class. If one asks why institutional care dominated the relationship between the state and family life until the late nineteenth century, the answer cannot be put in terms of the appearance of a new philosophy or idea. Boarding-out had a long history in England, and in Germany too this debate about the negative effects of institutions, together with attempts to 'empty the barracks', first appeared towards the end of the eighteenth century (Pinchbeck and Hewitt 1969: 140–1; Sauer 1979: 22–8).

Part of the answer would have to be that it would not have been possible before the 1870s because a respectable working class had not yet become either a political or an economic reality. The political idea that a majority of the working class was in fact respectable and able to be foster parents was in many ways a radical one that conservatives opposed; they still preferred the asylum as a strategy, and this preference was manifested in the continued and persistent support among Australia's elite for institutions like the Randwick Asylum. Given that well-to-do families were rarely inclined to take in other people's children, boarding-out was only workable once there was a sizeable proportion of the working class no longer living in desperate poverty. It was the economic fact of the poverty of foster families, together with the miserliness of their allowances, which had in the past undermined the success of boarding-out.

The reintroduction and survival of boarding-out is thus best explained in terms of, first, the political strength of both the liberal bourgeoisie (who would read about Wichern and de Metz) and the respectable working class, which laid the foundations for a liberal intellectual climate which could provide sufficient support for the idea. This, combined with the gradually improved economic position of at least a proportion of working-class families relative to the years prior to the 1850s, made boarding-out a realistic possibility.

Boarding-out in practice

The idea of boarding-out gained political support on the grounds that it would 'empty the barracks', and in Victoria it appeared to have that effect, closing down the nautical schools *Sir Harry Smith* and *Nelson*, as well as a number of reformatories and industrial schools (Ramsland 1974; Jaggs 1986: 43). In Hobart, too, the Queen's Asylum was closed by 1879. However, in New South Wales and South Australia the actual operation of the New South Wales State Children Relief Board (SCRB) and the South Australian State Children's Council (SCC) had a more limited effect. The barracks to be emptied in New South Wales were the orphan schools, which had closed their doors by 1886, and to some extent the Randwick Asylum; its numbers had dropped considerably, although it struggled on without government support until 1916.

The New South Wales legislation continued support for state-run industrial schools and reformatories, and the fact that the state could not claim guardianship over children supported privately meant that there was still considerable room for non-government asylums. The Anglicans and Roman Catholics established their own privately funded orphanages, although their aims and practices only occasionally diverged from those of the state institutions (Horsburgh 1982). Rather than 'the' barracks in general, the target of the boarding-out legislation in New South Wales and South Australia was much more specific: non-government institutions receiving government financial support.

In New South Wales the number of children in institutions was already declining relative to the population under the age of 20 from the high point in 1870 until it flattened out around 1886. Numbers increased again in the 1890s (van Krieken 1985). The increase between 1860 and 1870 can be attributed in institutional terms to the establishment of the *Vernon* and the Industrial School for Girls in 1866. There were also dramatic increases in the population of the Randwick Asylum, from 247 inmates in 1860 to 777 in 1870. These increases far outstripped population growth (57 per cent for those under 20 between 1860 and 1870), and the subsequent proportional decrease can in turn be attributed to the fact that neither the orphan schools nor the industrial schools grew in size as rapidly as the population (39 per cent between 1870 and 1880). That the Randwick Asylum's numbers shrank to 639 is perhaps due in part to the bad publicity emanating from the 1873–74 Royal Commission (van Krieken 1985).

In social terms, however, the decline is more difficult to explain. There is little evidence to suggest that general economic conditions were any better in the 1870s, or family life more stable than it had been in the 1860s. The prevalence of seasonal and casual labour, together with the continuing poor position of women in the labour market, continued to have precisely the kind of impact on family life which regularly brought children into child welfare institutions (Lee and Fahey 1986; Fitzgerald 1987). One can only speculate, therefore, on the fate of the children no longer able to be accommodated by the orphan schools, the *Vernon* and the Industrial School for Girls, or who were no longer being admitted to the Randwick Asylum.

Rather than emptying the barracks, the overall effect of boarding-out in New South Wales and South Australia was the more limited one of differentiating among the children coming under its control, providing another, cheaper and more effective way of dealing with the less troublesome children, and leaving the institutions, albeit smaller and often Church-run, to continue as before. For those considered to be in need of reformation, there remained basically the same form of asylum treatment as had operated since the opening of the Female Orphan School in 1801 (Dickey 1979: 49).

The main reason boarding-out did not replace asylums was that certain categories of children were seen as still very much in need of moral reconstruction. Poverty was, as always, the main force driving children into the SCRB's control and care. For the period 1881–91 the SCRB's annual reports indicate that only 13 per cent of the parents of children coming into its care fell into the category of moral destitution (drunken, prostitute, abusing the children), with by far the majority of cases—86 per cent—revealing simply the absence of one parent. Rather than parental neglect or abuse 'the general picture appears to be that of single parents unable to continue to care for their children, plus a large proportion of children without any available guardian' (Horsburgh 1977a: 26–7).

Nonetheless, while Arthur Renwick could speak no ill of his wayward waifs in his first report, this optimism quickly evaporated. The following year it was quite a different story, one of morally deformed creatures of the dark, Gollums not very different from the diseases springing from the cesspools Renwick was already familiar with in his capacity as a medical practitioner:

> The morally-diseased must be made whole in reformatories, wherein, as the cure proceeds . . . it may be possible to obtain fit subjects for boarding-out . . . Until some degree of soundness is imparted it would be wrong to place some children in decent homes at all. Such children are steeped in sin; they have breathed an atmosphere of it; when they come under the cognizance of the State their bodies are foul and their minds polluted (SCRB AR 1883:865).

In addition to disorderliness and an unwillingness to work, the objects of this medicalised Victorian moral outrage were largely things like swearing and sexual knowledge, not to mention activity. Usually the references were merely to vice, depravity and sin, but every so often we get a sense of what it was really about: 'vile sexual practices', and cases such as a boy taken from a brothel and committed to a large institution 'in which there are unlimited opportunities for enlightening nearly 200 other boys . . . as to his exploits' (p. 866).

Girls were given special attention, with greater social restrictions placed upon their everyday activity and especially on their 'modesty'. Not that it necessarily protected that modesty, for alongside the ideological concern about female sexuality, women, especially working-class women without a husband, were nonetheless often sexually exploited. At the time it was argued that they were better off in apprenticeship, i.e. domestic service, than they were on the street, but there is evidence to the contrary. While the younger girls boarded-out were supervised quite closely, girls in domestic service were sometimes raped by their masters or fellow workers. Rather than being protected from moral danger, a number of girls were subjected to a different, normalised form of it, inside instead of outside the home (Barbalet 1983: 88–94, 191).

The actual operation of boarding-out had the effect of intensifying the impact of the state on the children, their natural parents, and the families that took children in. The boarding-out of children, particularly in country areas, distanced them, socially as well as physically, from their previous environment more than the institutions did. This was the aim of the exercise: to replace the existing family with another, more respectable one. The object of state intervention was not to consolidate or undermine the family per se, but to support a certain kind of family life by breaking up unacceptable families and redistributing the children accordingly (Barbalet 1983: 191; Daniels 1977: xi). In return for the slight financial assistance they received from the SCRB, and of course the labour of the children they took in, foster families had to offer more than just board and lodgings. They also had to be willing to be visited, inspected, advised and reprimanded as to the proper way to run their homes. They were regularly visited by volunteer 'Lady Visitors' who wrote reports on the child's cleanliness, behaviour, treatment, accommodation and school attendance (SCRB AR 1882: 1129).

This regulation of foster families was intended to protect children from cruelty and ill-treatment. It is questionable how effective it really was, but it was an attempt at regulation nonetheless, by a group of volunteers accountable only to the SCRB in New South Wales and the SCC in South Australia. Alongside the protection of children, they hoped to reinforce a familial morality and set of moral norms which may or may not have made much sense of, or taken much account of, the conditions of working-class life.

The object of boarding-out was to reinforce a certain kind of family life in respectable working-class homes, and Donzelot's observations on the spread of a 'tutelary complex' are accurate enough in the sense that the attainment of this goal depended vitally on a further breaking down of the boundary between the private realm of the family and the public realm of the state. This was a qualitative change that went beyond what already applied to the natural families of state children to encompass a new population of foster families. The establishment of boarding-out had in fact changed the flow of the traffic in children: the decline in the number of children in asylums continued, going from 0.8 per cent of the population of New South Wales under 20 in 1868 to 0.2 per cent in 1891, while the total number of children either in institutions or supervised by the SCRB in foster homes increased from 0.5 per cent to 0.6 per cent (van Krieken 1985).

Economic development and political change

In order to adequately understand both the development towards a social policy of encouraging the transformation of children into 'good and useful men and women' and the responses to that policy, it is useful to say more about the overall context of changes in the social, political and economic conditions in nineteenth-century Australian cities. The concern about unsupervised street children, for example, followed a period of enormous growth in economic activity and population. The increase in immigration played an important role in raising the supervision of children as a social problem; the families of new arrivals did not yet have the network of kin and friends which could provide informal support during times of crisis, and were thus more vulnerable to breakdown, with the children more likely to require admission to the institutions.

In addition, the form taken by the labour market, together with the privacy and individuality of family life, was simply not very good at sustaining the raising of children among sections of the urban working class, especially when one parent was absent. This may seem merely a fancy way of saying that some people were poor, but it is important to specify why that was the case given the tendency of contemporary observers to attribute it to drunkenness, viciousness and improvidence.

The cost of housing, recurrent unemployment and the low level of wages for less skilled and casual labour meant that many workers could not claim to be earning a 'family wage'. This also made men less willing husbands and fathers; it is striking how many of the fathers of boys entering the *Vernon*, for example, had work, such as bullock driver, shepherd, sailor, that was casual or seasonal, or both. The frequent absences from home often required by such work 'in many marriages evolved into virtual or complete desertion' (Fisher 1985: 157; see also O'Brien 1979, 1988: 102–6; Lee and Fahey 1986: 27). Life was made particularly difficult for deserted wives by the fact that the conditions and rates of pay for the work available to them assumed the economic support of a male breadwinner: they simply did not allow for the existence of single working mothers.

The main occupation available to women—domestic service—usually required living-in, and thus excluded children. Many of the children admitted to the institutions had mothers who had to give them up in order to work as domestic servants. Washing and needlework were paid abysmally, and also suffered formidable competition from the charitable and government welfare institutions which set their inmates to work at precisely these forms of labour (Daniels and Murnane 1980: 5; Daniels 1977: viii). One effect of welfare asylums was to intensify the pauperisation of women, generating women paupers in need of assistance. It was not until 1896, for example, that the SCRB allowed children to be boarded out to their own (respectable) mothers, implementing an early form of deserted wives' pension.

A second consideration was the position of children within the labour market. Next to no systematic work has been done on the history of children's work in Australia, but Grimshaw and Willett have remarked that children were 'robbed' of 'traditional labour and pastimes' as industrialisation and urbanisation progressed (Grimshaw and Willett 1981: 149). The concern in the 1860s with children 'floating in the streets and lanes like fish in a pond' reflected the fact that population growth had outstripped the market for children's labour; it appears that there were just many more children, under the age of fourteen at least, than forms of work available to them.

This was to change in the 1880s and 1890s with the growth in demand for children's labour in factories (O'Brien 1988: 172–82), but for middle-class moral entrepreneurs this was no improvement on unsupervised larking about in the streets. Unemployment was in any case a persistent problem, and there seems to have been less scope for the smooth integration of children into the workforce than there had been in the convict period, an integration which has been used to explain the first generation's 'good' behaviour despite the viciousness of their convict parentage (McNab and Ward 1962: 289–308). Education was not yet compulsory, leaving only the streets for those who could not find work, which was often street-based work anyway, such as selling matches or newspapers.

There was also an important shift in political forces bound up with and following the introduction of responsible government in New South Wales and Victoria, which meant not only a change in the relationship with Britain, but also a change in political relationships within the colonies. A new arena of contention was produced through the shift of the financial burden for state activity to the colonies themselves, and overall the political change can best be summed up as the development of a 'middle-class' politics and the political ascendancy of the liberal bourgeoisie, revolving around the pursuit of mercantile interests within a framework of compromise between conservative forces and the demands of populist radicalism and the labour movement. Connell and Irving (1980), for example, have argued that the British Government saw their problem as achieving the right balance between democracy and class rule, which depended on 'the political leadership of the urban businessmen'. The support of movements and organisations of workers and small producers was thus useful to the liberal bourgeoisie both to establish a general consensus and to establish leadership within the ruling class (pp. 120, 105–10).

The focal point of this political development was the liberal–democratic state, a state of 'the general interest' which was meant to produce economic growth, propelled by and benefiting everyone willing to work. From the 1860s the maintenance and legitimacy of the ideal of a state of the 'general interest', as well as the political reality of an alliance between the liberal bourgeoisie and the respectable working class, became increasingly significant. By the turn of the century the strategy of the labour movement had crystalised into one which conceived state authority as 'a reservoir of power which could, by astute manipulation, be harnessed to provide a countervailing force to employers' industrial hegemony'. It aimed to 'extend state intervention in economic and social affairs to support wage earners' direct interests' (Macarthy 1967: 74).

Timothy Coghlan, who as New South Wales government statistician was to become 'the most influential public servant, if not the most influential political figure, of the period' (Deacon 1989: 108) was only the leading example of the working-class boys who had grown up assuming that the state should play an active interventionist role in economy and society, and that 'its strength and stability were essential to the well-being of the working class and the new middle class' (p. 110).

Mayne has also remarked on this in explaining the apparent acceptance of 'elite' views on urban reform; the social assumptions on which they were based 'matched the bourgeois aspirations of petty business and the marginal professions, and of working men and women proud in their accumulation of skills and possessions' (Mayne 1983: 558). Profits were supposed to mean prosperity for all, and the evidence that this was clearly not the case—poverty—was a political problem the resolution of which both the liberal bourgeoisie and the leadership of the working class were interested in, although for different reasons.

The elite response to poverty had in the past been divided between presenting it as part of the order of things, and explaining it in moral terms as individual rather than structural failure. This was not to change, but the political climate of consensus made the second mode of explanation, together with a social policy and some active state intervention based on it, more attractive to the liberal bourgeoisie as a strategic response to the flaws in the 'workingman's paradise'. From the working-class point of view, the process by which 'the poor' and 'the worker' gradually became separate categories also contributed to the specific form of the state's relationship to family life. The line between personal and collective improvement, as Eric Hobsbawm has observed for England, 'between imitating the middle class and, as it were, defeating it with its own weapons, was extremely thin for the nineteenth-century worker' (Hobsbawm 1975: 226–7).

An excellent example here is the upwardly mobile Henry Parkes, a driving force behind both the politics and the welfare reform of the period. In defence of the working man, he declared that workers had no reason to be ashamed of themselves, it was the non-working man, 'the man who rises late and consumes the day heedlessly and unprofitably to himself' who was 'unworthy' (Parkes 1896: 214). The workers who conformed to a respectable lifestyle either did, in fact, gain some material advancement, or believed that they eventually would (Cannon 1975; McCalman 1982), and this undermined their tolerance of those who appeared not to see a morally disciplined conformity as the best possible means of social and economic advancement.

The objections raised against child welfare institutions and agencies were rarely that they should not exist at all, or that state intervention into family life was in principle illegitimate, but revolved instead around the justice of particular cases or particular aspects of the procedures being followed. The ideal of marriage was firmly embedded within Australian working-class culture by the closing decades of the nineteenth century, so that 'most people, men and women, believed it to be in their own interests, and that it was both natural and necessary' (Fitzgerald 1987: 171). There was thus no cultural or political foundation for real resistance against the interventionist notion that children were best separated from parents who could be seen as improvident, violent, dirty, unchaste, or too frequently drunk.

While many workers did see their relationship to the state as one of opposition and resistance, 'desire for work, the willingness to appease authority and espousal of self-help and the work ethic also pierced deeply the minds of workers, many of whom have remained obscured from view by their more vocal and more militant brothers' (O'Brien 1988: 78). The effects of organised working-class struggles for equality, even the advances and successes of their struggles, were not simply to oppose everything bourgeois but, on the contrary, were often to produce overlap, compromise, even consensus on cultural issues like familial morality and respectability. Together with the interventionist zeal of middle-class moral reformers, this aspect of nineteenth-century working-class culture helped make 'objectively possible' (Weber 1949: 180–1) a state social policy of attempting to improve society through greater state involvement in the raising of at least some children as 'good and useful men and women' (Tholfsen 1971, 1976; Walkowitz 1980: 152).

5 The formation of a system, 1890–1915

The years between 1890 and 1915 were a period of extensive and formative change, involving a gradual rationalisation, systematisation and expansion of child welfare agencies, and a qualitative change in the power of the state over Aboriginal families. The watersheds in this process were, first, the passing of various Aborigines Protection Acts which gave specific powers to Aboriginal Boards to remove children from their families. Second, the establishment of Children's Courts and probation systems in the early 1900s significantly altered the character of both the agencies themselves and their work, as well as increasing the numbers (relatively as well as absolutely) of children and families under some form of state supervision.

This expansion of state involvement in the socialisation of children is usually explained in one of two ways: either as a process of modernisation and rationalisation, or as an expansion of state and professional control over the behaviour of both Aboriginal and white working-class families. The internal logic of 'rationalisation' can at times appear compelling: one thing just logically seems to have led to another. The state's active intervention into the lives of children and families through the establishment of reformatories and industrial schools in the 1860s, boarding-out in the 1870s and 1880s, and Aborigines Protection legislation from the late 1800s onwards, appears to constitute the major political turning point, leaving only the question of how to best achieve that goal. Any change and development can thus be seen as a matter of achieving the goal more effectively and economically, within changing surrounding conditions.

It is, however, this very obviousness, reasonableness and rationality itself which needs to be critically scrutinised. In practice some of the 'problems', such as children's street-trading, could have been defined differently (children supplementing their parents' inadequate income) and for changes to take place there had to be a range of political support extending beyond a small group of reformers. The supposed 'rationality' of an idea is by no means any guarantee of its implementation. A boys' reformatory, for example, was an 'obvious' development in New South Wales at the same time that the Shaftesbury Reformatory for Girls was established in 1866, and magistrates and newspapers were constantly arguing for one (StaNSW 4/901–1, Colonial Secretary's Special Bundle). But Henry Parkes was politically committed to the essential goodness and reformability of working-class boys, and did not consider a fully fledged reformatory necessary, arguing that the *Vernon* was adequate and that there were insufficient numbers of boys in adult gaols to warrant an additional institution.

Any process of rationalisation requires more than logic to be put into practice: it needs a political environment responsive to the ideas involved, a context which makes it possible. Rather than adopting a 'modernisation' perspective, then, it clearly makes more sense to ask what it was about the political and economic situation around 1900 that intersected with and encouraged the work of child welfare reformers.

The aim of this chapter is to examine the ways in which white working-class families often used the child welfare system for their own purposes, as well as identifying the source of whatever social control was exercised through child welfare.

State officials' arguments for change: 'the supply must be cut off at the source'

Boarding-out was established in the 1870s and 1880s in the context of a public debate about the appropriateness of institutional or asylum care for children, in which the public criticism of 'the barracks' played a central role. Although the original aim of boarding children out to foster families was to empty 'the barracks', this only happened in Victoria and Tasmania. The result in New South Wales and South Australia was an undermining of non-government institutions such as the orphan schools and larger institutions like the Randwick Asylum and Magill Industrial School, without much effect on the smaller-scale state-run institutions (Dickey 1979: 49). In New South Wales the SCRB also set up its own institutions, among them the Mittagong Farm Homes. Throughout the early twentieth century, smaller Church-run industrial schools admitted increasing numbers of children, so that in relative terms it is possible to argue that the institutionalised population stayed more or less stable after the 1890s.

Arthur Renwick was the SCRB's first President until 1900. A physician, he had been President of the Benevolent Society, and was constantly active in welfare reform. Charles Mackellar, another medical practitioner, was President from 1901 to 1915, and he was also an active social policy campaigner, heading the Royal Commission into the Decline of the Birth Rate and the Mortality of Infants. He published a comparative study of the treatment of mental defectiveness in children in 1913, and was generally a prominent writer and publicist in the areas of family life, education and child socialisation. Another influential administrator was Frederick Neitenstein, who went from being Superintendent of the *Vernon* and its successor the *Sobraon*, to the position of Comptroller-General of Prisons in 1896. He played an important role in shaping the debate on the prevention of delinquency, vagrancy and crime (Garton 1989).

During this period there was a lot of pressure being exerted by state officials for fundamental changes in the relationship between the state and children—not least because the existing system seemed not to be achieving its goals. As Presidents of the SCRB, Arthur Renwick and Charles Mackellar were constantly arguing for improvements and innovations in the organisation of its work. They were mainly concerned with ways to achieve more effectively what they saw as the Department's goals by transforming it from a boarding-out agency into a coherent system of reclaiming and reforming wayward children and youth: a system of intervention into and reconstruction of the families they thought were not socialising their children properly.

The SCRB's Annual Reports are a rich source of child welfare philosophy. Together with other writings on charity and child welfare, they show a gradual cumulation of themes in their arguments for changes to the legislation, themes which were echoed in the reports coming from other state bureaucracies. Whatever genuine concern or humanitarianism might have been present, the core issue around which everything revolved was the prevention of crime. 'Rescuing the rising generation' more effectively, efficiently and economically was always how the argument was posed. As George Guillaume said at the First Australasian Conference on Charity in 1890:

> The social reformer ... feels that his best hopes of success lie in
> rescuing and regenerating the young. If the ranks of the criminal and
> the vicious, whose unchecked growth would imperil the very
> existence of the commonwealth, are to be reduced, the one effective
> way of accomplishing this is by getting hold of and bringing under
> good influences the unhappy children who, if left unaided, must
> infallibly recruit those classes. The supply must be cut off at the
> source (*Proceedings*: 103).

This general concern was manifested in a number of more specific
ways.

First there was the problem of maintenance of children by their
parents, but more often of children by their father, with or without
their mother. The administrators of every child welfare institution
and agency since 1801 had worried, rightly or wrongly, about how
parents might be evading their responsibilities towards their offspring, but any provision for contribution towards support was
never very effectively enforced. Renwick and Mackellar pushed the
pursuit of this issue a little further, arguing for and getting political
support for the proposition that the state should more effectively
enforce a legal obligation on the part of parents, particularly
fathers, to contribute financially to the support of their children,
rather than leaving the state to foot the bill. While 'deserving'
widows and deserted wives (that is, those who were not defined as
prostitutes or drunkards) were to be allowed to keep their children
with state support, Renwick and Mackellar also believed that
fathers should be pursued to contribute towards the costs. Essentially the issue was one of the state at least attempting to force
parents to take financial responsibility for their offspring.

Secondly, child welfare reformers like Renwick and Guillaume
continued to urge the application of the family principle in institutional care: the principle that even in institutions life should
approximate the ideal family environment as much as possible.
More precisely, the idea was that institutional care should be on as
small a scale as possible, with only a small number of children per
'household', a substitute 'mother' and 'father' in the form of cottage homes, preferably in a rural setting, free from the moral
contagion of city life. However, in the absence of that principle
being taken up in the remaining industrial schools and reformatories, cottage homes were at least established for children regarded
unsuitable for boarding-out, especially crippled and invalid children and, later, children regarded as feeble-minded.

Thirdly, the idea of introducing a Children's Court and a probation system was also gaining support from a variety of sources.
The two changes were introduced simultaneously, but they were
separate issues. A system of probation, for example, could have

been introduced using the existing courts and, similarly, a Children's Court could have been established without introducing the option of putting children on probation. The argument for a Children's Court was a simple one: it was not conducive to their moral reformation to have children within an adult court. In his 1896 Report, the New South Wales Comptroller-General of Prisons, Frederick Neitenstein, said that there should be a special court and a special magistrate to deal with juvenile delinquents 'in a somewhat more private way'. Under the existing system 'the boys and girls are not edified or improved by contact with the persons with whom they unavoidably associate to a greater or lesser extent while awaiting trial in the Police Courts' (Prisons Report 1896:1377).

As well as this aspect of the Court's atmosphere, there was also the question of the type of judgement available to magistrates. Under existing legislation, magistrates could only determine whether or not children had committed an offence. The problem then was that magistrates might decide to acquit children of the offence but still regard them as 'neglected'. They would then have to acquit on the presenting charge, immediately charge under the Industrial Schools Act, and commit the child to an institution. Nor did they have the power to commit a child to the SCRB's care. A Children's Court with special legislation and special procedures would be more 'flexible' and do away with this administrative 'untidiness' (NSWPD 1902,7:3356).

In addition to the benefits of the centralisation and flexibility of the Children's Court, the new category in the classification scheme—probation—was also seen as having great reformative potential. The idea flowed logically from the principles underlying boarding-out as well as being derived from the example of the Massachussetts Juvenile Court: if institutions were bad for some children, they were bad for all, including those charged with criminal offences, and especially when the boundaries between delinquency and neglect were never very clear. If family life was the ideal context for children's moral development then, instead of sending them to an institution, it would naturally be preferable to devise a system which would keep children in a family setting. Reformation would ideally take place through the parents rather than apart from them (SCRB AR 1910: 315). Of course, to achieve this particular aim one could also have boarded-out children brought before the Court, but the already existing example of probation in North America provided a convenient formula, besides requiring less administration than boarding-out.

There were also arguments for a centralised package of measures which would be both more appropriate to the purpose of reformation and more 'flexible'. Basically the issue was one of improving both the classification and categorisation itself in relation to children, and of improving the mechanisms by which children were allocated to one or other categories. The process of allocation to, say, either an industrial school, a reformatory, or boarding-out was one which reformers like Neitenstein, if not the magistrates themselves, regarded as beyond magistrates' capacities, requiring more information and time than they had at their disposal. As Neitenstein put it in 1896:

> Committing magistrates are certainly not now in a position to perform the difficult and delicate task of defining the exact classification of the juvenile offenders who pass so hurriedly before them. The time allowed is not sufficient to admit of a correct estimate being arrived at, and the position is further complicated by the insufficient means at hand for identifying the youthful offender . . . In any case, classification before committal must be often liable to error. It can only be properly arrived at after observation, assisted by whatever particulars can be gleaned of home life, antecedents, and companions (Prisons Report 1896: 1305).

So he favoured committal to a depot '. . . until observation enabled the Minister, on the advice of his officer, to determine the ultimate destination, or to discharge on probation'.

Finally, various state officials were also concerned about truancy and children generally being 'on the streets', much as Henry Parkes had been in the 1860 Report from the Select Committee on the Condition of the Working Classes. The school system was only gradually exerting its influence, with the position of children in working-class family economics proving difficult to shift. Children's labour was still too important to the families of rural and industrial workers to allow them to waste their time and labour power in a schoolroom. The view from the heights of state administration was a long-term one, being concerned with the ultimate productivity, usefulness and moral condition of the labour force as a whole. For working-class families, though, immediate survival was the main concern, and it was important for children to be contributing to the family income as soon as possible.

Not that the ultimate usefulness and desirability of education was necessarily being rejected. Some working-class parents would have regarded all education as a waste of time, but there is no evidence to suggest what proportion saw education in this way. What evidence there is suggests that most children were sent to school whenever it fitted in with their work patterns (Wimshurst 1981). Nevertheless the economic significance of children's work was to remain until a 'living wage' was achieved for a majority of workers, and it is in this area that one can most clearly speak of working-class resistance to state intervention and the use of state coercion to enforce education among recalcitrant working-class families.

The police were responsible for enforcing truancy legislation. It is difficult to know how well they were doing their job, but we do know that they did not like being given the task. In his 1894 Police Report the New South Wales Inspector-General made the complaint that he was to repeat regularly over the next decade, drawing the Chief Secretary's attention to:

> ... the constantly increasing duties imposed upon the Police relating to matters entirely foreign to their legitimate functions ... constant complaints are made by the public of the protracted absence of constables from their stations, and the necessary neglect of patrols and other active measures for the detection of criminals and the prevention of crime (Police Report 1894/5: 760–1).

Although truancy in itself might not have been such a dramatic feature of Australian everyday life, it became a central issue within the general environment of public 'disorderliness' which characterised the period, and Neitenstein included it in his list of 'things to be done' about public order. In his 1896 Prisons Report he quoted English sources arguing that truancy was the main breeding ground of juvenile delinquency, along the lines of 'idle hands', and in this respect he was saying nothing very different from Parkes' reasons for introducing an education system in the first place (Prisons Report 1896: 1377; Parkes 1896: 216).

The accuracy of this view of what children were doing on the streets and out of school is debatable in a number of senses. Kerry Wimshurst argues for South Australia that 'far from aimlessly wandering the streets and acquiring "vicious" habits during their free time from school, the street children were engaged in meaningful and important casual labour' (Wimshurst 1981: 389). Nonetheless the police and the child welfare approach was to subsume all absence from school under the one definition. As Mackellar saw it in 1903, a 'large proportion' of children employed in street trades,

> ... are the children of idle or dissolute parents, and, being from infancy deprived of the restraining influence of healthy home surroundings, they are at an early age thrown onto their own resources, and in their effort to gain a livelihood exposed to the great moral dangers of the city. The excitement of their career creates in them a reluctance to work steadily, and a very large proportion of them soon become addicted to the practice of gambling, and readily lapse into a career of crime (SCRB AR 1903: 903–4).

The concern here is clearly not just developing a capacity to work in itself, but to work in a particular way. Children working on the streets selling matches, flowers or newspapers was the most visible form of truancy, so one element in the legislation introduced in this period was provision for the licensing of street trading and public performance, with the general aim of getting most street traders into school or at least fulfilling the minimum requirements.

These were main arguments for changes in child welfare coming from those in key positions in the state bureaucracy, the central focus being the police and their concern with crime prevention: that was the nucleus around which the thoughts of hard-headed administrators and politicians revolved. The more liberal way of describing it was developing 'citizens' with a proper sense of obligations as well as rights, but this line of argument tended largely to intersect with and support a more rigid law and order approach, in fact 'rationalising' it by arguing that a more humane approach to crime prevention among children was also more effective.

The reality of child welfare before and after the Children's Courts

It is, of course, important to examine more than just the arguments for change, given that they indicate primarily shifts in ideological orientation. We also need to examine the actual operation of the child welfare system. A difficulty which arises immediately is the paucity of sources; unlike many of the American Juvenile Courts, little of the Australian Children's Court records for this period has survived. However, there are still a number of observations one can make on the basis of the evidence that is available, which take us some distance beyond the arguments of state administrators.

To begin with, the entrance books of the New South Wales institutions (StaNSW 8/1740–1746, 8/1747–1751, 8/1753.2, 8/1758, 8/1755) reveal neither 'a quickening concern for the welfare of vulnerable children' (Dickey 1979: 53), nor a picture of an unruly working class being disciplined by the advance troops of bourgeois state intervention. That the children concerned were being disciplined and controlled, often in a cruel and senseless way, is beyond doubt; control was the whole purpose of the institutions. The issue of whether or not parents had lost control over their children was a central one, along with whether they were abusing them in some way and whether they could support them. As the language and procedures of child welfare authorities became routinised, the degree of a child's 'uncontrollability' became one of the main criteria determining the level and extent of state intervention.

However, the source and basis of that control varied. Firstly, there were cases where parents or relatives themselves actively sought or consented to the child being taken into the child welfare system. The proportions vary from time to time, and, of course, some doubt has to hang over the accuracy of the records, but for around 40 per cent of the admissions to the New South Wales institutions, the entrance books record the parent/relative's request or consent. There was a variety of reasons behind such an attitude. For example, the *Sobraon* entrance books record the case of a widower, with four children in the Benevolent Asylum around 1900, saying he could not control his son who regularly left home and did not attend school. He wanted his son put in a training school, and was willing to contribute to his upkeep. In 1898 another father, a labourer, said of his ten-year-old son: 'He is a good boy when at home but he takes these fits and runs away and I lose all control over him he has no means of support apart from me. I wish him to be sent to a training school.'

In another case in 1898 the police at Yass apparently went out of their way to trace the father of a fifteen-year-old boy caught stealing money, and the Balmain constable who found him reported the father as stating: 'The boy was sent on board the *Sobraon* in 1895 where he kept him for 18 months and after a lot of trouble obtained his release from this ship, since that time he says the boy's conduct has been bad and declines to have anything to do with him.'

Caring for an adolescent child often proved to be too much for a father or mother left alone and finding it difficult enough to provide for themselves, so that admission to an industrial school could be seen as a kindness, if a rather cruel one and forced by circumstance. In 1899 one mother wrote to her son:

> You must not think it either unkind, or cruel of me to let Mr. Reed lock you up, you know how many times in the last 9 months you have said you would not stay away . . . for me to take you back would be very foolish of me, I am very ill now, and I must do some easier work than washing.
>
> Now Gingie . . . you must do everything just as you are told to do it, . . . it is only doing what boys told you to do has put you where you are now . . . I am so tired and cannot write any more now. Now good bye, and God bless you. Try to be good.
>
> And believe me although I let you go I love you. I want you to be a good man, if you live, not a low bad man. I am and always shall be your loving mother (StaNSW 8/1753.2).

Institutions were also viewed as a kind of working-class boarding school, providing a stricter regime in which children would be straightened out, given their lack of responsiveness to the gentler family setting. The father of one boy admitted to the *Sobraon* in 1911 'says he has no control over him, and is willing, provided the boy improves under discipline, to have him back in the course of a few months'. An insufficient commitment to the work ethic could also make one 'uncontrollable': one boy admitted to the *Sobraon* in 1911 said: 'I was sent here for being uncontrollable. For not working I think it was' (StaNSW 8/1751). When picture shows caught the imagination of Australian youth, they also became an increasingly common reason for 'loss of control'. One ten-year-old boy was committed to the Mittagong Farm Homes for Boys (MFHB) in 1912 with the following entry: 'Uncontrollable, goes straight from school to the picture shows and comes home late at night. Mother wants boy sent institution' (StaNSW 8/1755).

For girls, however, uncontrollability focused primarily on their sexual behaviour; the New South Wales Industrial School for Girls, for example, was designated specifically for 'sexual delinquency' (Royal Commission into the New South Wales Public Service 1920: 461) and here, too, the parents themselves were often the initiators in having their daughters committed to the child welfare system. Girls suffered most from a sexual double standard in which they were blamed for being victims. In 1910 an entry for a thirteen-year-old girl admitted to the ISG recorded: 'Living under conditions lapsing into career of vice and crime. Man named Robinson was tried for carnally knowing girl on her evidence but was acquitted.'

So if under-age and raped, girls stood as good a chance of being institutionalised as if they had committed the crime. There was a sort of logic of 'protection' to it, but it was a rather appalling one. Similarly with cases of incest, the least powerful person, the girl, was often the one who was a punished. The record for another thirteen-year-old in 1914: 'Neglected, V & C ["in danger of lapsing into vice and crime"]. Brought to the Court on mother's complaint. Girl and step-father admitted reclining each night on stretcher on kitchen. Dr. Waugh deposed girl not *virgo intacto* and indicated more than one penetration. Has not been to school for 12 months.'

Alternatively, working-class girls who did not generally conduct themselves properly and buckle down to feminine domesticity and obedience, especially anywhere near the boundaries of sexual encounter, real or imagined, were subjected to state intervention. The ISG entries for some fifteen-year-olds speak for themselves:

> Uncontrollable. Stays out late in company of young men and boys. Will not obey parents.

> Associates with men and girl of bad character, has been cautioned by police. Admits immorality.

> Uncontrollable. Untruthful, disobedient, uses filthy language. Wants to promenade street at night with boys.

Roughly 80 per cent of the girls entering the ISG were admitted on this sort of charge, of 'lapsing into a career of vice and crime' (Sta NSW 8/1758). It should also be added, however, that far fewer girls entered the system than boys; in 1914 the Sydney Metropolitan Children's Court dealt with 1717 boys and 172 girls, most of the latter being under 'uncontrollable' charges (SCRB AR 1914: 877).

The second type of case involves that in which nothing at all is known about the parents' attitude—where they had, for example, committed suicide, been imprisoned or committed to a psychiatric institution, and where there are clearly no relatives or friends to help take care of the children. This type of intervention is central to child welfare's current public image of humanitarian assistance in times of crisis and family breakdown. It is most commonly used to support the benevolent image of social welfare in general, but it does nevertheless represent part of the truth. For example, two sisters, twelve and thirteen years of age, were admitted to the ISG in 1910 on a charge of neglect, with their entry declaring they had been 'wandering the streets and keeping company of young larrikins'. But the entry goes on:

> Parents living unhappily for some time. Last January mother left father for 4 months. The father states that she was living in adultery with a man who is now in gaol. She left home last Xmas and father attempted to commit suicide and was convicted. He was at one time a school teacher, but through his wife's behaviour was so worried that he resigned (StaNSW 8/1758).

The other two girls in the family were apparently boarded-out.

At other times the parents seemed confused as to what they really wanted done with their child; in 1898 one Newcastle constable said the following about a boy about to be committed to the *Sobraon*:

> I have seen him running about the streets at all hours of the day and night. On one occasion at half past eleven at night my attention was drawn to him by some ladies. He was lying asleep on the doorstep. I took him to the house where his mother and father lived. Neither of them were at home ... At one the next morning I saw his father and mother coming home under the influence of liquor, I said to L the adopted father: 'Why don't you look after the little boy I found him asleep on the doorstep at half past eleven last night.' He said 'you had better take him away.' Mrs L ... said 'The boy is all right and quite happy mind your own business' (StaNSW 8/1758.2).

The problem here is that it is not very clear, especially from this distance, what one should make of the mother's remark that the boy was 'quite happy'. Certainly to some extent cases like this slide over into the third category of case, in which there is an imposition of a morality and a set of norms by state officials which might actually be foreign to the parents, relatives and surrounding community. In this case, for example, the constable also remarked that 'the neighbours around the place . . . look after the child more than his adopted parents', indicating that there was some pattern of community support.

One does certainly come across some clashes of norms and values in the records: judgements about people's fitness as parents may or may not really have had anything to do with the child's well-being. Roughly 20 per cent of the admissions to the MFHB record the character of the parents in terms such as 'bad moral character; drunkard; living in adultery; addicted to drink'. The other 80 per cent were 'good, respectable, satisfactory, or nothing known against' (StaNSW 8/1755). Women's sexual behaviour and both parents' relation to alcohol seem to have been central criteria by which people were judged, alongside financial independence, cleanliness, ensuring school and church attendance and, for women, domesticity, although failure in one area seemed to go together with failure in all of them. In 1898, the Police Sergeant at Tumut had this to say about one family with three children:

> Their father died about 18 months ago and have since resided with their mother who is a simple minded person and of indolent and dirty habits and is without visible lawful means of support. For a number of years the family have been supported by charity and numerous complaints have been made to the Police by residents of the town and district about the children begging . . . I visited the place about a fortnight ago and found the place in a filthy dirty state and unfit for habitation of human beings. The house is occupied by the mother and eight children, brother-in-law, also Eliza S. who is a common prostitute. I consider the mother given to her dirty and indolent habits is quite unfit to have charge of the children and they have been much neglected (StaNSW 8/1753.2).

The two boys were sent to the *Sobraon* charged with 'living with a woman of no visible lawful means of support and also with a common prostitute'. We do not know what happened to the other six children.

The families seen by state officials to be in need of reform and re-education were 'usually found in the slums of the city, in the tent homes of the outlying suburbs, and in the numerous rude dwellings on the harbour foreshores' (SCRB AR 1906: 766). The

more remote rural districts were also regarded as dangerous
sources of improper family life:

> ... there is a very general tendency shown in country districts for an
> appreciable proportion of the poorer settlers to revert to primitive
> living improper or inadequate occupation and lodging—disregard of
> parental ties or obligations ... the result being frequently the
> degradation physical, mental and moral of their families and
> themselves (SCRB AR 1910: 310).

All Aboriginal families fell into the same category here, and were
by definition regarded as inappropriate and improper. The legislation introduced in Australia around the turn of the century was
intended to give enormous powers to the state in simply removing
children from their parents against their consent.

At first the legislation only covered illegitimate children, but
given that marriage was a white Christian social institution, clearly
many Aboriginal children fell into this category. Similarly, children
could be defined as neglected if there was no 'visible means of
support or fixed place of abode' (Read 1983: 5), and again in rural
areas this was likely to take in all Aboriginal children. In practice
even legitimate Aboriginal children and those who were more than
adequately supported by white standards were not really exempt,
as there are cases of such parents having had their children
removed and demanding their return. The authorities then 'reluc-
tantly relinquished the children' (Haebich 1988: 113), but how
many parents felt unable to assert their rights?

These were the types of family situations which bore the brunt of
state moralism, and could be most clearly regarded as being subject to control, surveillance and discipline involving the imposition
of an alien set of norms and values. It is in this area that indis-
criminate cruelty, intolerance of difference, particularly that
between whites and Aborigines, and the social effects of grinding
poverty manifest themselves most strongly in state action.

The great advantage of probation was said by its supporters to
be, rather than simply removing their children, the effective re-
education of the family as a whole. In a conference of probation
workers in 1912, Sydney Maxted made the following bold, and no
doubt exaggerated, claim about the effects of probation on the
'children who live with people of ill repute, whose parents and
relatives are drunkards, immoral, thieves, or ne'er do wells
generally':

> As a result of the probation officer's activity and the Special
> Magistrate's intercession, hovels have been transformed into
> presentable cottages, large families living in immorality have been

induced to amend their ways, intemperate parents have become temperate, indifferent relatives have been persuaded to come forward and assist indigent brothers and sisters, young women have been persuaded to abandon vicious habits, and in many other ways social reforms have been secured solely and directly through the sympathy and enthusiasm of Special Magistrates and probation officers (SCRB AR 1912: 818).

However, this type of case constituted a minority of the work of the Children's Courts. The 'great majority' of boys coming before the Children's Courts had engaged in offences 'common to boyhood', such as 'fighting in the streets, riding on the trams while in motion, bathing in public places, robbing orchards, playing football in the streets' (SCRB AR 1912: 818).

The general impression one gets is that the proportion of white families perceived as 'immoral and vicious' decreased as the twentieth century progressed. In the earlier *Vernon* entrance books there seems to be much more mention of a lack of parental respectability, drunkenness, prostitution and thieving than in the later *Sobraon* and MFHB entrance books. The apparent shift of focus from reforming children to reforming their environment, which was central to the introduction of the Children's Court, did conceal the fact that the strategy for those institutionalised was not to change, and the reformation of environment took place for children previously not 'reformed' at all. Nonetheless, instead of being denounced as drunkards, thieves and prostitutes, working-class families were now given lectures on ensuring school and church attendance, keeping their sons out of their neighbours' houses, their daughters at home at night, and so on (*Sydney Morning Herald* 6 June 1913: 8).

By 1915 the kind of moral disapproval which had in 1880 been freely heaped on the lower classes in general had been given a new object—Aboriginal families, especially those with half-caste children. The following comment on the Aboriginal camps on the outskirts of country towns was part of a much longer diatribe by Mackellar on the Aboriginal 'problem':

Paternity is casual and conjectural, and promiscuous association is the rule; sanitation is ignored. Dirt is the dominating element. In this mire of moral and physical abasement, tended by semi-imbecile mothers, children are allowed to wallow through the imitative stages of childhood (SCRB AR 1915: 878).

Again this kind of attitude and the practices associated with it clearly involved the state's imposition of a morality intolerant of the social effects of poverty. Nevertheless, the bulk of child welfare work involving white children seems to have dealt with cases of destitution and those of parents simply not being very successful—often in their own judgement as well as that of the authorities—in socialising their children. Put another way, in relation to the issue of social control, while it is true that once they 'went so far' they were, of course, subject to state control, the coercion driving the majority of children to the Children's Court and state control came not from state officials and agencies, but from other quarters: force of circumstance, relatives, neighbours, or the parents themselves.

A closer look at the operation of probation also reveals that the public claims made about it both before and after its introduction gave a false impression of what it really involved. Rather than liberalising and humanising child welfare practices, it was the aspect of centralisation and improvement of classification which in fact determined the real changes brought about by the legislation. Perhaps it was an unintended consequence—one can only speculate whether the reformers predicted how it would actually work—but instead of the 'welfare' view of probation leading to an alternative to institutionalisation being realised, probation and the Children's Court tended to add to the range of children being brought under state supervision.

In the 1907 review of the working of the New South Wales 1905 Act, for example, the Sub-Inspector at Balmain Police Station wrote: 'The constitution of the Children's Court is another very laudable provision, for before its establishment a considerable number of juvenile offenders were handed over to their parents by the Police for chastisement rather than identifying them with other offenders ...' (StaNSW 5/7750.2, Attorney General and Justice Department Special Bundle).

This leniency, he complained, 'failed to inspire either child or parent with any renewed sense of duty towards each other or towards the State', but the activities of the Children's Court 'have aided considerably in restoring neglectful children and parents to a better sense of their respective duties than heretofore'. The Children's Court, in other words, encouraged the police to charge children they would previously have merely warned or admonished.

Even in relation to the children brought before the Court prior to the introduction of probation, most were charged with petty theft or riotous behaviour, and in the six months to 30 August 1901, for example, only 56 of the 243 children convicted in Sydney courts were committed to an industrial school or reformatory. The rest, about 75 per cent, were either fined or detained for brief periods of 24–48 hours. It was this population of children, who would previously have been released after a brief spell in a court room or a prison cell, who were to be the ones put on probation and supervised at home for much longer periods of time. Although there was a slight drop after 1905, the proportion sent to reformatory and industrial schools recovered to its previous level by 1909 and remained roughly the same until the 1930s (van Krieken 1985).

There was also no place given to church involvement in the rhetoric, but in some states it did recover from the 'emptying of the barracks' which boarding-out was meant to signify. The Catholic Church in particular, ever fearful for its flock, responded to the closure of its Sydney orphan school by opening other, smaller orphanages. Five orphanages had been opened by 1886—in Manly, Singleton, Bathurst, Goulburn and Albury—and by 1899 another five were opened in or near Sydney (Horsburgh 1982: 275). Protestant involvement was to follow later with the Burnside Homes at Parramatta, and the Church of England also opened homes for girls. The church institutions were in turn incorporated into the SCRB's work: they were an alternative location for specific categories of children, and Mackellar in particular regarded church homes as ideal for girls, given what he saw as their greater resistance to moral reform once they had 'fallen'. As he put it in 1913:

> Many authorities ... are emphatic in their view that certain classes of girls—namely, those who are sexually immoral and those of a hysterical, incorrigible type—cannot be reformed in reformatories. Stress is everywhere laid on the necessity for the intervention in this work of religious organisations, and with this I am in hearty agreement (Mackellar 1913: 1224).

Not that this view was necessarily shared by, say, the administrators of the Industrial School for Girls—in fact there was quite some opposition—but it did exert a significant influence on relations between church and state institutions, and in turn on their relations with government agencies.

Church organisations also became involved through the probation system. In 1908 the St Vincent de Paul Society was approached to provide Honorary Probation Officers. A meeting of the Society was told that: '... officers, owing to their other duties, could only visit each boy once a month, and that, while they might satisfy themselves that the boys attended school they could not watch over their attendance at Church and Sunday School' (St Vincent de Paul Miscellaneous Material, MI K15498).

The brothers were exhorted to help in the reformation of Catholic boys—apparently Catholic girls did not require this assistance—and the brothers responded to the call, as did Protestant and Church of England groups.

Economic reality, ideological change and family life

The growth of child welfare was part of a broad range of developments generally affecting relations between the state, children and the family in industrial societies around the turn of the century. First, the political characteristics of Australian society in this period which distinguished it from the previous 50 years, and which seem particularly significant in relation to child welfare, were the continuing change in class relations and the increasing degree of state intervention, both into the structure of economic relations and into civil society as a whole. Although it is important to emphasise that any increasing affluence among skilled workers was accompanied by either continued or increasing poverty for the unskilled (Fisher 1982), it is also true that in general terms the increasing political organisation and activity of the labour movement from the 1870s on was to produce a working class which, even if it did not achieve improved wages and conditions, had a leadership which believed they could be achieved through parliamentary reform and state intervention.

As the labour movement became more organised, its leadership slowly penetrated parliament and the organisations of party politics, and continued to operate in terms of class integration and consensus, despite the occasional outbreak of serious and overt class conflict in particular disputes. Connell and Irving speak of the 'institutionalisation' of working-class intellectuals and argue that by 1900 'there was a single intellectual milieu, where liberal and labour intellectuals met to produce the discourse of labourism' (Connell and Irving 1980: 201). The state was regarded as the agency which could redress the grievances workers had with employers, the main one being the lack of a living wage for many workers. As Macarthy puts it:

> The broad strategy of labour's policy was to act on governments as an alternative source of strength. State authority was increasingly conceived as a reservoir of power which could, by astute manipulation, be harnessed to provide a countervailing force to employers' industrial hegemony. In effect, labour worked to extend state intervention in economic and social affairs to support wage earners' direct and immediate interests (Macarthy 1967: 74).

This is not to deny that the bourgeoisie also regarded the state as a potential troubleshooter, particularly through the legal system and police action like breaking up strikes. Certainly the sort of state regulation and intervention being proposed by the labour movement and liberal reformers did not threaten their essential interests enough to produce coherent and effective opposition.

The period was thus characterised by a statism, a political reliance on the state as problem-solver, and it was not until the 1960s that the dominance of this philosophy of state intervention was to be challenged. As Stephen Garton has put it, around the turn of the century 'there was a general agreement, across a broad political spectrum, that the state was a tool that should be used more extensively for the reconciliation of social conflict and the amelioration of its consequences' (Garton 1982: 161; see also Roe 1976a). This was clearly a political context very favourable to updating and renovating strategies for old issues, like crime and social order, which refused to go away.

The political environment of state expansion encouraged not only reforms in child welfare itself, but also in other areas which would in turn have their own impact on child welfare agencies. The stricter enforcement of compulsory education, for example, gave child welfare authorities the work of chasing truants, running truant schools and licensing street-trading and child performances in order to get most of them back into school. School attendance also became an important criterion by which the suitability of a family environment was judged.

Not that things all went the one way: various community associations, committees and church groups continued attempting to curb state expansion. The churches in particular were engaged in a running battle with the government, especially in areas like child welfare and education. In more recent debates it has been suggested that the associations of civil society persist largely because they are in many ways useful to state agencies, forming a flexible communications link between the bureaucracy and the electorate, and there seems little reason to doubt this view (Mowbray 1980).

The probation system in its early days, for example, gave religious bodies, like the St Vincent de Paul Society, a significant role to play through the use of an Honorary Probation Officer system. Charles Mackellar, in a dispute with the New South Wales Minister of Public Instruction, argued for the appropriateness of church homes for reforming girls, and the state continued to support non-government bodies in one form or another. State officials may attempt to control the form and activity of non-government organisations, but few seemed to have either the inclination or the ability to abolish them altogether. The general pattern was nonetheless one of a definite tendency towards centralisation and state expansion, of a blurring of the boundary, a sort of osmosis, between the state and civil society, with minor undercurrents of private and church associations tugging the other way which have never been completely eliminated. In fact one could argue that they are currently experiencing a revival.

This general environment of state interventionism was one of the key political conditions allowing for expansion and development in child welfare. A second one was what John Gillis calls the 'institutionalisation of adolescence', with institutionalisation used loosely to include supervision and organisation. Discussing juvenile delinquency in England between 1890 and 1914, Gillis makes the point that for working-class youth, the increasing organisation of their lives, in the form of schools and youth organisations, was both unnecessary and illegitimate. In Australia their street-trading was a much needed supplement to the family income, and schools certainly did not appear to have much immediate purpose or promise.

Child welfare agencies also had their own contribution to make: by 1915 the proportion of the New South Wales' population under 20 either institutionalised or supervised by child welfare institutions and agencies was nearly double that of 1881—1 per cent—with probation and boarding-out accounting for most of the increase (van Krieken 1985). It was equally true for Australia that resistance to being organised and supervised in turn,

> ... came to be interpreted as evidence of anti-social tendencies on the part of all adolescents, thereby justifying further protective legislation. A reinforcing cycle of organization and resistance continued for almost two decades until the model of organized adolescence became more widely accepted (Gillis 1975: 97).

If one asks why adolescence became institutionalised, one has to turn to the major transformations taking place in the experience of childhood and youth, especially for the working class, which had both economic and political underpinnings.

In economic terms the picture is an untidy one. One could argue that with industrialisation the nature of work was changing such that the 'distance' between a child and a competent adult worker was increasing, forcing working-class children and youth out of work and into a socially detached existence, which encouraged delinquency and attracted attempts to organise youth. The trouble is that things were not so straightforward. Complaints about aimless youth date back much further (Pinchbeck and Hewitt 1969, 1973; Pearson 1983), and at this time school only affected children up to the age of fourteen. According to Keating, the workforce participation rate of 15–19 year olds in 1911 was 85 per cent for males (until the mid 1930s) and 42 per cent for females (rising gradually) (Keating 1973: 340–1). Even for those under fourteen, in unskilled areas like factory work it made sense to employ juveniles, and there was a demand for child labour. In 1910, for example, the Minister for Labour and Industry was told that with respect to child labour ' . . . competition was perhaps never so keen as at present, and the demand for boys and girls is very great' (Report to the Minister of Labour . . . on the Factories and Shops Act 1910: 575).

On the other hand, Keating's workforce participation rates for 10–14 year olds belie this assessment, being 15 per cent for boys and 2 per cent for girls (Keating 1973: 340–1). Even allowing for an under-representation in the figures, the great majority of 10–14 year olds appear not to have been working. Similarly, the sectors of the workforce where educational requirements were rising (the service sector, shops and offices) were growing: the service sector accounted for 48 per cent of employment by 1910–11 and 51 per cent in 1920–21. Unfortunately, I cannot obtain figures for the period prior to 1910, but one would assume they would have been lower (Industries Assistance Commission 1977: 4).

Very tentatively, then, one can argue that the overall trend was that heavier demands were being made on the workforce, so that it made increasing economic sense to put children and youth through some sort of 'preparation' imposed compulsorily by the state before they entered the workforce. One has to be tentative about this, however, given that it does not explain what the delinquency problem was supposed to be with 15–19 year olds, and given the counter-tendency of de-skilling: within a given capitalist economy it is always possible to find sectors requiring little or no education. Besides, we do not know whether schooling really did 'prepare' children for work any better than no schooling at all. My own assessment is that for working-class youth this argument about delayed adulthood only gains real strength around the 1920s, for that was when the workforce participation of 15–19 year olds declined dramatically (Keating 1973: 340–1).

We can afford to be less tentative if we look at the matter in political terms, with the idea that the state should be 'doing something' about children and youth gaining support from a number of quarters. For the middle class the period was a high point in its attempts to shape society and 'the nation' in its own image, with the working class, and especially working-class children, being the main focus of its attention. The health of the nation had to be improved, if not for the sake of science in itself, then for reasons such as disease. Ill-health could spread and, besides, it was unpleasant to look at. Stunted, unhealthy boys made poor soldiers, and the poor health of mothers and babies was worrying to those who saw a connection between population size and a nation's capacity to fight and win wars.

Alongside infant mortality, the declining birth rate also became a target of investigation and concern with Mackellar, at the head of the Royal Commission into the declining birth rate, lamenting the spreading use of contraception (Hicks 1978). The Boer War had revealed the extent of ill-health among British slum children, and this in turn generated anxiety among some intellectuals about the health of working-class youth within a general theory of 'urban degeneration' (Davison 1983: 143–74).

Another aspect of this degeneration was juvenile crime and delinquency, with factory work now being blamed for the delinquency and larrikinism of youth over the age of fourteen (Connell and Irving 1980: 206). This concern and the anxiety about urban degeneration was not in itself new: it was as old as cities themselves. What was new was the willingness of middle-class groups to do something about it. Kindergartens, playgrounds and baby health centres were established, particularly in working-class areas. Workers' housing was built and supervised, and slums were cleared. Child protection legislation was passed and various youth organisations—such as the YMCA, YWCA, the Boys' Brigade, the Scouts and Girl Guides—were established to 'keep them off the streets' (Maunders 1984).

Intellectual developments like Social Darwinism, eugenics, the genesis of child psychology and psychological measurement, as well as the psychiatric profession's own interest in expanding its territory, fed into this kind of concern, so that medically and psychologically 'scientifically' supervising and restructuring the working class became an obvious course of action for the state and its officials (Garton 1982; for a discussion of Social Darwinism in Australia, see Goodwin 1964). It was in this period, for example, that Mackellar became interested in feeble-mindedness, coming back from overseas trips with a lengthy report and recommendations about what should be done about the feeble-minded: psychological measurement and intervention almost took on the appearance of a panacea which would solve the more intractable child welfare problems, much as boarding-out was to have done before it (e.g. SCRB AR 1914: 819; Mackellar 1913: 1224).

While working-class families were the target of most of this reform and improvement, it is difficult to pin down a uniform and coherent working-class response to it all. For a great deal of the respectable working class, education was seen as a means of upward mobility. In the interests of equality it was to be made available to all, with 'making available' in practice being experienced as coercion by some. The labour movement itself required organisation, and working-class adults as much as bourgeois ones saw value in channelling youthful energy into useful pursuits. If there was argument along class lines, it was more about what was useful and how the organisation was achieved, rather than being about the idea of organisation and social control itself. Hence the attitude of the working class to the institutionalisation of youth was largely ambivalent—there were both drawbacks and advantages, which explains the combination of overall accommodation, with sporadic resistance, against initiatives like schooling, kindergartens, youth organisations and child welfare.

This point is illustrated even more vividly in relation to the third question of the familial morality—the norms and values around what constitutes a 'good', 'appropriate' family environment—which surrounded child welfare intervention. The respectable working class was itself aspiring to a 'bourgeois' family form of getting married and having fewer children, a sexual division of labour and a suburban lifestyle—the agitation of both male labour and feminist groups converged on this ideal (Game and Pringle 1983). The evil of capitalism, it seemed, was not that it imposed this family form, but that it did not allow the material conditions of its existence. The focus of labour movement politics was thus the attainment of a (male) living wage, one which would support a whole family, and the regulation of children's and women's work to fit with that primary concern—at a heavy cost, of course, to those women wanting economic independence for any reason.

If we agree with Connell and Irving that the significance of the 1907 Harvester Judgement on the basic wage 'was that it enshrined the concept of the family wage, thus confirming that the working-class woman's place was in the home, where she was expected to produce at least three children' (Connell and Irving 1980: 204), we can hardly go on to agree with their general picture of the working-class family being 'renovated' by the bourgeoisie, given that the family wage was precisely a long-awaited victory for the labour movement. The impetus towards a 'bourgeois' family form, in other words, came as much if not more from within the working class itself—albeit for different reasons for men and women—as from bourgeois attempts to remould working-class families.

The point is that as the working class's standard of living increased, albeit unevenly, its desire for a more comfortable life was, as Ali de Regt says for the Netherlands, partly 'preformed' (de Regt 1984: 101) by the example of a middle-class family lifestyle. Far from being imposed through state intervention, it came to be seen as equivalent to a higher standard of living, as well as being structured by the material conditions of working-class life. The times when working-class families had cause to resist and rebel were largely when middle-class reformers and social workers tried to insist on conformity to the standards of middle-class family life prior to its material, economic basis being laid—that is, in a situation where their wage and working conditions made cultivated

domesticity a nonsense. Jane Lewis, for example, emphasises that
in the English situation:

> All women's groups recognized the importance of economic
> assistance to mothers ... if they were to be able to improve their
> own health and that of their families. Feminist groups were anxious
> to increase the status of motherhood by securing a financial reward
> for mothers' services (Lewis 1980: 190).

This is, of course, why the object of the male labour movement and
feminists' struggles ranged between improving their wages and
conditions and securing state economic assistance for families, so
that they too could enjoy a respectable lifestyle.

These general developments are evidenced in child welfare in a
number of ways. Throughout the period the general tone of the
official references to the working-class family changed. More and
more emphasis was laid on 'rescuing the rising generation' by
working through the family, supporting existing families, rather
than simply removing their children to an institution. The pattern
of state intervention also became more supportive of a particular
family form. After the introduction of boarding-out to one's own
mother—in effect a (meagre) Deserted Wives' and Widows'
Pension—the number of children so supported by the state grew
considerably and significantly, in both relative and absolute terms
(up to nearly 1 per cent of the population under 20 by 1915 (van
Krieken 1985). The state was thus making the lives of families
without a male breadwinner somewhat easier, but doing so within
the overall framework of women's economic weakness and dependency. It acted more to substitute for the absent father—the state
as father—than to establish the conditions under which single
parent families could survive independently.

As well as these general developments—statism, institutionalisation of youth, increasing popularity of the nuclear family—there
were the forces from within child welfare agencies themselves: the
reformers' zeal, the interest of those working in the area to expand
their territory, the fact that the agencies had to expand in absolute
terms just to keep up with the population increase. However, it is
difficult to ascribe as much weight to the influence of reformers
like Guillaume and Mackellar's project of 'reform through legislation' on the development of child welfare as some historians have
in the past (Dickey 1977; Jaggs 1986: 45–59), as there was a whole
network, extending beyond those reformers themselves, at work in
the development of child welfare. Although it is difficult to establish with any precision, it seems more plausible to argue that it was
the political context of the period which laid the ideological foundations for the rationalisation and reform of child welfare through-

out Australia. One need not argue that the general context 'produced' child welfare reform, or made it 'necessary', but it did establish a social environment which enabled, and certainly did not prevent, key individuals like Mackellar and Guillaume to bring about change.

The general increase in state intervention into family life was thus part of a wider range of political, economic and social developments, which were to continue into the 1920s and 1930s. As far as the precise role that the state played is concerned, can we conclude, as Connell and Irving do, that the family and the community 'was a source of weakness for the working class', which was why it 'became a site of cultural intervention by the state' in order to 'reconstruct bourgeois culture' (Connell and Irving 1980: 202)? Can we see child welfare, as some writers have recently, as part of the assertion of state control over family life, a process of social 'gardening' in which the state brought about the 'embourgeoisement' of working-class family life?

The evidence available on Australian child welfare leads me to reject these kinds of approaches for white Australian families, and accept them with major modifications for Aboriginal families. As was said before, the coercion driving white children and families to child welfare came far less from state officials than from either poverty itself or the parents, relatives and neighbours of the children concerned. One can easily produce dramatic examples of the heartless and cruel things done by state officials to some impoverished families, but the problem is that these constituted a minority of cases.

On the whole, the criteria of intervention corresponded too much with more widespread norms and values to be considered simply as 'bourgeois'. The families dealt with by child welfare authorities lay on the outskirts of the working class as a whole: the heartland was already well and truly captured by the 'bourgeois' family. The white working class shared a range of familial morals with the middle class for some very good and practical reasons: cleanliness, for example, was more than a mere bourgeois obsession. If nothing else it was an important means of maintaining one's pride in the face of poverty (McCalman 1984: 20–9), and it was important that one's neighbours also maintained certain standards:

> The dirty and the unrespectable were far more of a trial for the
> people who had to live near them. Dirty households harboured
> vermin and respectable families waged constant war against lice, bed
> bugs and rats that were not of their making. And they were forced
> to live under a moral stigma that was equally not of their making
> (p. 46).

Sobriety, too, was as practically important to working-class wives as it was in ideological terms to the middle class, given that it was largely their husbands who drank away their meagre earnings and made keeping a family together even more difficult (p. 29).

In relation to the white population, the child welfare system relied heavily on the cooperation of parents, relatives, neighbours and civic-minded citizens, most of whom one would have difficulty calling 'bourgeois'. Events in Australia paralleled those in England where in 1896–97, 58 per cent of the child abuse complaints made to the National Society for the Prevention of Cruelty to Children (NSPCC) came from the general public, 24 per cent from salaried officials like police officers and teachers, and 18 per cent from the personal investigations of the NSPCC. A decade later, the proportion of cases discovered by the NSPCC itself had fallen to 10 per cent. English working-class men and women 'did confide in the cruelty men', and although the work of NSPCC inspectors did often involve imposition and coercion, 'they were much more likely to be regarded as useful allies in the struggle of the poor to maintain neighbourhood respectability' (Behlmer 1982: 172).

The Australian evidence on child welfare supports this view. The state operated not as a bourgeois gardener or social engineer, restructuring working-class families, but in an alliance with the working class's 'struggle for respectability'. That many would resist that move to respectability, especially children and youth, and that men and women defined it differently, does not detract from its overall strength as a tendency within the working class as a whole, nor from the fact that state intervention into family life was more another product of general cultural and political developments than an instrument in bringing those changes about.

For Aboriginal families and children, however, the story is different, as we cannot speak of a similar convergence of views on how social progress would best be achieved, or an overlapping of value systems. Their position remained a marginal one, and they were given no place in white society except when their cultural and familial identity and social forms were left behind. Children were removed almost entirely against the will of their parents, to be brought up in white families and apprenticed to white employers. Unlike white children who came into the state's control, far greater care was taken to ensure that they never saw their parents or family again. They were often given new names, and the greater distances involved in rural areas made it easier to prevent parents and children on separate missions from tracing each other. Reformers had long espoused the virtue of rural settings in more effectively separating children from their 'vicious' urban environment, particularly their parents, but this philosophy was most efficiently realised in relation to Australia's Aboriginal population. Between 1909 and 1916 the New South Wales Aborigines Protection Board had removed 400 such children, and although similar figures are not available for other parts of Australia, one can only assume that they were at least similar, and probably higher in states such as Queensland and Western Australia. In their case state intervention did bring about a radical and wholly unwanted change in family relationships.

6 The system consolidated, 1915–1940

Australian historians of child welfare have shown least interest of all in the period after 1915, creating the general impression that it was somehow less interesting, the landscape flatter and duller than it had been between the introduction of boarding-out in the 1870s and the establishment of the Children's Court and a probation system in the early 1900s. John Ramsland and Joan Brown stop their studies of New South Wales and Tasmania around 1900, (Ramsland 1986; Brown 1972) and Brian Dickey's very cursory treatment of the inter-war years (Dickey 1980: 153–6) contrasts with his detailed discussions of the events between 1850 and 1915 (Dickey 1968, 1977, 1979). It is as if all the really meaningful and dramatic things had been said and done by the child-saving reformers, leaving only faceless bureaucrats to either crank the machinery set up in 1905 or to replace 'all by rule and account' (Dickey 1980: 154). Barbalet's work on the South Australian experience stands out as the most serious and detailed discussion of the period, and it is worth examining whether her more nuanced observations on boarding-out are applicable to the parallel developments throughout Australia (Barbalet 1983).

To say that child welfare 'took on an increasingly bureaucratic air' (Dickey 1980: 153) does take us some of the way towards capturing the atmosphere of the period, but it is more precise to say that child welfare gradually became absorbed and integrated into the administrative apparatus of the state bureaucracy as a whole. There was ongoing conflict over organisational territory and power between the old guard, such as Catherine Spence and

Charles Mackellar, and the new generation of public service bureaucrats, and one could argue that in the end the bureaucrats and the push for integration into the state bureaucracy 'won'. In New South Wales, for example, the SCRB and the office of President had been abolished by 1923, and a Child Welfare Department (CWD) created which was much more clearly subordinate to the Minister of Public Instruction. The lack of secondary historical literature on this period also means that in this chapter I will be necessarily more dependent on my own work on New South Wales, so you will have to forgive a neglect of what has to be assumed were similar developments in other states.

Bureaucracy, social science and Australian historiography

Two historiographical points will emerge from my discussion of the period up to 1940. The first relates to the temptation to equate the evolution of state welfare bureaucracies with expansion in size, centralisation and an increasing degree of intervention into social and family life. To understand adequately the specifics of the historical development of child welfare, one needs to draw on a wider range of concepts than 'increased state intervention' or an expanding 'tutelary complex': economic and political conditions changed in a very particular way, as did theories of juvenile delinquency and how to prevent it, but the effects of these changes were also varied and complex. For example, in this period the proportion of the New South Wales population under the age of 20 declined in child welfare institutions, both government and non-government, from 0.31 per cent in 1915 to 0.19 per cent in 1940, and there was also a decline in absolute numbers from 2320 in institutional care in 1915 to 2017 in 1940 (van Krieken 1985).

It is also true that youth leisure was organised more systematically, largely in order to prevent delinquency, but more by non-government organisations than state agencies. Equally important was the shift in the state's activity towards more mundane matters like cash transfers to single mothers, in the form of the boarding-out allowance, as well as the ongoing critique and discussion of the violence apparently integral to the treatment of children in institutional care. Together with the very basic question of administrative competence, these issues were the focus of the political attention paid to child welfare in the 1920s and 1930s.

The second point concerns the question of the impact of scientific and technical rationality on Australian social life since 1900. The wider ideological and political context was one of an emphasis on social efficiency, rationality, and a scientific approach to the

management of social problems. One of the more notable characteristics of child welfare between 1923 and 1940 was the attempt
to render it more scientific, systematic and efficient. The political
atmosphere of the period has been described as one of a 'faith in
the power of an expert bureaucracy to apply technological and
scientific skills for the betterment of all society' (Roe 1976: 184), a
faith which resonated with American Progressivism as well as
English Fabianism. Social Darwinism constituted a very flexible
sociological and political utilisation of natural scientific concepts,
with its arguments being used to support both laissez-faire policies
and the notion of a strong, interventionist state (Goodwin 1964;
see also Laurent 1986). Carol Bacchi argued that the hard-headed,
deterministic emphasis on heredity and biology in the harsher
inter-war years—with leading intellectuals like R.J.A. Berry influential in disseminating a concern with 'mental defectiveness' and
'feeble-mindedness' as a solution to social problems (Cawte
1986)—was preceded by a more optimistic environmentalism
before World War I (Bacchi 1980). However, Stephen Garton has
pointed out the prior appearance of concerns with 'mental defectiveness' in the early years of the twentieth century (Garton
1986b). Further afield, other writers have traced the characteristics
of a scientific approach in sociology (Bourke 1981), education
(Connell 1980: 24–35, 63–75; McCallum 1983; Cashen 1985),
urban reform (Davison 1983), psychiatry (Garton 1988), criminal
law (Garton 1986a) and child welfare (Garton 1986b).

A major problem with this literature is its concentration on
supposedly influential 'men of ideas' and the ways in which particular ideas about a scientific approach circulated around the
intellectual networks of Australia's leading doctors, lawyers, psychiatrists and politicians, without going on to deal with the more
difficult problem of identifying how those ideas, strategies and
institutional forms were translated into practice. In Stephen
Garton's examination of Charles Mackellar's reception of eugenicist ideas, for example, he emphasises the role and impact of 'a
small but influential group of doctors and social reformers influenced by prevailing medical and psychiatric theory', arguing that
these reformers 'had the means to introduce eugenic schemes into
their areas of operation' (Garton 1986b: 34, 28). The difficulty
here is that the evidence on the actual impact of such schemes on
the day-to-day workings of the organisations concerned is far from
secure.

While Garton is persuasive about the impact of psychiatry on
criminal law (Garton 1986a), in relation to child welfare in the
period 1900–1914 he is less so. He suggests the impact of
Mackellar's concern with feeble-mindedness is demonstrated by

the increased numbers of children in cottage homes intended to be oriented towards mentally defective children, in 'specialised residential care'. However, he does not examine the practical reality of that so-called specialised care (Garton 1986b: 33). One needs to go some way beyond the history of ideas, discourses and institutional forms to examine the reality of everyday practices.

While the advocates of the new scientific rationality may have thought that 'they held the key to grounding social policy in "science" rather than "morality" ' (Garton 1986b: 28), we cannot go on to assume that their ideas correspond to what actually took place. As well as identifying the ways in which movements to effect a rational, scientific management of personal relationships and domestic life have developed and perhaps succeeded, it is also worth identifying their limits, and discovering what happens when one approaches the new discourses of rational management with some scepticism (Reiger 1985).

In relation to education, the turn from morality to science was often seen as a form of naive sentimentalism. There was 'considerable public disquiet over what were seen as attempts to explain away delinquency and end punishment for juvenile offences' (Cashen 1985: 80). This reinforces Jill Roe's more general observation on social policy in this period, that nineteenth-century attitudes 'did not merely survive; they were actively reinforced' (Roe 1976b: 106). The South Australian Education Department's truancy officers continued to see their everyday practices as a response to breakdowns in parental control, and 'the psychological "paradigm" ... applied in the assessment and treatment of the "problem" [of truancy] emerges as crude, ill-conceived and generally directionless' (Cashen 1985: 83). It is therefore essential to investigate the possibility that the changes which did occur operated primarily at the level of language and terminology, while everyday institutional practices either remained roughly the same, or changed in response to other and quite distinct social developments.

Organisation, control and administration

A central feature of the mechanics of the process of incorporation of child welfare into the larger state bureaucracy was the Inquiry or Royal Commission. In New South Wales there was a conflict over the administration of the SCRB immediately after Charles Mackellar's departure as President, with a Public Service Board (PSB) inquiry which in 1915 reported 'an unsatisfactory condition

... as to methods of organisation' (Report on the General Organisation, Control and Administration. ... Welfare Institutions, 1934/5, 1:176). The system of boarding children out to foster families was also criticised in 1918, with allegations of both ill-treatment of boarded-out children and cruelty in the Mittagong Farm Homes.

Responsibility for the institutions was split between the SCR Department and the Department of Public Instruction, and there was still a range of separate Acts to be administered, which generated constant conflict between the SCRB and Public Instruction in relation to the running of the child welfare institutions, with an Inquiry in 1915–17 and a Royal Commission in 1920. The Royal Commissioner, G. Mason Allard, examined all the institutions in detail and reported on their conditions, administration and classification of inmates. However, instead of producing what Mackellar sought, a condemnation of Public Instruction, Allard produced the exact opposite: a damning critique of the SCRB which effectively sounded its death-knell; a fine example of unintended consequences.

A part of the Mittagong Farm Homes had been gazetted as an Industrial School for Boys, and there Allard found 'considerable looseness in respect to the reception of inmates'. They contained boys who had committed no offence, and in his view 'there should be no children in the industrial school section who have not been committed from the children's courts'. He found different cases of children 'improperly ... associated', and felt that they 'might be grouped in separate homes very much more appropriately and in fairness to the boys concerned'. The Home for Cripples contained a wide variety of types of cases, and Ormond House also mixed girls who had committed no offence with those who had, leading Allard to complain that 'it is incomprehensible how the mixing of children in this fashion was ever permitted, and how it can ever have been allowed to continue for so long'.

The boys' civil liberties were clearly being infringed: there were delays in their release when no 'suitable' relative or guardian could be found, and if the boys misbehaved or did not get on with their foster parents, rather than being dealt with by the courts they were sometimes simply returned to the MFHB, 'and thus the delinquent is condemned for some alleged new offence to what he regards as penal detention without the benefit of a trial in the courts provided' (p. 179).

Allard had even more to say about the Raymond Terrace Home for 'feeble-minded' boys, in what amounts to a telling criticism of the practical application of the concept 'feeble-minded'. He found that although the inmates were classified as 'mentally weak', they

had been given no medical examination and 'an important witness' had stated 'that these inmates are by no means all feeble-
minded, but that the authorities apparently consider that if a boy
has been guilty of some immorality, he must be regarded as such'.
Allard also found that their records were so poorly organised that
it was impossible to say where they should be sent.

At this point Allard could contain himself no longer, and said
that 'it would be much better—strange enough though it may seem
that the recommendation should have to be made—if more for-
mality were to be observed' (Royal Commission into the Public
Service 1920: 476). Remarks like these cannot be taken at face
value, but at the very least they indicate that the SCRB was not
held in very high regard by important sections of the New South
Wales state bureaucracy. Allard recommended the establishment of
a separate department, administered in a manner similar to Public
Health, and shortly after Thomas Mutch became Minister, Walter
Bethel became the first Secretary of the Child Welfare Department
(CWD) in 1923.

Jack Lang and Widows' Pensions

The CWD appeared to be in administrative paralysis in its first
years, with no Annual Report appearing until 1927. However, the
appearance of this Report coincided with a new upheaval which
threw child welfare in New South Wales into turmoil for another
three years. Lang argued in 1926 that the Widows' Pension Act
had relieved the CWD of 'considerable work' (*NSWPD* 111, 10
March 1927: 2223). Lang's Treasury Under-Secretary, Chapman,
asked the Auditor-General, Coghlan, to provide a special report on
the extent of the decrease in the CWD's workload, the cause of a
number of overpayments to widows, and 'whether proper precau-
tions are taken to ensure that payments ... are made only to
genuinely deserted wives or widows' (Inquiry into the Child Welfare Department 1927: 676).

The subsequent Auditor-General's report claimed that the CWD
had been deficient on all these points, but it was subsequently
defended in a Public Service Report which attributed any overpayments to the CWD being understaffed. The dispute spilled over
into Parliament, and Lang appointed a Royal Commissioner who
also reported to Lang along lines similar to the PSB's report
(Report on the General Organisation ... etc. 1934: 182).

The closer one looks at Lang's role, the more central it appears,
and the more the inquiry seems to have been politically rather
than economically motivated. Mutch considered Lang to be

responsible for initiating the investigation, and in Parliament he made the point that Lang could easily have approached him before sending Coghlan off on the hunt, and that the questions the inquiry centred on implied maladministration in themselves. Lang adopted a posture of lofty detachment, saying it was all Chapman's idea (*NSWPD* 111, 10 March 1927: 2233), but this makes little sense in terms of how he otherwise dealt with bureaucrats and Cabinet Ministers. He held senior public servants in contempt, being of the opinion that they were there simply to do their Minister's bidding, and he prided himself on the absolute control he had over them (Dixson 1976: 227–8). He had sacked two previous Treasury Under-Secretaries (Lang 1980: 171–7; 1970: 60), and no doubt Chapman was his personal choice. Lang was certainly never innocent about anything he put his name to (Lang 1980: 173). It is really very improbable that the initiative and motivation came from anyone other than Lang himself.

The fact that Lang approved of Coghlan's inquiries, focusing as they did on the deservedness of women receiving aid, casts an interesting light on his stated concern for widows and deserted wives. In *I Remember* he tells us how when his father was made an invalid, 'I realised just how hard the world could be on a mother bringing up young children', and that he would attempt to ensure that widows were properly supported. One day 'the widow was to be freed from the haunting spectre of destitution' (Lang 1980: 219–20), and he saw the 1926 Widows' Pensions Act as the fulfilment of that objective. Miriam Dixson refers to Lang's 'eternal wariness' as to whether bureaucrats were humiliating widows or subjecting applicants to inquisitorial questions (Dixson 1976: 37), but it was precisely this inquisitorial spirit which lay at the heart of the inquiry Lang initiated.

In public at least, Mutch was less severe than Lang about the policing of morals and deservedness. He regarded the payment of boarding-out allowances to children's own mothers as discretionary rather than as an entitlement, but only within the framework of the Department's general responsibilities. So if a mother were 'drunk and dirty and disreputable', the Department's policy 'would be to take the child away from her as an incompetent person' rather than pay her the allowance, but the Children's Court would take that attitude in any case. In general, said Mutch, it was problematic to set oneself up as moral censor. 'Even if a mother is immoral,' he said, 'the child has to be fed, and the child's welfare is the thing that concerns us.' For Mutch, the mother's morals were only relevant to the extent that they clearly had a negative effect on the child. Asked whether an allowance would be paid to a woman living with another man, Mutch said that it should 'so long as the

mother is a clean, decent woman . . . the home conditions are good
. . . the mother keeps them clean and well clothed and fed, and
sends them to school' (Inquiry into Child Welfare Department
1927: 682).

Similarly, the Victorian CWD Secretary argued in 1924 that
they 'consider the saving of the mother as of as much importance
as that of the child' (Vic. CWD AR 1924: 11). Mutch placed less
emphasis on the mother's marital status and sexual relations than
Lang, who focused on a case where a widow had been unjustly
accused of living with a man who was really her brother-in-law, the
implication being that if the accusation were just, the allowance
should not be paid. Lang had a much more selective view of
'genuine deservedness'.

More important than Lang's principles, however, is the light this
episode throws on a number of important aspects of the changes
which had taken place in child welfare by the 1920s. Firstly, the
pattern of finances had changed significantly from the early days of
boarding-out, with a rapidly growing number of women receiving
cash assistance. The figures for New South Wales almost doubled
from 7310 in 1915 to 12 839 in 1920 (Statistical Register of NSW;
SCRB Annual Reports; CWD Annual Reports). In Victoria they
increased similarly from around 5000 in 1917 to roughly 10 000 in
1930 (Jaggs 1986: 112–5). The granting of cash assistance had
become a major aspect of child welfare systems, alongside the
more traditional aspects like fostering and adoptions, running the
institutions and probation.

Secondly, the conflict with Lang in New South Wales was to a
large extent a demarcation dispute over how such a process of
providing cash should be administered. It was a battle between two
parts of the state bureaucracy over a new piece of territory, with
Lang determined to have it administered by the Treasury. Rather
than seeing his Widows' Pensions Act as 'merely an extension of
the current relief system administered by the Child Welfare and
Education Departments' (Nairn 1986: 157), Lang thought of it as a
partial alternative to that system, one which would police
deservedness more effectively. This episode illustrates nicely the
basic historical and theoretical point that 'the state' is not a mono-
lithic entity; disputes, conflicts and contradictions arose within the
state bureaucracy about exactly how state intervention into family
life should operate and what kind of morality it should embody. In
this area, at least, the state was very much contested terrain.

Thirdly, and partly due to the particular way the contest has
worked in Australian society and politics, state departments of
child welfare and education consistently had difficulty gaining the
resources they required for their expanding workload, with funds

and staff constantly below the level necessary to match performance to objectives. In his speech to Parliament in 1927 (*NSWPD*
111, 1926–27: 2221-33), Mutch gave an impassioned account of
how tight finances were for the CWD and how much pressure it
was being put under to cut and keep cutting its expenditure. What
might today be called a 'crisis' in the welfare state had become an
institutionalised feature of child welfare's incorporation into the
state bureaucracy. This in turn had long-term effects on the character of all the CWD's work, including the quality of its staff and
the manner in which its institutions were run.

Institutionalised violence

Violence had always been part of everyday life in child welfare
institutions, and in New South Wales it resurfaced again as the
object of a 1934 inquiry (*Sydney Morning Herald* 23 January 1934:
9), which supported allegations of brutality and bashings dating
back to 1928. Of more far-reaching significance, however, were the
questions raised about the administration of the CWD as a whole,
which were dealt with in a subsequent, wider-ranging inquiry into
the CWD by J.E. McCulloch (Report on the General Organisation
. . . Welfare Institutions, 1934/5).

McCulloch made a number of points about the administration of
the CWD. Firstly, he was surprised at the persistence of complaints about specific kinds of problems which appeared never to
be resolved and simply resurfaced time and again at regular inter-
vals. After surveying all the inquiries that had taken place since
1874, he remarked that 'in view of so many inquiries, the organisation and administration of the Child Welfare Department
should be nearly perfect' (Report on the General Organisation . . .
etc. 1934: 154). Instead, many of the current problems, which
included inadequate training and staff levels, cruel and excessive
punishment, and poor organisation, were old ones and many of his
recommendations had already been anticipated and simply not
adopted. Faced with explaining why the CWD was not in fact
perfect, McCulloch focused on the lack of training, and went on to
make the case for some professionalisation in the CWD, or at least
more extensive training of its staff.

Secondly, it was a particular individual, Alex Thompson, the
Secretary of the CWD, who bore the brunt of McCulloch's criticisms. McCulloch drew attention to the fact that Thompson had
cheerfully declared his disinterest in becoming familiar with child
welfare practices either overseas or in other Australian states, and

this lack of interest in the world beyond New South Wales ran counter to the tradition established by the early child welfare reformers (p. 144). McCulloch's assessment effectively put an end to Thompson's career, and he was replaced by C.T. Wood in 1935. Wood fared no better. In 1938 he was transferred back to the Department of Attorney-General and Justice, with the Minister, Drummond, saying that Wood was well-intentioned but not capable of dealing with the abuses under him. Drummond then went on to try and reorganise the whole Department and to draw up a new Child Welfare Act, which was not introduced until 1939 (*NSWPD* 145, 18 September 1935: 174).

McCulloch's assessment of Thompson was probably accurate, but his report nevertheless paid little attention to the CWD's financial state and its overall status within the Public Service. Thompson was the Secretary because he had been appointed to the job, and if he had indeed been promoted beyond his capacities, the question is how and why that had happened. That was a broader structural and political question which McCulloch was unable or unwilling to address. It was far easier to argue for some administrative reorganisation than to examine the underlying factors which produced the situation in the first place, and which would probably reproduce it: the promotions process in the Public Service, with its emphasis on seniority, and the overall status of child welfare in terms of its political significance, the level of funds and the quality of staff it could attract.

Scientific child welfare?

At a conceptual level there was a gradual development in this period towards what was presented as a more scientific understanding of child welfare practice. The nineteenth-century welfare reformers saw their reforming work as 'social science' and regarded it as being based on knowledge derived from experience, aiming at changing particular social conditions. However, the explanations remained at the rather homespun level of discussions of exemplary overseas institutions like Mettray and Rauhe Haus, the superiority of familial over institutional care, and the importance of school attendance and the child's moral environment. It was Mackellar who first added to that the contribution of psychology. In his 1913 report, 'The Treatment of Neglected and Delinquent Children in Great Britain, Europe and America', Mackellar emphasised the significance of mental defectiveness, its role in the production of delinquency, as well as the importance of doing something about it through systematic testing and psychological supervision of children passing through the SCRB's shelters, as well as the provision of a wide range of specialised institutions.

In his report Mackellar lent on the authority of a lecturer in psychological medicine from Sydney University, Andrew Davidson, who was attached to the Sydney Boys' Shelter in 1913. There the boys were given IQ tests by the Superintendent and then examined more generally by Davidson; the girls did not require an IQ test, as their problem was usually defined as 'sexual depravity'. Although psychological testing became a permanent feature of child welfare, given the prevailing notion of an intimate relation between immorality and mental deficiency it is very likely that testing operated in a rather haphazard fashion. We should here recall Allard's observations in his 1920 report, in which he found that in practice children were often committed to an institution for the feeble-minded without having been tested at all, and the children regarded as immoral were often automatically considered to be 'mentally weak'.

By the 1930s there was a 'Psychological Clinic' attached to the Children's Court in Sydney. Boys were examined there 'to determine the causes of delinquency and to provide information to the Department's Officers and Social Workers of a nature to assist them in the work they have to perform' (CWD AR 1930–31: 535). Again, what real use the information might have had is unclear; for example, the 1930–31 CWD Annual Report informs us that among boys of 'superior' intelligence are usually found thieves and car-thieves, 'as it usually found that such lads possess a fund of information beyond the ordinary, and are well above average intelligence' (CWD AR 1930–31: 535). Beyond this sort of thing we get little idea of the substantive role, if any, that IQ testing really played. By the mid 1930s vocational guidance and testing—again, for boys only—had been absorbed into the CWD's routine, and superintendents and departmental officers made increasing use of the tests to inform and justify their decisions and practices (for South Australia, see Barbalet 1983: 129–30).

The theoretical basis for psychological and vocational testing came from outside child welfare agencies, usually via education departments (Cashen 1985), but from within child welfare a body of theory was also being developed around a topic it could consider uniquely its own: probation. Probably the main vehicle for the production of probation theory was the conference, and the first conference of probation officers in New South Wales was held in March 1912, at the Metropolitan Boys' Shelter. Sydney Maxted's paper was largely a public relations morale-boosting exercise on the history of probation and the wonderful effect it was having on family life in New South Wales, but the one by Jenkins was a more practical piece on the dos and don'ts of probation.

The basic argument was a variation on the old 'rescuing the rising generation' theme: in order to produce good citizens effectively one had to educate children rather than punish them, and this would be achieved largely through educating the parents, especially the mother. 'Where good mothers are there will be good children. The mother has to bear the brunt of the battle.' Turning a boy 'debased by the appalling effect of Saturday night's drunken brawls' into a 'healthy moral citizen' was only possible if the home environment was put on 'a higher plane'. Jenkins was aware of the economic constraints involved: 'No one, unless positively vicious, would live in a squalid home if it could be avoided; but the demand above the supply of homes renders it impossible to obtain classy houses for the industrious people'. Still, he continued, 'all homes might reasonably be expected to be kept clean; and a home is generally what the inmates make it' (SCRB AR 1912: 810–22).

This basic goal of educating good mothers was also supplemented with some principles of practising probation. To paraphrase:

- 'There is good in every child—a successful probation officer will discover it and work on it.'
- Reform is best achieved through gentle encouragement rather than compulsion—it is important to secure the child's and the parents' commitment to and willing participation in the whole process.
- A bit of mucking-up is a common phase in boyhood, which they grow out of.
- It is important to find a release for the boy's physical energy and aggression—preferably through sport.

This last principle was at the heart of the education and organisation of boys through the twentieth century, in schools, the Boy Scouts, the Surf Life Saving Clubs, the Police Citizens Boys Clubs and the YMCA.

Partly because of the far greater number of boys being put on probation, and partly because of the masculine bias of male probation officers, the attention was focused on how one dealt with boys on probation. Some of the principles could equally be applied to girls, but the main difference was that the boys were seen as 'full of energy', requiring the release provided by sporting activity. The girls, on the other hand, could stay at home, as it was their sexual behaviour which required supervision.

It was roughly a decade later, in the 1920s, when this basic ideological framework was fleshed out as a 'youth' literature began to develop in America, with titles like *Reconstructing Behaviour in Youth* (Healy et al. 1929) and *Youth in Conflict* (van Waters 1926). These two books are worth mentioning in particular because they represent the major streams in the youth literature of the period, begun in 1905 with G. Stanley Hall's work on adolescence, but especially because they were used within the New South Wales CWD to extend the theoretical and scientific training of CWD inspectors in the wake of the 1934 Inquiry. In 1936 the CWD's inspectors began to meet regularly on Fridays between 4 and 5 pm. Wood outlined the purpose of the meetings as follows:

> I want our standard of work to assume a higher plane than it has in the past ... we will have to realise that, with the advancement in ideas in regard to Child Welfare all over the world and the great attention that is being paid to it in Geneva, we have now arrived at the point when we must conduct our work on a scientific basis (YACS Misc.Cor., StaNSW 9/6153).

The 'science' of child welfare would consist of the knowledge derived from the departmental officers' practical experience and a study of overseas practices, as well as simply being systematic and orderly, a notion central to any bureaucracy. The meetings followed the pattern of the earlier Probation Officers' Conferences, raising complaints about obstacles to their work, such as: certain categories of children being released on probation, lack of training and overwork, probation officers being given duties other than probation work itself, lack of understanding of the CWD among teachers and the police, a lack of detailed reports on children from magistrates and probation officers.

The meetings would also discuss chapters from Healy's book, which dealt with 'modifying undesirable behaviour tendencies' in foster placements, such as stealing, running away from home, truancy, 'excessive' sexual activity, bed-wetting, and behavioural problems like being 'stubborn, unmanageable or very disobedient' and 'quarrelsome'. After an eclectic theoretical chapter which discussed the behaviourists, Adler, Freud and Jung, the second half of the book outlined how one went about setting up and maintaining a foster home placement. Healy revealed his behaviourist leanings in this part of the book in a discussion of an 'experiment' with 501 children which sought to identify how 'human raw material' might be modified with a foster home placement.

'Success' in a foster home placement was loosely defined as occurring when an individual 'has made a steady gain in his ability to master his difficulties and maintain his position as a desirable member of a family and a community' (Healy et al. 1929: 232). What 'desirable' meant was left unexplained, and in essence a successful foster placement was simply one where order had been restored. Healy and his associates concluded that fostering was dependent upon 'the introduction of scientific methods and discrimination', which meant an extensive use of psychological and psychiatric testing. They argued that '90 percent of the mentally normal succeeded' in their foster placement, whereas only 45 percent of 'those who showed mental abnormality' succeeded, so that accurate identification of the child's mental condition was central to the success or failure of the placement.

Miriam van Waters' book, *Youth in Conflict*, represented the environmentalist wing of the new scientific approach—it dealt more with the Juvenile Court and probation, concentrating less on psychological testing and more on the social context of 'modern youth in conflict'. It discussed the effects of schooling, work, marriage and family life, pleading for a shift of emphasis from 'transitory economic goals and seeking for power', to the 'primary biological goals of healthy childhood' (van Waters 1926: 284). Her position was basically a critique of modernity and consumerism, of the ways in which 'the satisfaction of earning and spending money outrun the earlier and more fundamental goals of our race'. However, the recovery of community and family ties would have to take place with the aid of a thoroughly modern phenomenon, science:

> We must in truth turn to science for our salvation ... Goodwill will
> not solve the problem, nor is philosophy or art sufficiently devoted
> to weaker and handicapped forms of life to effect a solution. Science
> with all its mistakes and false values, still remains the fittest
> instrument with which to delve into the secrets of human behaviour.
> It alone possesses requisite impersonality and far-sightedness (Waters
> 1926: 283).

The goal was thus a scientifically informed and controlled human warmth, genuineness and community—a clearer illustration of the replacement of religion by science would be difficult to find.

Child welfare administrators also had a clear sense of the political role that being scientific could play. In New South Wales, child welfare agencies had been under almost constant public siege over the past 20 years. Their image in the eyes of the public and the rest of the state bureaucracy had been poor from the start, but the introduction of science would change all that. It would strengthen the image of state child welfare agencies and their ability to counter criticism and attack, as well as protecting its appointments and promotions from outsiders. Science would help defend and maintain its organisational boundaries:

> Let us have our own science and let us bring it to as high a scale as possible. I want to be able to say when I leave this Department that we do not want any outsiders to take executive positions ... I want you to be able to satisfy the general public and the Public Service Board that they cannot obtain any officers outside the Department who are as expert to deal with Child Welfare problems as the officers that act within the Department (YACS Misc.Cor., StaNSW 9/6153).

Science was their 'salvation' not just in the sense of improving the quality of the CWD's work, saving youth, the family and the community from alienation and breakdown, but also in the much more pragmatic and political sense of strengthening the CWD's position in relation to other occupations, the rest of the public service, the press and the public. This is a central element in processes of professionalisation. The development of a specific body of knowledge is vital to any occupational group defending its boundaries, and a measure of Wood's and the CWD's vulnerability was their inability to do so in a convincing way.

Despite the lip-service being paid to modernity and science, a major feature of the role of science, psychological or social, in child welfare was in fact its minimal impact. There was a shift towards trying to explain things more in terms of psychological mechanisms and broader social structures and processes, but in a way so crude that in fact it did not get far beyond the earlier analyses. In the weekly Inspectors' meetings in Sydney, any theoretical discussion confirmed and remained within the framework of the Inspectors' existing attitudes and ideas, and there was rarely any attempt at challenge or innovation; the most one would get was criticism of some inefficiency in the system. In the end one would always fall back onto 'good old fashioned' ideas, such as the importance of a 'good, clean, healthy home' (CWD AR 1926-29: 778). At one weekly meeting Wood explained his theory of the 'fog-horn voice':

> ... we must not disregard the methods of the old sea captain [who] had a voice like a fog-horn, and did not forget to use it on occasions to let somebody know what he thought of him. There are times and there are youths when the 'fog-horn voice' and a sudden outburst might be very effective (YACS Misc.Cor., StaNSW 9/6153).

The scientific literature, limited as it was in any case, appears to have played a relatively minor role compared to this sort of home-spun wisdom.

Overall there was a potent mixture of nineteenth-century moralism and commonsense, with attempts to explain things in terms of psychology and the environment. In 1930 Thompson could both plead for 'the very maximum of scientific and systematic attention' being paid to child welfare, and also explain the CWD's approach to delinquency in the following terms:

> One delinquent child recovered and guided into correct paths means a better family and a healthier neighbourhood. One family cleansed of sordidness and carelessness and beautified and lifted into a cleaner and healthier atmosphere where every thought and action is devoted to the good and lasting things in life means a better and happier community (CWD AR 1929: 762).

Probation was consistently seen in terms of a combination of a search for social antecedents with notions of 'cleanliness': 'Why the child did wrong in the first instance is the important question to be answered, and when this is ascertained a beginning is made to instil into his mind clean thoughts and healthy habits that will give him a fresh start in life (p. 772). The nineteenth-century child welfare reformers would have been at home with language like this.

The Depression years did, however, introduce some significant changes in the way child welfare was perceived, from within the state bureaucracy at least. In the CWD's 1930–31 Annual Report there was a heightened awareness of the role that economic conditions played. Alex Thompson warned that the whole tone of his report would 'necessarily be affected by the severe industrial crisis and financial crisis through which the State is passing', and went on to mention issues like inequality of income and opportunity, and 'the dreaded spectre of unemployment' and how it undermined the work of the CWD (CWD AR 1930–31: 533).

On the one hand Thompson was saying that the prevailing economic conditions were increasing the CWD's workload; institutions like the Industrial School for Girls were becoming overcrowded, 'as parents have refrained from applying for the discharge of girls because of the difficulty of placing them in situations or keeping them occupied in the homes where other members of the family were already unemployed'. He did not want to put pressure on the parents to take their girls, as that might only exacerbate their poverty (p. 547). On the other hand, the Minister, David Drummond, also pointed out that in general the CWD's workload appeared to be decreasing. Unemployment, 'idleness and increased leisure combined with the increased strain of poverty' was expected to increase the numbers brought before the Children's Court, but:

> Strange to say the reverse was the case, and a search for probable causes for this decrease suggests that the presence in the homes of unemployed fathers, and in many cases unemployed mothers, who were previously absent at work during the day, led to an

> improvement in the home government enabling the parents to
> exercise better supervision over the actions of their children (p. 547).

A rather novel theory was being put forward here, that unemployment could prevent instead of produce juvenile delinquency, by strengthening family ties, encouraging solidarity in the face of hardship and reinforcing family life in opposition to the public world of work. Certainly the proportion of New South Wales' children in the Department's care was decreasing overall, and Drummond's explanation fits with the critiques of the effects of 'modern industrial society' on family life, but we need not accept it as the right one. The Police, the Court and the CWD's officers may simply have been operating differently, applying the law with different standards. Whatever the explanation, at the very least it is clear that the relationship between hardship and juvenile delinquency is not a straightforward one.

Those who ran the CWD saw the first 40 years of the twentieth century as a period in which the conditions of family life, childhood and youth had changed dramatically from those of the nineteenth century. Child-rearing had become more tolerant and kindly, children sought more of their 'amusement and training' outside the home, and the state played a larger role in the 'education and moral training' of children. These changes had produced mixed results, Thompson thought: on the one hand, 'the average community, today is brighter, more cheerful, more discriminating and possibly more artistic', and modern children appeared to be more 'self-reliant'. On the other hand, Thompson lamented that 'the lure of cheap pleasure and the tendency to selfishness and self-indulgence are antagonistic to the cultivation of that discipline of character which is most evidenced in the sense of duty' (CWD AR 1930–31: 529).

A basic problem was thus being posed: how to maintain social discipline and order in the face of both a more tolerant approach to child-rearing and encroaching consumer culture: the 'lure of cheap pleasure' and 'self-indulgence' such as picture shows and dance halls. The concept 'idleness' had not disappeared, but it was complemented by a more sophisticated notion of 'leisure' and how the leisure time of young people ought to be filled—how to keep them off the streets.

The solution was the child-centredness which we now take to be a central defining feature of modern family life, but which received a strong boost in this period, in which it became important for parents to 'get in touch' with their children. The expanding role of the state and other organisations in family life had the effect of increasing the ideological emphasis on the centrality of the family rather than undermining it, as family life had more to compensate for. As Thompson argued:

Good children, and in their turn, good citizens are in the main the product of good homes, where all the love and devotion and the sense of service and self-sacrifice, all true pride and idealism and worthy ambitions are born, moulded and encouraged. The State, the Church and the School may educate, inspire and guide the way, but they can rarely, if ever, create, and the home must ever remain the source of all the great social virtues that are worthwhile.

But Thompson did not view all families and homes as being the same:

... the term 'home' as used here was not meant to apply to the apology for home, the travesty for home or the sort of hell upon earth that sometimes masquerades under that name; rather what is meant is that wonderful social unit in which the strength and inspiration of a good man, and the love, devotion and sacrifice of a noble woman hold sway, and in which a family is reared in the spirit and likeness of the Great Father of all (CWD AR 1930–31: 530).

These final lines of his foreword to the 1930–31 Report indicate that Thompson had lost none of that implacable hostility toward 'improper' families which characterised the nineteenth-century child savers (Barbalet 1983: 191), nor any of their sense that the political dominance of the state over the family was something desirable and necessary. Although the individuality of family life was important, the form that it should take would be determined collectively, by the officers of the state.

In terms of explanation and analysis, there was a shift away from the moral concerns of the nineteenth century to an emphasis on psychological development, family dynamics and social pressures on family life. However, this represented more a change in tone than a fundamental change in approach. Families and children were still being described as being 'good, clean and healthy', and it is questionable whether everyday child welfare practices were much affected. For example, instead of simply condemning masturbation as excessive sexual activity indicating either moral pollution or mental deficiency, Wood declared in 1936:

It should be understood that, because a boy gives way to masturbation, this is not conclusive evidence that he is a sexual pervert by any means. It is a very general failing ... although the masturbating type must, of course, be kept under observation to determine whether there are also leanings towards the serious side of perversion (YACS Misc. Corr., StaNSW 7/7584).

The very fact that Wood had to oppose the idea that masturbation equals perversion means it was in circulation, and while he was introducing some nuances, the basic disgust at sexual behaviour in children and youth remained. Any rationalisation or 'disenchantment' which was going on in this part of the state bureaucracy was thus deeply flawed; official rhetoric and language had become scientific in a sense, but largely through the formation of a relatively thin layer grafted on top of an essentially nineteenth-century moral and pragmatic discourse.

A little digging below the surface to everyday practices in child welfare institutions reveals little evidence of science or rationality—the New South Wales 1934 Inquiry certainly indicated that institutional life had changed very little, and the training CWD officers received, if any, was still very rudimentary. What was going on in the CWD was much more a rather haphazard rationalisation of language and discourse than of practices and structures.

Kerreen Reiger has already pointed out the fundamental contradiction between technical rationality as applied to the domestic sphere and dominant notions of the naturalness of femininity. The evidence on the operation of child welfare indicates that there were other, equally fundamental contradictions at work between pragmatism, commonsense, bureaucratic imperatives and inertia, and an underlying nineteenth-century view of human nature which employed profoundly unscientific concepts like 'goodness', 'health', 'cleanliness' and 'pollution'. Barbalet makes similar observations of the work of the officers of the South Australian State Children's Department, who 'despite their practical approach . . . sometimes clung to beliefs more at home with Victorian charity than twentieth century social welfare' (Barbalet 1983: 217–18). The impression generated by most of the Australian treatments of the role of science in this period is one of a break or transformation, a shift in paradigms from 'morality' to 'science', and David Rothman explains the failure of progressive reform in terms of 'administrative convenience' (Rothman 1980). However, the evidence here suggests more of a mixing of currents, a laying of strata one on top of the other. Child welfare workers operated very much like Carlo Ginzburg's miller, Menocchio, overlaying their own deeply rooted pre-rational models of the world and human behaviour with new terminology and concepts rather than simply exchanging one for the other (Ginzburg 1980).

The policies with regard to Aboriginal children also speak volumes about the darker side of 'science', in that it unleashed the eugenicism inherent in the Social Darwinist ideas on feeble-mindedness and biological inferiority, kept in check by sheer inefficiency in relation to white children, and turned it into a fully blown exercise in social engineering backed by legal authority and state force. Between 1915 and 1940, the removal of Aboriginal children accelerated rapidly throughout Australia, with roughly 1600 children passing through the hands of the Aborigines Protection Board in New South Wales alone. In 1915 the New South Walses Aborigines Protection Act was amended to allow children to be removed without parental consent 'if the Board considered it to be in the interests of the child's moral or physical welfare'. The onus was on the parents to show that their child should stay with them (Read 1983: 6).

To save expense, the smaller Church-run missions in Western Australia had gradually been phased out and replaced with larger settlements like the Moore River Settlement (Haebich 1988: 167), where large numbers of children were separated from their parents, with no relatives to turn to. They were given new names, and many children grew up not knowing their real names or who their parents were. Many parents 'attempted in vain to have their children returned to them or to at least obtain permission to visit them, while the white staff told their children that their parents were no longer interested in them' (p. 208). In fact, where children had been sent in by their parents, they understood that their children would return on completion of their schooling, but the Department simply dishonoured such agreements (p. 171). The children's desperation would on occasion erupt in attempts to escape, as some children did on one mission by cutting through their canvas-walled dormitories in an attempt to find their parents (p. 175).

By 1936 the West Australian Commissioner for Native Affairs had become the legal guardian of *all* Aboriginal children up to the age of 21. The Native Administration Act empowered the state to forcibly take all Aboriginal children from their families and place them in government institutions 'to be trained in the ways of "white civilization" and "society" ' (p. 350). Throughout Australia this training appeared to consist primarily of brutality, contempt and an attempt to train into the children an abhorrence of Aboriginal culture.

Youth leisure and child welfare in 1940

If we return to the urban economic context within which the white child welfare system operated, a number of patterns emerge in the work available to children and youth (Keating 1973: 340–1). First, the workforce participation of 10–14 year old boys had declined steadily from about 10 per cent in 1915 to a low of 3 per cent in 1932, where it stayed from then on. The rate for girls similarly declined from about 3 per cent to around 1 per cent. For 15–19 year old boys, the rate remained steady at about 85 per cent, except for 1928–35, when it dipped to a low of 70 per cent in 1932. For girls, however, their workforce participation rate rose steadily, dipping less dramatically than the boys in 1928–35, from 45 per cent in 1915 to 60 per cent in 1940. The picture is not a uniform one: 10–14 year olds were gradually being eased out of the workforce, so that they might be said to have had more leisure time, but for 15–19 year old boys, it was mainly the crisis years of 1928–35 which affected them particularly badly, and increasing numbers of girls went out of the home to work.

There were thus a number of different types of leisure: that which could be bought with the money a job brought in—picture shows, dance halls, the theatre; that which was generated by unemployment; that which affected younger boys finding it difficult to get work, probably because of the conflict with school. This meant that the official concern with leisure as a breeding ground for delinquency was an ideological response to a varied set of phenomena: the increasing economic independence of girls from their families, the transition from schooling to working for a proportion of 10–14 year olds, and the conjunctural unemployment of 1928–35.

The few fragments of the New South Wales Children's Court records which survive indicate frequent conflicts between parents and children over how their leisure time—the time spent neither at home nor at school or work—ought to be spent (Children's Court Deposition, StaNSW 3/12486–93). The terms used were not the nineteenth-century ones of children 'wandering', but the issue was the same—children being where their parents wanted them to be. The Court assumed a parental right to determine the hours children kept, and children who refused to recognise that right were defined as uncontrollable. Parents who did not assume the right themselves were seen as unable to control their children and 'not respectable'.

The fact that fewer children were brought before the Court in the Depression years, together with a decline in the number of children being fostered, on probation and in the institutions, means that one cannot explain the changing relationship between the state and family life simply in economic terms. One cannot say, for example, that the more unemployment and poverty there is, the more family disintegration and social disruption, the more juvenile delinquency, the more call for state intervention. In reality the connections are much more complex; the general tendency towards more stability in the network of relationships between families, schools, working children and youth, as well as a more routinised organisation of young people's leisure time, seems to have over-shadowed the effects of economic downturn.

By 1940 the picture which emerges is one of both increasing and decreasing intervention into and involvement with children and family life. Together with the decline in numbers of children in the CWD's care, there was greater organisation of youth leisure, partly as a response to the high unemployment of 1928–35, with various groups aiming to keep children off the streets, more counselling and guidance through Vocational Guidance and Child Guidance Clinics, as well as Baby Health Centres. All these sorts of ventures were intended to be preventative—of crime, delinquency, family breakdown, and even communism—particularly when the scarcity of work seemed to be creating a crisis in the socialisation process: a gap between school and work which would have all sorts of dire consequences.

As well as the increase in this sort of activity, some of it state-run, some of it not, there was also an increase in the volume of funds going directly into providing the economic support for families that would keep them away from child welfare agencies: first through 'boarding-out to own mother' allowances, and then through Deserted Wives' and Widows' Pensions. At the same time, however, there was a decline in the level of state child welfare activity overall. There were a number of possible reasons for this: funding restrictions making it impossible to expand with the population; increasing stability in working-class families, despite (or because of?) the Depression; and changing practices on the part of the Police, the Children's Courts and child welfare inspectors.

There was in any case a shift away from child welfare originating within the state bureaucracy to other forms of organising children and youth which were based on the initiative of groups based in 'the community' or civil society—the YM and YWCA, the Boy Scouts and Girl Guides, the Police Citizens Boys Clubs, and so on. Rather than simply expanding, the whole field of child welfare was changing form: being diversified, going beyond the basic state-run structure of fostering, adoption, probation and institutions, towards a less structured and more varied, although also more extensive, organisation of childhood and youth, both inside and outside the home.

As for the impact of scientific ideas on the operations of child welfare, whether they consisted of the psychiatrists' emphasis on feeble-mindedness, or the environmentalists' hopes of fostering the forms of family life and the urban environment which would prevent juvenile delinquency, the evidence indicates that it took a very specific form. On the one hand, the structural shift of emphasis away from concentrating on managing the institutions and fostering system appears to be partly attributable, whether intended or not, to the environmentalist concern with prevention of delinquency. On the other hand, there was also more attention paid to the question of a child's mental and physical state, and at least some attempt was made to tailor their treatment accordingly.

However, to a large extent it is also fair to say that while the rhetoric changed, as did some of the practices, they did so in a manner which retained so much of the pre-scientific moral approach to child welfare, and left intact so much of the everyday violence of institutional life, that the scientific content of the new practices—child guidance, psychological testing, classification of inmates, prevention of delinquency—was effectively neutralised. Margaret Barbalet has said of South Australia that 'morality and mission lay at the core of the methods of the Departmental staff', changing only 'right at the end of the 1930s' (Barbalet 1983: 215), and the evidence for New South Wales is similar.

Certainly the 'child welfare' that Aboriginal families were subjected to was largely a vehicle for the destruction of Aboriginal culture, an effective program of cutting ties between one generation and the next, perhaps the most brutally efficient realisation of the 'rescuing the rising generation' idea originally intended for the industrial working classes. It may be putting it too strongly to say that the coming of science to child welfare was a case of old wine in new bottles, but by the time scientific approaches to child welfare had entered the belly of 'that rough beast' and been subjected to some of its digestive processes, one can only wonder whether their authors would have recognised the final product.

Conclusion: beyond social control

The book began with an argument for the necessity of a historical perspective in understanding contemporary issues. In this final chapter I would like to draw out the implications of my discussion for more current problems concerning the state's involvement in family life. Examining the history makes it possible to put child welfare in its social and historical context, allowing for an evaluation of its continuities and developments in relation to wider social stability and change.

The theoretical issues I have examined are not confined simply to 'the past' with no relevance to present-day problems: Lasch's and Donzelot's analyses are intended to apply as much to current child welfare practices as to their historical antecedents, and Aaron Cicourel's detailed study of the American juvenile justice system in 1968 revealed patterns of relationships between parents, their children and state agencies strikingly similar to those uncovered in my own examination of the Australian historical material (Cicourel 1976). My comments will refer in the first instance to white Australian society, and I will return to the very specific case of Aboriginal family life and state intervention towards the end of the chapter.

State expansion in context

A central issue raised by a consideration of child welfare history is what role should be attributed to the state in explaining the apparent 'embourgeoisement' of working-class family life. Contrary to

133

the view that the state 'reconstructed' working-class family life in a bourgeois image, the historical evidence is that current patterns of family life developed in response to given economic and ideological environments, independently of, as well as in response to, state action, and state agencies and policies are themselves products of both broader social processes and human agency. This makes it necessary to return to theories of ideology and cultural change, and analyse the nature of 'civil society' in addition to the state, engaging in historical and sociological investigations of the fabric of everyday social life and the meaning of social events to their human participants.

The development of working-class respectability and adherence to a nuclear family ideal continues to resist simple historical explanations. There is still considerable debate among historians of the family about whether working-class family life really experienced much of a transformation during industrialisation and the rise of capitalism *at all*, particularly in England. It is possible to argue that the 'traditional' English working-class family was precisely 'the privatised, home-centred domestic unit based on the nuclear family', and historical demographers have demonstrated the long history of such households in pre-industrial England (Pahl 1984: 321–2). Well before the industrial revolution, Pahl maintains, 'ordinary English people' were committed to . . . an overall set of values concerned with homeliness, cosiness, domesticity and a belief that, if one can control just a small part of this large and threatening world, then one has achieved something worthwhile (p. 324). Even if we regard this as too radical an interpretation, the state was not at the centre of social and cultural change, and we have to look for the social foundations of state expansion. In other words, while state action clearly has some independent impact on social life, it also occurred within the context and on the basis of social and cultural developments in civil society unattributable to the effects of state intervention.

The material conditions of the working class gradually improved during the second half of the nineteenth century, very unevenly, with large sections of the working class remaining in dire poverty, depending on their position in the labour market (Fisher 1982: 32–50). Industrialisation introduced new skills, and established a distinction between those who had mastered these skills and those who possessed them to a lesser extent or not at all. As Peter Stearns sums it up, 'in the very long run industrialisation set up a modest mobility ladder, in which many traditional unskilled learned that they, or their children, could rise a notch or two higher' (Stearns 1976: 250).

What this meant *politically*, among other things, was that for an increasing proportion of the working class, the attainment of moral improvement, respectability and education became both economically possible and ideologically desirable, as a cultural means of leaving their poverty behind them, which often included leaving their poor neighbours behind them as well. Domesticity was a means of responding to the lack of control male workers experienced in the workplace. As Daunton puts it:

> Negotiation tended to be limited to the economics of the wage bargain, and to exclude issues of control over work. The changing life-style of the working class is thus seen not only as a response to a rising standard of living, but also as a defensive reaction to the onslaught of employers upon work-based culture. The working class turned away from dependence in their experience of work, towards a search for purpose in life of the family and home, which came to be seen as a source of assertive dignity (Daunton 1983: 266).

The support given by both the labour and the women's movements to the notion of a family wage—the setting of male wages to a level intended to support a wife and children—also said a great deal about working men and women's aspirations for family life, combining a feminist valorisation of motherhood with male workers' emphasis on economic self-sufficiency. As Zaretsky points out, the ethical and social origins of support for a family wage 'certainly included traditions of community more characteristic of working-class than middle-class life, and probably drew upon expectations of co-operation and sharing between the sexes' (Zaretsky 1982: 217).

Hence the strong emphasis in working-class organisations on respectability and self-discipline: economic improvement may be slow in coming, but one could attempt either to speed it up or to compensate for its slowness by attaining respectability, dignity and self-worth, which in themselves did not necessarily mean deferring to bourgeois domination and control (McCalman 1984: 20). The effects of organised working-class struggles for equality, even the advances and successes of those struggles, were not simply to oppose everything bourgeois, but on the contrary to often produce overlap, compromise, even consensus on issues like the work ethic, familial morality and respectability.

The very forms of collective political action which were to improve the position of the working class, perhaps even defeat the bourgeoisie and bring about socialism, demanded precisely the qualities that the social control theorists argue have been, and continue to be, imposed on the working class: self-discipline, delayed gratification of immediate needs, order, industriousness, sobriety, cleanliness, and so on (Green and Cromwell 1984). This is the fundamental point which the historical evidence makes clear, and which undermines the logic at the heart of the arguments that child welfare is a form of 'class control'.

If we perceive the ideology underlying social welfare as bourgeois or middle-class, and by definition alien to working-class culture, we come uncomfortably close to suggesting that the working class as a whole wanted, and perhaps still wants, to be dirty, drunk, poor, unemployed, unmarried, and to bash and abandon each other to destitution. One can of course argue that these labels were often attached unfairly, and this was often what welfare clients objected to in the way that social welfare operated, but the notion of a *just* social control remains quite some distance away from the current social control paradigm. Child welfare agencies did not deal with the working class as a unified whole, but primarily with the families on its outskirts, often geographically as well as ideologically. Even if the parents did not share the state officials' view of how their children should behave, many of their working-class neighbours probably did.

There were thus a number of factors underlying the shift by working-class families towards a familial lifestyle similar to that of the middle class well prior to any possible effect of state action. The two major innovations in state child welfare—the establishment of boarding-out, and the Children's Court and probation— were both premised on the existence of a substantial proportion of working-class families who already adhered to the respectable norms and values the reformers hoped to develop in the rising generation, and depended on the overall cooperation of many working-class families. Boarding-out and probation could not have operated without that cooperation—in taking children in, in working together with probation officers to supervise their children, in reporting cases of neglect, in supplying the police and child welfare officers with information.

This is not to deny the conflict that often took place, nor that coercion was exercised on many families, but relations between child welfare agencies and working-class families were universally marked not by outright hostility and entrenched opposition, but most often by ambivalence and sullen cooperation. The form of 'working-class child welfare' which operated wherever possible was simply the temporary care of the child by relatives or neighbours, and children were brought to charitable or state institutions largely when this kind of informal support network did not exist (Ross 1983; McCalman 1984). The coercion in these situations came from the economic vulnerability of working-class families, especially women left solely responsible for a family, not from the state. In fact both charitable and state agencies were more often *reluctant* to intervene, and only did so under political and ideological pressure,

Ironically, it was Christopher Lasch who pointed out that egalitarianism itself seems to have produced the sort of intolerance of diversity, the sort of concern to hold everyone to similar values and norms of behaviour that characterised the child welfare system's 'policing of families':

> The rise of egalitarianism in western Europe and the United States seems to have been associated with a heightened awareness of deviancy and of social differences of all kinds, and with a growing uneasiness in the face of those differences—a certain intolerance even, which expressed itself in a determination to compel or persuade all members of society to conform to a single standard of citizenship. On the one hand, egalitarian theory and practice insisted on the right of all men (and logically of all women as well) to citizenship and to full membership in the community; on the other hand, they insisted that all citizens live by the same rules of character and conduct (Lasch 1973: 17).

Clearly we should not see society as a harmonious organism in which everyone is controlled for the common good, but at the same time the *source* of social control has to be conceptualised not as 'the state', 'capitalism' or 'middle-class professionals', but as the *intersection* of those forces with the independent effects of working-class political action and cultural change. It is thus accurate enough to say that the development of state intervention had a lot to do with state officials' interest in improving the apparatus of social control, making 'wider, stronger and different nets' (Cohen 1985: 38), as well as the expansion of bureaucratic and professional territory and power, but that is by no means the whole story. As E.P. Thompson argues, to see the state as imposing ideology 'is to mistake the whole social and cultural process': 'This imposition will always be attempted, with greater or lesser success, but it cannot succeed at all unless there is some *congruence* between the imposed rules and view of life and the necessary business of living a given mode of production' (Thompson 1978: 367).

Probably the major failing of the social control approach is that it overlooks this 'congruence' and reduces the working class to the passive object of historical change. If we are to understand the material basis for political and cultural stability within a basically unequal economic system, we have to recognise the *active* role that working-class men and women played in participating in, supporting and extending a respectability and social control which should be seen as bourgeois only in its historical origins. The so-called

'embourgeoisement' of working-class families should therefore be
regarded as a workable response to the material conditions of
working-class life, predating organised attempts to reform
working-class familial relations and morals on any sort of mass,
and therefore effective, scale (Houlbrooke 1984; Macfarlane 1986).
It was only one among many possible responses, to be sure, and
one partly based on emulation of the apparent success of the
bourgeois familial strategy (Pelling 1960: 10), but it was still one
which 'made sense' within their overall social and economic situation (Hearn 1978), rather than being something alien and antithetical to working-class interests imposed from above.

Interaction and (other) structural constraints

The consequence of developing a sensitivity to the agency of
groups other than state officials and middle-class social pathologists is to see the events which make up the whole phenomenon of
'child welfare' as the product of processes of social *interaction*
rather than simply an imposition by one group over another, and
one where the meaning of the events concerned varies for different
members of a family (Joffe 1979: 253; de Swaan 1988: 248). The
child welfare system was clearly embedded within a class structure
and class conflict, but political and cultural class conflict is not a
zero-sum game of domination and resistance in which every
advance on one side is a loss to the other. Working-class men,
women and occasionally children often found something to gain in
the child welfare system—most frequently as slight compensation
for their weaker position in the class structure and the labour
market, to be sure, but the dynamics of that lay not in what state
agencies did, but in the broader political and economic system, the
most important aspect of which was, and continues to be, women's
employment prospects and wages.

Throughout the second half of the nineteenth century it was the
economic vulnerability of women, especially when left without a
male breadwinner, which produced the largest proportion of child
welfare cases. One of the most significant developments from
around the turn of the century onward was thus the gradual extension of both women's employment opportunities and status, and
the state economic support given to women left to care for their
children on their own. This gradually reduced sheer poverty as a
force driving children to child welfare agencies, and the balance
shifted towards attempts at a greater regulation of childhood
within their original families.

In the early decades of the twentieth century there was a shift from removal of children from their families towards more subtle forms of involvement in family life by both youth leisure organisations and what Lasch calls the 'social pathologists' in the form of social casework, counselling, therapy and so on. However, their activity should in turn be seen not as taking over the socialisation of children from their parents, or as male professionals redefining the role of mother and wife, but as a complex set of processes of negotiation and alliance. The little material that survives on the Children's Court in New South Wales indicates that parents were using the Court to manage their children's behaviour, as the industrial schools and reformatories had been used before. Similarly in relation to child care, although twentieth century women did pay a price in terms of anxiety and stress about their proper fulfilment of the role of mother and wife, they also achieved significant gains in raising the status of women and their own position within the family (Jones 1983; Reiger 1985).

Once one sees 'the family' as a collection of people with different, perhaps conflicting, interests rather than as a unified whole, it becomes clear that what might be the imposition of control to one can be a way out of an untenable situation for another (see especially Gordon 1988 concerning family violence). In an analysis of conflict management in medical encounters, Abram de Swaan has extended this interactionist argument to suggest a three-cornered model which helps us grasp the relationship between child welfare workers, state agencies and the families they dealt with. He argues that the interaction 'rests on a collusion, a secret complicity between the parties to the conflict, with each other and with the doctors':

> The weakest party in the conflict gains from having its wants
> re-defined as medical necessities; the strongest party gains by the
> 'individualization' thus realized, by the social isolation of the
> conflict ... The gain for the third in this alliance, the doctor, comes
> from the chances of prestige, income, and the realization of
> occupational ideals (de Swaan 1990: 69).

Other studies support such an 'asymmetrical alliance' model of the relationship between professionals and clients: in an examination of homeopathy and psychoanalysis, William Rothstein points out that doctors' professional autonomy and control was severely limited and directed by clients' demands and expectations (Rothstein 1973: 159–78). Philip Wilkinson and Clive Grace also argue that the client–social worker relationship is not simply one of redefinition by the social worker, but of negotiation (Wilkinson and Grace 1975). It is certainly *asymmetrical* negotiation, in that both the social worker and their employing agency has access to far greater resources, but it is negotiation nonetheless, and not simply one-sided control and domination.

If one applies this model to child welfare, the gain for the parent(s) would be the resolution of a crisis or problem, either temporary or permanent, and the objectification of that crisis or problem as an issue that someone else had to do something about. For state officials the gain was the *possible* prevention of crime, delinquency, and other 'drains on the public purse', as well as the public moral capital gained from being seen to assist children, deserted wives and widows. For the third party, child welfare workers and administrators, the gain was income, status, a piece of bureaucratic and occupational territory and 'the realisation of their professional ideals'. The *difference* with de Swaan's account of medical encounters is that there was a fourth party—the child— who usually had very little to gain at all.

The problem with seeing 'the family' as the weakest party is that there was often a conflict *within* the family in that parents and children often had opposing interests. With every new generation adult society faces another invasion of the 'barbarian hordes' (Tawney 1964: 81), and the history of parent–child relations illustrates quite clearly that the raising of children was often a conflict-ridden process (Aries 1973; Pollock 1983). Rather than seeing things in purely class or gender terms, as Geoffrey Pearson has recently argued in relation to hooliganism, it often makes more sense to see the more oppressive aspects of child welfare as the manifestation of a *generational* conflict (Pearson 1983). It thus becomes impossible to understand the dynamics of child welfare unless one examines the intra-familial conflicts both between men and women, and between parents and their children.

The perceived needs, aspirations and strategies for improvement of working-class men, women and children did not, of course, drop from the sky, but developed in response to changes in surrounding social conditions. However, state expansion was only one aspect of those changes, and it is also necessary to examine the possible determining effects on family life of the social changes brought about by industrialisation, the rise of capitalism, urbanisation, and their very particular expression in Australia. People experience constraints not just from the state, but also from the nature of their social circumstances and from each other. It is this structural constraint characterising the denser social networks of modern societies which leads Norbert Elias (1982a; 1982b) to see the phenomenon focused on by the social control theorists more as an overall change in social relationships. In this change the constitution of social order moved gradually from the public and external

exercise of authority, often through physical violence, to the more
privatised internalisation of coercion, the development of a self-
discipline and regulation of people's behaviour through mutual
negotiation.

Behind the therapists, social workers, counsellors, clinics, community 'treatment' programs and halfway houses, therefore, lies a
particular kind of society which produced them, a particular pat-
terning of social relations characterised by phenomena such as
working-class respectability, the egalitarian emphasis on adherence
to a unified set of norms and moral principles alongside an intolerance of diversity and deviance. All of this was borne of an
increasing recognition of mutual interdependence, of the impact
that the education and socialisation of your neighbour's children
could have on that of your own, and more indirectly on the destiny
of any organised attempts to shape the form that Australian society
was to take. It led, as we have seen, to a general working-class
acceptance of state expansion as the means to the realisation of the
labour movement's ends, and this assent to the notion of a state of
'the general interest' played an integral part in laying the ideological and political foundations for a more active, interventionist
state.

The social control theorists are right to emphasise that these
modern forms of deliberate socialisation are not at all as liberating
as they are made out to be, that they necessarily involve the
calculated management of our behaviour and perhaps our very
identity (Cohen 1985), but where they lead us astray is in not
seeing that in relation to the forms of social control which preceded them. The greater regulation of personal and family life by
welfare state bureaucrats and social workers went together with
pensions and benefits which made it easier for families to survive
temporary crises and escape the more immediate controlling
effects of poverty itself.

The limiting and constraining effects of state action on individuality are usually its most visible and prominent aspect, but the
problem is that the object of state intervention has always been
precisely to *guarantee* and *support* both family life and individuality against the arbitrary constraint of, among others things, market
forces (Zaretsky 1982). State expansion thus involved the
formalisation and *rationalisation* of social control rather than
simply its extension. State agencies might be experienced as, and
appear to be, intruding on individual and family life, but the two
are in fact mutually dependent on each other. They are two sides
of the same social configuration.

The historical change referred to as state expansion was not
simply a transformation in the relationship between 'the state' and

'the family' (or 'the community'), for this captures only the form, the appearance of the real change, which was an overall transformation in our relations with each other, a transformation of the relationship between public and private life (Sennet 1978). In the process we gradually unchained ourselves both from the constraints inherent in family and community control, and from the limiting effects of the inability of family and community to deal adequately with poverty and family breakdown—very *unevenly* of course, given that 'we' referred and continues to refer to a deeply divided population in terms of class, gender, age and race. We also paid a certain price for that in the *abstraction* of that control into the public authority we call the state, which consequently confronts us as an *alienated* authority.

While the effects of state action are often violent and unjust, and certainly controlling and dominating (Lüdtke 1979), there are accompanying long-term benefits: the creation of 'pacified social spaces' free of physical violence, and the potential for individuality and diversity within an overall framework of state-sanctioned coercion and constraint (Elias 1982b: 235), so that the pressures we experience become more subtle and inter-active (de Swaan 1981). The disappearance of pre-welfare state forms of support, as Abram de Swaan puts it, '. . . is above all a change: neighbourly love has been succeeded by social consciousness, and one is to the other what craftsmanship is to industrial production. No use mourning, no point in rejoicing' (de Swaan 1983: 2). The changes in the forms of social control which this study of the history of Australian child welfare has identified are thus tied up with changes in the nature of Australian society itself.

State intervention, family life and justice

The final problem which emerges from a consideration of child welfare history concerns how current forms of state intervention into family life might be critically evaluated. Writers such as Lasch and Donzelot are widely read, and are often regarded as providing the only theoretically informed perspective on the welfare state, making it necessary to take up a position in relation to the larger historical thesis they put forward, that the welfare state constitutes the destruction of an otherwise intact social fabric, so that 'the citizens's entire existence has now been subjected to social direction, increasingly unmediated by the family or other institutions to which the work of socialization was once confined' (Lasch 1977: 189). The vision is a common one, tellingly captured in novels such as *1984* and *Brave New World*, and centres on a romantic view of a somehow more natural social world rendered artificial to the point of meaninglessness by the intrusive meddlings of an artificial state apparatus.

This meta-narrative on the historical origins and contemporary nature of the modern social world suggests that the other forms of social control within the family or the community, which preceded or operate alongside state intervention, are somehow preferable, less controlling, less intrusive and less oppressive. The problem in relation to childhood is that although state agencies may not be very good at parenting (Rothman 1978), neither are parents. In her critique of the 'poisonous pedagogy' of both past and present parenting practices, Alice Miller makes the important point that the central problem with child-rearing advice and instruction, all the expert and professional intervention that distresses Lasch, is that it fulfils the needs of adults rather than children (Miller 1983: 97–8).

Similarly, it is difficult to sustain a romantic view of the 'community', given that neighbourhood justice is often crueler and harsher than the state (Greenberg 1983: 323); frequently state agencies operate precisely to *protect* people from the justice of their peers. The nurturing aspects of community have a darker underside, an over-arching normative consensus maintained at the expense of diversity and difference. The attempt to create social institutions free of structure and control—such as free schools—is an inherently unstable contradiction in terms, and ultimately only possible, as Punch argues, because of 'the immense normative power exercised by the group over the individual'. Ironically, he goes on to say, it produces a situation where 'social control over the deviant may be exercised as thoroughly as in the most sophisticated police state' (Punch 1974: 323).

Comparing current forms of social control to their historical antecedents, it is by no means clear that we are nowadays *more* socially controlled than we were at any other time, as some commentators seem to think (White 1990: 2). Support and assistance invariably have a cost of one sort or another, and in the pre-industrial forms of community and family support, the price one paid was greater regulation, surveillance and inspection of one's behaviour by family and neighbours than we would now consider acceptable (van Krieken 1990: 154). Power and control are exercised within all social relations; infancy, childhood and socialisation in particular are by definition experiences of submission to authority, the subjection of individual human beings to the power of social institutions, and an integral part of family dynamics is the imposition of control and the exercise of power. All one can say is that the development of child welfare reflected *changes* in the forms of social control, rather than the expansion or extension of social control through state agencies.

Although it was worth pointing out the aspects of social control built into social welfare in order to counteract the 'Whig' view of history, there is little further mileage to be gained from that 'unmasking' endeavour. The more useful exercise is to detail the social and material bases of various forms of social control, how they have changed within their surrounding social contexts, what its oppressive and unjust aspects have been, and to suggest what lessons might be learnt from its past and present for the making of future political choices.

The history of child welfare gives no ready answers to questions about whether or not the extension of state involvement in family life was or remains 'a good thing'. In short, it depends. For the Aboriginal children who were taken from their families against the wishes of their parents it was clearly not 'a good thing', and there can be no question of justice for them or their families. The 'child welfare' system set up specifically for them early in the twentieth century was by definition a system of domination deliberately designed to eliminate their parents' culture and society. For them the social control arguments *do* apply, as it was a wholly unwelcome system designed by members of an alien culture to radically transform theirs, through the systematic removal and resocialisation of the rising generation. The questions this history raises for us to contemplate today, at the very least, are what implications it has for relations between Aboriginal and white Australians, and what traces of that systematic attempt at social and biological engineering remain in current child welfare practices and institutions (Read 1983; Chisholm 1985).

In relation to the general issue of de-institutionalisation, however, the problem is that the alternatives to institutional care for particular children may be experienced by them as no less if not more oppressive (Sauer 1979; Lee and Pithers 1980). Unless we think clearly about alternative strategies of state intervention and specify the ways in which issues such as family breakdown and abuse can be responded to, a critique of state social control leads by default to the idea that the family is always the best place for a child to be, an odd position after all the effort sociologists have put into exposing and criticising the oppressiveness of family life.

The striking thing about the opposition between institutions and family life is its persistence as a theme running throughout child welfare history. Every generation of welfare reformers thought they were the first to criticise 'the barracks'. Time and again, though, the alternatives did not quite match the expectations, and some sort of return to institutional care took place. This historical persistence indicates a need to look further afield at what it is about the nature of family life, and especially family breakdown, in Western culture and society which keeps the opposition between 'the barracks' and the 'family principle' alive, rather than treating it as the product of current developments in welfare ideology and politics.

Another crucial lesson to be drawn from the history is that any critical evaluation of state intervention in family life will begin to have a real impact at the point where it goes beyond identifying the mere existence of a lofty rhetoric of social control accompanied by brutalising bureaucracies and institutions, and deals with the question of *justice* in social control. The focus of our critical attention should therefore not simply be power and control in themselves, but the *forms* they take, the point at which we can genuinely say they have turned into *domination*, as well as how we could turn a cruel, self-serving and unjust authority into one which is humane, accountable and just: what Richard Sennet calls a visible, legible authority (Sennett 1981: 165–90).

It is the *injustice* of child welfare institutions, agencies and bureaucracies which is a worthwhile target of criticism, rather than their role in the maintenance of capitalism, patriarchy, or social control generally, for that role was a minimal one. Labels such as neglect, drunkenness, immorality and abuse were often attached unfairly and with little intelligence, especially in relation to Aboriginal parents. For the remainder their preceding family life was nothing other than sad, and many were in fact neglected and abused by any criteria. Once in the child welfare system, their fate was too often both mindlessly routine and brutal, a cruel waste of human life.

It is not necessary to wait for the arrival of a socialist society, however, or in the case of Lasch, the return of a truly bourgeois society, to argue that children and their parents should be treated fairly and humanely, and there is no reason why we should define either these ideals or their abuse as particularly 'bourgeois'. We have to assume that various forms of social control are constitutive of all social relationships, and the object of critical social theory can then become not only 'the state' or 'middle-class professionals', but also how and why particular social institutions have cruelty and injustice built into their walls, as well as, perhaps most importantly, what it is about the rest of us that allowed and continues to allow those cruelties and injustices in the construction of childhood to exist.

Bibliography

Abele, A. and Stein-Hilbers, M. (1978) 'Alltagswissen, öffentliche meinung über Kriminalität und soziale Kontrolle' *Kriminologisches Journal* 10(3): 161–73

Abrams, P. (1982) *Historical Sociology* Shepton Mallet: Open Books

Alford, K. (1984) *Production or Reproduction? An Economic History of Women in Australia, 1788–1850* Melbourne: Oxford University Press

Aries, P. (1973) *Centuries of Childhood* Harmondsworth: Penguin

Austin, A.G. (1958) *George William Rusden and National Education in Australia 1849–1862* Melbourne: Melbourne University Press

Bacchi, Carol L. (1980) 'The nature-nurture debate in Australia, 1900–1914' *Historical Studies* 19(75): 199–212

Badie, B. and Birnbaum, P. (1973) *The Sociology of the State* Chicago: University of Chicago Press

Bailey, R. and Brake, M. (eds) (1975) *Radical Social Work* London: Edward Arnold

Barbalet, J.M. (1985) 'Power and resistance' *British Journal of Sociology* 36(1): 521–48

Barbalet, M. (1983) *Far From a Low Gutter Girl. The Forgotten World of State Wards: South Australia 1887–1940* Melbourne: Oxford University Press

Becker, C.L. (1932) *The Heavenly City of the Eighteenth-Century Philosophers* New Haven: Yale University Press

Behlmer, G.K. (1982) *Child Abuse and Moral Reform in England, 1870–1908* Stanford: Stanford University Press

Bellingham, B. (1983) 'The 'Unspeakable Blessing': street children, reform rhetoric, and misery in early industrial capitalism' *Politics and Society* 12(3): 303–30

Benjamin, J. (1988) *The Bonds of Love. Psychoanalysis, Feminism, and the Problem of Domination* New York: Pantheon

Bessant, B. (1987) 'Children and youth in Australia 1860s–1930s' in B. Bessant (ed.) *Mother State and Her Little Ones. Children and Youth in Australia 1860s–1930s* Melbourne: Centre for Youth and Community Studies, pp. 7–30

Betts, K. (1986) 'The conditions of action, power and the problem of interests' *Sociological Review* 34(1): 39–64

Bignell, S. (1973) 'Orphans and destitute children in Victoria up to 1864' *Victorian Historical Magazine* 44(1–2): 5–18

Boswell, J. (1984) '*Exposito* and *Oblatio*: the abandonment of children and the ancient and medieval family' *The American Historical Review* 89(1): 10–33

Bourke, H. (1981) 'Sociology and the social sciences in Australia, 1912–1928' *Australian and New Zealand Journal of Sociology* 17(1): 26–35

Braudel, F. (1973) *Capitalism and Material Life 1400–1800* New York: Harper & Row

Brenzel, B. (1983) *Daughters of the State. A Social Portrait of the First Reform School for Girls in North America, 1856–1905* Cambridge, Mass.: Massachussetts Institute of Technology Press

Bridges, B.J. (1973) The Sydney Orphan Schools, 1800–1830, MEd thesis, Sydney: University of Sydney

Brown, J.C. (1972) '*Poverty is Not a Crime': The Development of Social Services in Tasmania 1803–1900* Hobart: Tasmanian Historical Research Association

Burke, P. (1980) *Sociology and History* London: Allen & Unwin

Burns, A. and Goodnow, J. (1979) *Children and Families in Australia* Sydney: Allen & Unwin

Burns, T.R. (1986) 'Actors, transactions and social structure' in U. Himmelstrand (ed.) *Sociology: From Crisis to Science? Vol 2: The Social Reproduction of Organization and Culture* London: Sage, pp. 8–37

Calhoun, C. (1982) *The Question of Class Struggle* Chicago: University of Chicago Press

Callon, M. (1986) 'Some elements of a sociology of translation: domestication of the scallops and the fishermen of St Brieuc Bay' in J. Law (ed.) *Power, Action and Belief: A New Sociology of Knowledge?* London: Routledge & Kegan Paul, pp. 196–232

Cannon, M. (1975) *Life in the Cities* Melbourne: Nelson

Carpenter, M. (1851) *Reformatory Schools for the Children of the Perishing and Dangerous Classes, and for Juvenile Offenders* London: C. Gilpin

Cashen, P. (1985) 'The truant as delinquent: the psychological perspective, South Australia, 1920–1940' *Journal of Australian Studies* 16: 71–83

Castel, R., Castel, F. and Lovell, A. (1982) *The Psychiatric Society* New York: Columbia University Press

Cawte, M. (1986) 'Craniometry and eugenics in Australia: R.J.A. Berry and the quest for social efficiency' *Historical Studies* 22(86): 35–53

Chisholm, R. (1985) *Black Children: White Welfare? Aboriginal Child Welfare Law and Policy in New South Wales* Sydney: Social Welfare Research Centre, University of New South Wales

Cicourel, A.V. (1976) [1968] *The Social Organization of Juvenile Justice* London: Heinemann

Clarke, J., Critcher, C. and Johnson, R. (eds) (1979) *Working Class Culture* London: Hutchinson

Clegg, S.R. (1989) *Frameworks of Power* London: Sage

Cleverley, J.F. (1971) *The First Generation: School and Society in Early Australia* Sydney: Sydney University Press

Cohen, J. and Arato, A. (1989) 'Politics and the reconstruction of the concept of civil society' in A. Honneth, T. McCarthy, C. Offe, and A. Wellmer (eds) *Zwischenbetrachtungen: Im Prozess der Aufklärung* Frankfurt a.M.: Suhrkamp, pp. 482–503

Cohen, S. (1979) 'The punitive city: notes on the dispersal of social control' *Contemporary Crises* 3: 339–63

——— (1985) *Visions of Social Control* Cambridge: Polity Press

——— and Scull, A. (eds) (1983) *Social Control and the State: Historical and Comparative Esays* Oxford: Basil Blackwell

Connell, R.W. (1983) *Which Way Is Up? Essays on Class, Sex and Culture* Sydney: Allen & Unwin

——— and Irving, T.H. (1980) *Class Structure in Australian History* Melbourne: Longman Cheshire

Connell, W.F. (1980) *The Australian Council for Educational Research, 1930–80* Melbourne: Australian Council for Educational Research

Corrigan, P. and Leonard, P. (1978) *Social Work Practice Under Capitalism* London: Macmillan

Crew, D.F. (1986) 'German socialism, the state and family policy, 1918–33' *Continuity and Change* 1(2): 235–63

Crow, G. (1989) 'The use of the concept "strategy" in recent sociological literature' *Sociology* 23(1): 1–24

Dahl, T.S. (1985) *Child Welfare and Social Defence* Oslo: Norwegian University Press

Daniels, K. (1977) *Women in Australia: An Annotated Guide to the Records, Vols 1 and 2* Canberra: Australian Government Publishing Service

——— and Murnane, M. (1980) *Uphill All the Way: A Documentary History of Women in Australia* St Lucia: University of Queensland Press

Daunton, M.J. (1983) *House and Home in the Victorian City. Working-Class Housing 1850–1914* London: Edward Arnold

Davis, J. (1984) 'A poor man's system of justice: the London Police Courts in the second half of the nineteenth century' *The Historical Journal* 27(2): 309–35

Davison, G. (1983) 'The city-bred child and urban reform in Melbourne 1900–1940' in P. Williams (ed.) *Social Process and the City: Urban Studies Yearbook 1* Sydney: Allen & Unwin, pp. 143–74

Dawe, A. (1979) 'Theories of social action' in T. Bottomore and R. Nisbet (eds) *A History of Sociological Analysis* London: Heinemann

De Mause, L. (1974) 'The evolution of childhood' in L. De Mause (ed.) *The History of Childhood* New York: Harper and Row, pp. 1–73

de Regt, A. (1982) 'Unacceptable families: on the origins of social maladjustment' *Netherlands Journal of Sociology* 18(2): 139–56

——(1984) *Arbeidersgezinnen en Beschavingsarbeid. Ontwikkelingen in Nederland 1870–1940; Een Historisch-Sociologisch Studie* Amsterdam: Boom

de Rooy, P. (1982) 'Kinderbescherming in Nederland' in B. Kruithof, J. Noordman and P. de Rooy (eds) *Geschiedenis van Opvoeding en Onderwijs* Nijmegen: Socialistische Uitgeverij Nijmegen, pp. 105–26

de Swaan, (1981) 'The politics of agoraphobia' *Theory and Society* 10: pp. 337–58

——(1983) 'In care of the state. The social dynamics of public health, education and maintenance' *Verzorging* 1(2): 1–14

——(1988) *In Care of the State. Health Care, Education and Welfare in Europe and the USA in the Modern Era* Cambridge: Polity Press

——(1990) *The Management of Normality. Critical Essays in Health and Welfare* London: Routledge

Deacon, D. (1989) *Managing Gender. The State, the New Middle Class and Women Workers 1830–1930* Melbourne: Oxford University Press

Dekker, J.J.H. (1985) *Straffen, Redden en Opvoeden: Het Onstaan en de Ontwikkeling van de Residentiele Heropvoeding in West-Europa, 1814–1914, met Bijzondere Aandacht voor 'Nederlandsche Mettray'* Assen/Maatricht: Van Gorcum

Dickey, B. (1968) 'The establishment of industrial schools and reformatories in New South Wales, 1850–1875' *JRAHS* 54(2): 135–51

——(1977) 'Care for deprived, neglected and delinquent children in New South Wales, 1901–1915' *JRAHS* 63(3): 167–83

——(1979) 'The evolution of care for destitute children in New South Wales, 1875–1901' *Journal of Australian Studies* 4: 38–57

——(1980) *No Charity There: A Short History of Social Welfare in Australia* Sydney: Allen & Unwin

——(1986) *Rations, Residences, Resources. A History of Social Welfare in South Australia Since 1836* Netley: Wakefield Press

Dingwall, R., Eekelaar, J.M. and Murray, T. (1983) *The Protection of Children. State Intervention and Family Life* Oxford: Basil Blackwell

Dixson, M. (1976) *Greater than Lenin? Lang and Labour 1916–1932* Melbourne: Melbourne Politics Monographs

Donzelot, J. (1979a) *The Policing of Families* London: Hutchinson

——(1979b) 'The poverty of political culture' *Ideology and Consciousness* 5: 73–86

—— and de Swaan, A. (1984) ' "Social life has been destroyed, that is the essence of the crisis". A dialogue on the crisis of the welfare state' *De Groene Amsterdammer* 108 (5): 10–11

Downs, S.W. and Sherraden, M.W. (1983) 'The orphan asylum in the nineteenth century' *Social Service Review* 57(2): 272–90

Driver, F. (1990) 'Discipline without frontiers? Representations of Mettray Reformatory Colony in Britain, 1840–1880' *Journal of Historical Sociology* 3(3): 272–93

Earnshaw, B. (1979) 'The convict apprentices, 1820–1838' *Push from the Bush* 5: 82–97

Edwards, A. (1988) *Regulation and Repression. The Study of Social Control* Sydney: Allen & Unwin

Elias, N. (1982a) *The Civilizing Process, Vol 1: The History of Manners* New York: Pantheon
—— (1982b) *The Civilizing Process, Vol 2: Power and Civility* New York: Pantheon
Elster, J. (1983) *Explaining Technical Change* Cambridge: Cambridge University Press
Evans, P.B., Rueschemeyer, D. and Skocpol, T. (1985) *Bringing the State Back In* Cambridge: Cambridge University Press
Faler, P. (1974) 'Cultural aspects of the Industrial Revolution: Lynn, Massachussetts, shoemakers and industrial morality, 1826–1860' *Labor History* 15(3): 367–94
Fisher, S. (1982) 'An accumulation of misery? in R. Kennedy (ed.) *Australian Welfare History: Critical Essays* Melbourne: Macmillan, pp. 32–50
—— (1985) 'The family and the Sydney economy in the late nineteenth century' in P. Grimshaw, C. McConville and E. McEwen (eds) *Families in Colonial Australia* Sydney: Allen & Unwin
Fitzgerald, S. (1987) *Rising Damp. Sydney 1870–90* Melbourne: Oxford University Press
Foucault, M. (1977) *Discipline and Punish* London: Allen Lane
—— (1979a) 'Governmentality' *Ideology and Consciousness* 6: 5–21
—— (1979b) 'Truth and power' in M. Morris and P. Patton (eds) *Michel Foucault. Power, Truth, Strategy* Sydney: Feral Publications
—— (1980) *Power/Knowledge* Brighton: Harvester
—— (1982) 'The subject and power' in H.L. Dreyfus and P. Rabinow *Michel Foucault: Beyond Structuralism and Hermeneutics* Brighton: Harvester Press, pp. 208–26
—— (1986) 'Disciplinary power and subjection' in S. Lukes (ed.) *Power* Oxford: Basil Blackwell, pp. 229–42.
—— (1988) 'Technologies of the self' in L.H. Martin, H. Gutman and P.H. Hutton (eds) *Technologies of the Self. A Seminar with Michel Foucault* London: Tavistock, pp. 16–49
Fox, R. (1976) 'Beyond "social control": institutions and disorder in bourgeois society' *History of Education Quarterly* 16(2): 203–7
Frost, N. (1989) *The Politics of Child Welfare: Inequality, Power and Change* Brighton: Harvester Wheatsheaf
Game A. and Pringle, R. (1983) 'The making of the Australian family' in A. Burns, G. Bottomley and P. Jools (eds) *The Family in the Modern World* Sydney: Allen & Unwin, pp. 80–102
Gandevia, B. (1978) *Tears Often Shed: Child Health and Welfare in Australia from 1788* Sydney: Pergamon
Garrick, P. (1988) 'Children of the poor and industrious classes in Western Australia, 1829–1880' in P. Hetherington (ed.) *Childhood and Society in Western Australia* Perth: University of Western Australia Press, pp. 13–27
Garton, S. (1982) 'The melancholy years: psychiatry in New South Wales, 1900–1940' in R. Kennedy (ed.) *Australian Welfare History. Critical Essays* Sydney, Allen & Unwin, pp. 138–66
—— (1986a) 'The rise of the therapeutic state: psychiatry and the system of criminal jurisdiction in New South Wales, 1890–1940' *Australian Journal of Politics and History* 32(3): 378–88

——(1986b) 'Sir Charles Mackellar: psychiatry, eugenics and child welfare in New South Wales, 1900–1914' *Historical Studies* 22(86): 21–34

——(1988) *Medicine and Madness. A Social History of Insanity in New South Wales, 1880–1940* Sydney: New South Wales University Press

——(1989) 'Frederick William Neitenstein: juvenile reformatory and prison reform in New South Wales, 1878–1909' *JRAHS* 75(1): 51–64

Gerstenberger, H. (1985) 'The poor and the respectable worker: on the introduction of social insurance in Germany' *Labour History* 48: 69–85

——(1990) *Die subjektlose Gewalt. Theorie der Entstehung bürgerlicher Staatsgewalt* Münster: Westfälisches Dampfboot

Gettleman, M.E. (1974) 'The Whig interpretation of social welfare history' *Smith College Studies in Social Work* 44: 150–57

Giddens, A. (1982) *Profiles and Critiques in Social Theory* London: Macmillan

Gillis, J.R. (1975) 'The evolution of juvenile delinquency in England 1890–1914' *Past & Present* 67: 96–126

Ginzburg, C. (1980) *The Cheese and The Worms. The Cosmos of a Sixteenth Century Miller* London: Routledge & Kegan Paul

Godden, J. (1982) ' "The work for them and the glory for us!" Sydney women's philanthropy, 1880–1900' in R. Kennedy (ed.) *Australian Welfare History. Critical Essays* Melbourne: Macmillan

Goode, W. (1968) *World Revolution and Family Patterns* New York: Macmillan

——(1973) 'Functionalism: The empty castle' in *Explorations in Social Theory* New York: Oxford University Press, pp. 64–94

Goodwin, C.D. (1964) 'Evolution theory in Australian social thought' *Journal of the History of Ideas* 25: 393–416

Gordon, L. (1986) 'Family violence, feminism and social control' *Feminist Studies* 12(3): 453–78

——(1988) *Heroes of Their Own Lives: The Politics and History of Family Violence* New York: Viking Penguin

Gough, I. (1979) *The Political Economy of the Welfare State* London: Macmillan

Govan, E. (1951) Public and Private Responsibility for Child Welfare in New South Wales, 1788–1887, PhD thesis, Chicago: University of Chicago

Grabosky, P.N. (1977) *Sydney in Ferment* Canberra: Australian National University Press

Gramsci, A. (1971) *Selections from the Prison Notebooks of Antonio Gramsci* edited by Q. Hoare and G.N. Smith, New York: International Publishers

Gray, R. (1977) 'Bourgeois hegemony in Victorian Britain' in J. Bloomfield (ed.) *Class, Hegemony and Party* London: Lawrence & Wishart, pp. 73–93

Green, D. and Cromwell, L. (1984) *Mutual Aid or Welfare State. Australia's Friendly Societies* Sydney: Allen & Unwin

Greenberg, D.F. (1983) 'Reflections on the justice model debate' *Contemporary Crises* 7: 313–27

Grimshaw, P. and Willett, G. (1981) 'Women's history and family history: an exploration of colonial family structure' in N. Grieve and

P. Grimshaw (eds) *Australian Women: Feminist Perspectives* Melbourne: Oxford University Press, pp. 134–55

Habermas, J. (1984) *The Theory of Communicative Action Vol 1: Reason and the Rationalisation of Society* London: Heinemann

——(1987) *The Theory of Communicative Action Vol 2: Lifeworld and System: A Critique of Functionalist Reason* Cambridge: Polity Press

——(1989) *The Structural Transformation of the Public Sphere* Cambridge: Polity Press

Haebich, A. (1988) *For Their Own Good. Aborigines and Government in the Southwest of Western Australia, 1900–1940* Nedlands: University of Western Australia Press

Hall, G. S. (1905) *Adolescence. Its Psychology and Its Relation to Physiology, Anthropology, Sociology, Sex, Crime, Religion and Education, Vols 1 & 2* New York: D. Appleton & Co

Hall, P.A. (1986) *Governing the Economy: the Politics of State Intervention in Britain and France* Cambridge: Polity Press

Harris, R. and Webb, D. (1987) *Welfare, Power, and Juvenile Justice* London: Tavistock

Healy, W. et al. (1929) *Reconstructing Behaviour in Youth. A Study of Problem Children in Foster Families* New York: Alfred A. Knopf

Hearn, F. (1978) *Domination, Legitimation and Resistance. The Incorporation of the Nineteenth-Century English Working Class* Westport, Connecticut: Greenwood Press

Hegel, G.W.F. (1976) *The Phenomenology of Mind* New York: Harper and Row

Henry, S. (1983) *Private Justice: Towards Integrated Theorising in the Sociology of Law* London: Routledge & Kegan Paul

——(1987) 'The construction and deconstruction of social control: thoughts on the discursive production of state law and private justice' in J. Lowman, R.S. Menzies, and T.S. Paly (eds) *Transcarceration: Essays in the Sociology of Social Control* Aldershot: Gower, pp. 89–108

Hewitt, M. (1983) 'Bio-politics and social policy: Foucault's account of welfare' *Theory, Culture and Society* 2(1): 67–84

Hicks, N. (1978) *'This Sin and Scandal': Australia's Population Debate, 1891–1911* Canberra: Australian National University Press

Higgins, J. (1980) 'Social control theories of social policy' *Journal of Social Policy* 9(1): 1–23

Hill, F. (1868) *Children of the State. The Training of Juvenile Paupers* London: Macmillan

Hirst, P. (1981) 'The genesis of the social' *Politics and Power* 3: 67–82

Historical Records of Australia (HRA) Series III, Vols 2, 3, 4, 6 Canberra: Library Committee of the Commonwealth Parliament

Historical Records of New South Wales (HRNSW) Vol. 2 Sydney: Charles Potter, Government Printer

Hobsbawm, E. (1975) *The Age of Capital* London: Weidenfeld & Nicolson

Horn, M. (1984) 'The moral message of child guidance, 1925–1945' *Journal of Social History* 18(1): 25–36

——(1989) *Before It's Too Late: The Child Guidance Movement in the US, 1922–1945* Philadelphia: Temple University Press

Horsburgh, M. (1976) 'Child care in New South Wales in 1870' *Australian Social Work* 29(1): 3–24

—— (1977a) 'Child care in New South Wales in 1890' *Australian Social Work* 30(3): 21–40

—— (1977b) 'Randwick Asylum: organizational resistance to social change' *Australian Social Work* 30(1): 15–24

—— (1980) 'The apprenticing of dependent children in New South Wales between 1850 and 1885' *Journal of Australian Studies* 7(1): 33–54

—— (1982) 'The churches of New South Wales and the care of neglected children' *Church Heritage* 2(4): 271–88

Houlbrooke, R.A (1984) *The English Family, 1450–1700* Longman: New York

Humphries, J. (1977) 'Class struggle and the persistence of the working-class family' *Cambridge Journal of Economics* 1: 241–58

Humphries, S. (1981) *Hooligans or Rebels? An Oral History of Working-Class Childhood and Youth, 1889–1939* Oxford: Basil Blackwell

Ignatieff, M. (1983) 'State, civil society and total institutions: a critique of recent social histories of punishment' in S. Cohen and A. Scull (eds) *Social Control and the State* Oxford: Basil Blackwell, pp. 75–105

Industries Assistance Commission (1977) *Structural Change in Australia* Canberra: AGPS

Jaggs, D. (1986) *Neglected and Criminal. Foundations of Child Welfare Legislation in Victoria* Melbourne: Centre for Youth and Community Studies, Philip Institute of Technology

James, A. and A. Prout (eds) (1990) *Constructing and Reconstructing Childhood* London: The Falmer Press

James, J.S. (1969) *The Vagabond Papers* Melbourne: Melbourne University Press

Jamrozik, A. (1983) 'Changing concepts and practices in child welfare and options for the future' in J. Jarrah (ed.) *Child Welfare: Current Issues and Future Directions* Sydney: Social Welfare Research Centre, University of New South Wales, pp. 65–89

Jessop, B. (1982) *The Capitalist State* Oxford: Martin Robertson

Jevons, W.S. (1929) 'Sydney in 1858. A social survey' *Sydney Morning Herald* 9 November 1929

Joffe, C. (1979) 'Symbolic interactionism and the study of social services' *Studies in Symbolic Interaction* 2: 235–56

Johnson, R. (1970) 'Educational policy and social control in early Victorian England' *Past and Present* 49: 96–119

Jones, G. (1986) *Social Hygiene in Twentieth Century Britain* London: Croom Helm

Jones, G.S. (1974) 'Working-class culture and working-class politics in London, 1870–1900: notes on the remaking of a working class' *Journal of Social History* 7(4): 460–508

—— (1977) 'Class expression versus social control' *History Workshop* 4:162–70

Jones, K. (1983) 'Sentiment and science: the late nineteenth century paediatrician as mother's advisor' *Journal of Social History* 17(1): 79–96

Jones, M.B. (1987) 'The benefits of benificence' *Social Service Review* 61(2): 183–217

Kadushin, A. (1976) 'Child welfare services—past and present' *Children Today* 5(3): 17–19

Kaestle, C. (1983) *Pillars of the Republic* New York: Hill & Wang

Katz, M.B. (1976) 'The origins of public education: a reassessment' *History of Education Quarterly* 16(4): 381–407

——(1978) 'Origins of the institutional state' *Marxist Perspectives* 1(4): 6–22

——(1986) *In the Shadow of the Poorhouse. A Social History of Welfare in America* New York: Basic Books

Keating, M. (1973) *The Australian Workforce 1910–11 to 1960–61* Canberra: Australian National University Press

Kett, J.F. (1977) *Rites of Passage: Adolescence in America, 1790 to the Present* New York: Basic Books

King, H. (1956) 'Some aspects of police administration in New South Wales, 1825–1851' *JRAHS* 42: 205–30

Kittrie, N. (1971) *The Right to Be Different* Baltimore: John Hopkins Press

Knapp, P. (1984) 'Can social theory escape from history? Views of history in social science' *History and Theory* 23(1): 34–52

Kociumbas, J. (1984) 'Childhood history as ideology' *Labour History* 47: 1–17

——(1988) 'The best years?' in V. Burgmann and J. Lee (eds) *Making a Life* Melbourne: McPhee Gribble/Penguin, pp. 133–51

Kumar, K. (1983) 'Class and political action in nineteenth-century England' *European Journal of Sociology* 24(1): 3–43

Lang, J. (1970) *The Turbulent Years* Sydney: Alpha Books

——(1980) *I Remember* Leura: McNamara's Books

Laqueur, T. (1976) *Religion and Respectability: Sunday Schools and Working-Class Culture, 1780–1850* New Haven: Yale University Press

Lasch, C. (1973) 'Origins of the asylum' in *The World of Nations: Reflections on American History, Politics and Culture* New York: Alfred Knopf

——(1977) *Haven in a Heartless World: The Family Besieged* New York: Basic Books

——(1980) 'Life in the therapeutic state' *New York Review of Books* 27 (10): 24–32

Latour, B. (1986) 'The powers of association' in J. Law (ed.) *Power, Action and Belief: A New Sociology of Knowledge?* London: Routledge & Kegan Paul, pp. 264–80

Laurent, J. (1986) 'Tom Mann, R.S. Ross and evolutionary socialism in Broken Hill, 1902–1912: alternative Social Darwinism in the Australian Labour Movement' *Labour History* 51: 54–69

Law, J. (1986) 'On power and its tactics: a view from the sociology of science' *Sociological Review* 34(1): 1–38

Lawson, R. (1972) 'Class or status? The social structure of Brisbane in the 1890s' *Australian Journal of Politics and History* 18(3): 344–59

Lee, J. and Fahey, C. (1986) 'A boom for whom? Some developments in the Australian labour market' *Labour History* 50: 1–27

Lee, P. and Pithers, D. (1980) 'Radical residential care: Trojan horse or non-runner?' in M. Brake and R. Bailey (eds) *Radical Social Work and Practice* London: Edward Arnold, pp. 86–122

Levy, B.-H. (1977) 'Power and sex: an interview with Michel Foucault' *Telos* 32: 152–61

Lewis, J. (1980) *The Politics of Motherhood. Child and Maternal Welfare in England, 1900–1939* London: Croom Helm

———(1986) 'The working-class wife and mother and state intervention' in J. Lewis (ed.) *Labour and Love. Women's Experience of Home and Family, 1850–1940* Oxford: Basil Blackwell, pp. 99–120

Lis, C. and Soly, H. (1979) *Poverty and Capitalism in Pre-Industrial Europe* Atlantic Highlands, NJ: Humanities Press

Lloyd, C. (1989) 'Realism, structurism, and history: foundations for a transformative science of society' *Theory and Society* 18(4): 451–94

Lubove, R. (1965) *The Professional Altruist* Boston: Harvard University Press

Lüdkte, A. (1979) 'The role of state violence in the period of transition to industrial capitalism: the example of Prussia from 1815 to 1848' *Social History* 4(2): 175–221

Luhmann, N. (1982) *The Differentiation of Society* New York: Columbia University Press

Macarthy, P.G. (1967) 'Labor and the living wage, 1890–1910' *Australian Journal of Politics and History* 13: 67–89

MacCann, P. (1977) 'Popular education, socialization and social control: Spitafields, 1812–24' in P. McCann (ed.) *Popular Education and Socialization in the Nineteenth Century* London: Methuen, pp. 1–40

Macfarlane, A. (1978) *The Origins of English Individualism* Oxford: Basil Blackwell

———(1986) *Marriage and Love in England, 1300–1840* Oxford: Basil Blackwell

Mackellar, C. (1913) 'The treatment of neglected and delinquent children in Great Britain, Europe, and America, with recommendations as to the amendement of administration and law in New South Wales' *New South Wales Parliamentary Papers* 1913, 4: 1207–1349

Mackinlay, J. (1973) 'The professional regulation of social change' in P. Halmos (ed.) *Professionalisation and Social Change* Keele: Sociological Review Monographs, pp. 61–84

Manton, J. (1976) *Mary Carpenter and the Children of the Streets* London: Heinemann

Marks, R.B. (1973) 'Institutions for dependent and delinquent children: histories, nineteenth-century statistics, and recurrent goals' in D.M. Pappenfort, D.M. Kilpatrick and R.W. Roberts (eds) *Child Caring: Social Policy and the Institution* Chicago: Aldine Publishing Co, pp. 9–67

Martin, A.W (1977) 'Drink and deviance in Sydney: investigating intemperance, 1854–55' *Historical Studies* 17: pp. 342–60

Marx, K. (1975) [1845] 'The holy family' in *Collected Works, Vol 4* London: Lawrence & Wishart

———(1979) [1852] 'The 18th Brumaire of Louis Bonaparte' in *Collected Works, Vol 11* London: Lawrence & Wishart

────and Engels, F. (1976) [1846] 'The German ideology' in *Collected Works, Vol 5* London: Lawrence & Wishart

Mathieson, T. (1987) 'The eagle and the sun: on panoptical systems and mass media in modern society' in J. Lowman, R.J. Menzies and T.S. Palys (eds) *Transcarceration: Essays in the Sociology of Social Control* Aldershot: Gower, pp. 59–75

Matthews, J.J. (1984) *Good and Mad Women. The Historical Construction of Femininity in Twentieth Century Australia* Sydney: Allen & Unwin

Maunders, D. (1984) *Keeping Them off the Streets* Melbourne: Phillip Institute of Technology

Mayne, A.J.C. (1982) *Fever, Squalor, Vice: Sanitation and Social Policy in Victorian Sydney* St Lucia: University of Queensland Press

────(1983) ' "The question of the poor" in the nineteenth-century city' *Historical Studies* 20(81): 557–73

McCallum, D. (1983) 'Eugenics, psychology and education in Australia' *Melbourne Working Papers* 4: 17–33

────(1990) *The Social Production of Merit. Education, Psychology and Politics in Australia, 1900–1950* London: Falmer Press

McCalman, J. (1982) 'Class and respectability in a working-class suburb: Richmond, Victoria, before the Great War' *Historical Studies* 20(78): 90–103

────(1984) *Struggletown. Public and Private Life in Richmond, 1900–1965* Melbourne: Melbourne University Press

McCullagh, C.B. (1984) *Justifying Historical Descriptions* Cambridge: Cambridge University Press

McDonald, D.I. (1966) 'Henry Parkes and the Sydney Nautical School' *JRAHS* 52(3): 212–27

McGovern, C.M. (1986) 'The myth of social control and custodial oppression: patterns of psychiatric medicine in late nineteenth-century institutions' *Journal of Social History* 20(1): 3–23

McIntosh, M. (1978) 'The state and the oppression of women' in A. Kuhn and A. Wolpe (eds) *Feminism and Materialism* London: Routledge & Kegan Paul, pp. 254–89

McNab, K. and Ward, R. (1962) 'The nature and nurture of the first generation of native-born Australians' *Historical Studies* 10(39): 289–308

Mead, G.H. (1925) 'The genesis of the self and social control' *International Journal of Ethics* 35: 251–77

Melossi, D. (1990) *The State of Social Control. A Sociological Study of Concepts of State and Social Control in the Making of Democracy* Cambridge: Polity Press

────and Pavarini, M. (1981) *The Prison and the Factory. Origins of the Penitentiary System* London: Macmillan

Merton, R.K. (1984) 'The fallacy of the latest word: the case of "Pietism and Science" ' *American Journal of Sociology* 89(5): 1091–121

Meyer, P. (1983) *The Child and the State. The Intervention of the State in Family Life* Cambridge: Cambridge University Press

Michielse, H.C.M. (1990) 'Policing the poor: J.L. Vives and the sixteenth-century origins of modern social administration' *Social Service Review* 64(1): 1–21

Miliband, R. (1969) *The State in Capitalist Society* London: Weidenfeld & Nicolson

Miller, A. (1983) *For Your Own Good. Hidden Cruelty in Child-Rearing and the Roots of Violence* New York: Farrar-Straus-Giroux

Miller, P. (1987) *Domination and Power* London: Routledge & Kegan Paul
―― and Rose, N. (1988) 'The Tavistock programme: the government of subjectivity and social life' *Sociology* 22(2): 171–92

Mills, C.W. (1943) 'The professional ideology of social pathologists' *American Journal of Sociology* 49(2): 165–80
―― (1959) *The Sociological Imagination* New York: Oxford University Press

Mitchell, W. and Sherington, G. (1985) 'Families and children in nineteenth-century Illawarra' in P. Grimshaw,C.McConville and E. McEwen (eds) *Families in Colonial Australia* Sydney: Allen & Unwin, pp. 108–10

Moore, B.J. (1958) 'Strategy in social science' in *Political Power and Social Theory* Cambridge, Mass.: Harvard University Press

Mowbray, M. (1980) 'Non-government welfare: state roles of the Councils of Social Service' *Australian and New Zealand Journal of Sociology* 16(3): 52–60

Mulvany, J. (1989) 'Social control processes, activities and ideologies—the case of school non-attendance in Melbourne' *Australian and New Zealand Journal of Sociology* 25(2): 222–38

Muraskin, W.A. (1976) 'The social control theory in American history: a critique' *Journal of Social History* 9(4): 565–68

Nairn, B. (1986) *'Big Fella': Jack Lang and the Australian Labor Party* Melbourne: Melbourne University Press

Neustadter, R. (1989) 'The politics of growing up: the status of childhood in modern social thought' *Current Perspectives in Social Theory* 9: 199–221

O'Brien, A. (1979) 'Left in the lurch. Deserted wives in NSW at the turn of the century' in J. Mackinolty and H. Radi (eds), *In Pursuit of Justice. Australian Women and the Law, 1788–1979* Sydney: Hale & Iremonger, pp. 96–105
―― (1982) The Poor in New South Wales, 1880–1918 PhD dissertation, Sydney: University of Sydney
―― (1988) *Poverty's Prison: The Poor in New South Wales, 1880–1918* Melbourne: Oxford University Press

O'Brien, P. (1982) *The Promise of Punishment: Prisons in Nineteenth-Century France* Princeton, NJ: Princeton University Press

O'Connor, J. (1973) *The Fiscal Crisis of the State* New York: St Martin's Press

O'Donnell, C. and Craney, J. (eds) (1982) *Family Violence in Australia* Melbourne: Longman Cheshire

Pahl, R.E. (1984) *Divisions of Labour* Oxford: Basil Blackwell

Parkes, H. (1896) *Speeches on Various Occasions Connected with the Public Affairs of New South Wales, 1848–1874* Melbourne: George Robertson

Parr, J. (1980) *Labouring Children* London: Croom Helm

Parsons, T. (1951) *The Social System* New York: Free Press
Parton, N. (1985) *The Politics of Child Abuse* London: Macmillan
Patton, P. (1989) 'Taylor and Foucault on power and freedom' *Political Studies* 37(2): 260–76
Pearson, G. (1975) *The Deviant Imagination* London: Macmillan
—— (1983) *Hooligan: A History of Respectable Fears* London: Macmillan
Pelling, H. (1960) *Modern Britain, 1885–1955* Edinburgh: Nelson
—— (1979) *Popular Politics and Society in Late Victorian Britain* London: Macmillan
Peukert, D. (1986) *Grenzen der Sozialdisziplinierung. Aufsteig und Krise der deutschen Jugendfürsorge von 1878 bis 1932* Köln: Bund Verlag
Peyser, D. (1939) 'A study of the history of welfare work in Sydney from 1788 till about 1900' *JRAHS* 25(2–3): 89–128, 169–212
Philips, D. (1977) *Crime and Authority in Victorian England: The Black Country, 1835–1860* London: Croom Helm
Piliavin, I. (1964) *Institution or Foster Family. A Century of Debate* New York: Child Welfare League of America
Pinchbeck, I. and Hewitt, M. (1969) *Children in English Society, Vol 1* London: Routledge & Kegan Paul
—— (1973) *Children in English Society, Vol 2* London: Routledge & Kegan Paul
Piven, F.F. (1984) 'Women and the state: ideology, power and the welfare state' *Socialist Review* 14(2): 11–19
—— and Cloward, R.A. (1972) *Regulating the Poor. The Functions of Public Welfare* London: Tavistock
Platt, A.M. (1969) *The Child Savers* Chicago: University of Chicago Press
—— (1977) *The Child Savers* 2nd edition, Chicago: University of Chicago Press
Polanyi, K. (1944) *The Great Transformation* New York: Rinehart & Co
Pollock, L. (1983) *Forgotten Children. Parent-Child Relations from 1500 to 1900* Cambridge: Cambridge University Press
Proceedings of the First Australasian Conference on Charity (1890) Melbourne, 11–17 November, Melbourne: Government Printer
Procter, I. (1990) 'The privatisation of working-class life: a dissenting view' *British Journal of Sociology* 41(2): 157–80
Punch, M. (1974) 'The sociology of the anti-institution' *British Journal of Sociology* 25(3): 312–25
Qvortrup, J. (1987) 'Introduction to the sociology of childhood' *International Journal of Sociology* 17(3): 3–37
Radi, H. (1979) 'Whose child? Custody of children in New South Wales, 1854–1934' in J. Mackinolty and H. Radi (eds) *In Pursuit of Justice: Australian Women and the Law, 1788–1979* Sydney: Hale & Iremonger, pp. 119–30
Ramsland, J. (1974) 'The development of boarding-out systems in Australia: a series of welfare experiments in child care 1860–1910' *JRAHS* 60(3): 186–98
—— (1980) 'Mary Carpenter and the child-saving movement' *Australian Social Work* 33(2): 33–41
—— (1982) 'The Sydney Ragged Schools: a nineteenth-century voluntary approach to child welfare and education' *JRAHS* 68(3): 222–37

—— (1984) 'An anatomy of a nineteenth-century child-saving institution' *JRAHS* 70(3): 194–209

—— (1986) *Children of the Backlanes. Destitute and Neglected Children in Colonial New South Wales* Sydney: New South Wales University Press

Read, P. (1983) *The Stolen Generations: The Removal of Aboriginal Children in New South Wales, 1883 to 1969* Sydney: Ministry of Aboriginal Affairs

Reese, W.J. (1986) *Power and the Promise of School Reform: Grass Roots Movements During the Progressive Era* London: Routledge & Kegan Paul

Reiger, K. (1985) *The Disenchantment of the Home* Melbourne: Oxford University Press

Roach, J. (1978) *Social Reform in England, 1780–1880* London: Batsford

Rodger, J.J. (1988) 'Social Work as social control re-examined: beyond the dispersal of discipline thesis' *Sociology* 22(4): 563–81

Roe, J. (1976a) 'Leading the World? 1901–1914' in J. Roe (ed.) *Social Policy in Australia* Sydney: Cassell, pp. 3–23

—— (ed.) (1976b) *Social Policy in Australia. Some Perspectives, 1901–1975* Sydney: Cassell

Roe, M. (1976) 'The establishment of the Australian Department of Health' *Historical Studies* 17(67): 176–92

Roeland, D. (1980) *Kinderbescherming in de Maatschappij, 1905–1980* Baarn: Ambo

Rooke, P.T. and Schnell, R.L. (1982) 'Childhood and charity in nineteenth Century British North America' *Social History* 15(29): 157–79

Rose, N. (1987) 'Beyond the public/private division: law, power and the family' *Journal of Law & Society* 14(1): 61–76

Rose, N. (1990) *Governing the Soul. The Shaping of the Private Self* London: Routledge

Ross, E. (1983) 'Survival networks: women's neighbourhood sharing in London before World War I' *History Workshop* 15: 4–27

Ross, E.A. (1901) *Social Control* New York: Macmillan

Rothman, D. (1971) *The Discovery of the Asylum: Social Order and Disorder in the New Republic* Boston: Little, Brown

—— (1978) 'The state as parent: social policy in the progressive era' in W. Gaylin et al. (eds) *Doing Good: The Limits of Benevolence* New York: Pantheon, pp. 67–96

—— (1980) *Conscience and Convenience. The Asylum and its Alternatives in Progressive America* Boston: Little, Brown

Rothstein, W.G. (1973) 'Professionalization and employer demands: the cases of homeopathy and psychoanalysis in the United States' in P. Halmos (ed.) *Professionalization and Social Change* Keele: Sociological Review Monograph, pp. 159–78

Sauer, M. (1979) *Heimerziehung und Familienprinzip* Neuwied: Luchterhand

Scarre, G. (ed.) (1989) *Children, Parents and Politics* Cambridge: Cambridge University Press

Schmitt, C. (1985) *The Crisis of Parliamentary Democracy* Cambridge, Mass.: MIT Press

Sennett, R. (1978) *The Fall of Public Man. On the Social Psychology of Capitalism* New York: Vintage
———(1981) *Authority* New York: Vintage
Shaw, A.G.L. (1974) '1788–1810' in F. Crowley (ed.) *A New History of Australia* Melbourne: William Heinemann, pp. 1–44
Shorten, A.R. (1976) 'Nautical School Ships in Australia, 1850–1920' *Australian and New Zealand History of Education Journal* 5(2): 19–32
Sieder, R. (1986) 'Vata, derf i aufstehn? : childhood experiences in Viennese working-class families around 1900' *Continuity and Change* 1(1): 53–88
Simmel, G. (1971) *On Individuality and Social Forms* Chicago: University of Chicago Press
Simon, B. (1960) *Studies in the History of Education, 1780–1870* London: Lawrence & Wishart
Sinclair, W.A. (1976) *The Process of Economic Development in Australia* Melbourne: Longman Cheshire
Skocpol, T. (ed.) (1984) *Vision and Method in Historical Sociology* Cambridge: Cambridge University Press
Sommerville, C.J. (1982) *The Rise and Fall of Childhood* Beverley Hills: Sage
Spierenburg, P. (1984) *The Spectacle of Suffering* Cambridge: Cambridge University Press
Spitzer, S. (1987) 'Security and control in capitalist societies: the fetishism of security and the secret thereof' in J. Lowman, R.J. Menzies and T.S. Palys (eds) *Transcarceration: Essays in the Sociology of Social Control* Aldershot: Gower, pp. 43–58
Stansell, C. (1982) 'Women, children, and the uses of the streets: class and gender conflict in New York City, 1850–1860' *Feminist Studies* 8(2): 309–35
Staples, W.G. (1990) *Castles of Our Conscience. Social Control and the American State, 1800–1985* Cambridge: Polity Press
Stearns, P.N. (1976) 'The unskilled and industrialization: a transformation of consciousness' *Archiv für Sozialgeschichte* 16: 249–89
Sturma, M. (1983) *Vice in a Vicious Society: Crime and Convicts in Mid-Nineteenth Century New South Wales* St Lucia: University of Queensland Press
Sydney Labour History Group (1982) *What Rough Beast? The State and Social Order in Australian History* Sydney: Allen & Unwin
Synnott, A. (1983) 'Little angels, little devils: a sociology of children' *Canadian Review of Sociology and Anthropology* 20(1): 79–95
Tawney, R. (1964) [1914] 'An experiment in democratic education' in *The Radical Tradition* London: George Allen & Unwin, pp. 70–81
Taylor, I., P. Walton and J. Young (1973) *The New Criminology* London: Routledge & Kegan Paul
———(eds) (1975) *Critical Criminology* London: Routledge & Kegan Paul
Thane, P. (1984) 'The working class and state "welfare" in Britain, 1880–1914' *The Historical Journal* 27(4): 877–900
Tholfsen, T.R. (1971) 'The intellectual origins of mid-Victorian stability' *Political Science Quarterly* 86: 57–91

——(1976) *Working Class Radicalism in Mid-Victorian England* London: Croom Helm

Thomas, W.I. and Znaniecki, F. (1927) *The Polish Peasant in Europe and America* 2 volumes, New York: Knopf

Thompson, E.P. (1967) 'Time, work discipline and industrial capitalism' *Past and Present* 38: 56–97

——(1978) *The Poverty of Theory and Other Essays* London: Merlin Press

——(1980) *Writing by Candlelight* London: Merlin Press

——(1982) *The Making of the English Working Class* Harmondsworth: Penguin

Thompson, F.M.L. (1981) 'Social control in Victorian Britain', *The Economic History Review* 34(2): 189–208

——(1988) *The Rise of Respectable Society: A Social History of Victorian Britain, 1830–1900* London: Fontana

Thomson, D. (1986) 'Welfare and the historians' in L. Bonfield, R.M. Smith and K. Wrightson (eds) *The World We Have Gained. Histories of Population and Social Structure* Oxford: Basil Blackwell, pp. 355–78

Tiffin, S. (1982) 'In pursuit of reluctant parents', in Sydney Labour History Group (eds) *What Rough Beast? The State and Social Order in Australian History* Sydney: Allen & Unwin, pp. 130–150

Tilly, C. (1981) *As Sociology Meets History* New York: Academic Press

——and Tilly, L. (1980) 'Stalking the bourgeois family' *Social Science History* 4(2): 251–60

Titmuss, R. (1976) *Essays on the Welfare State* London: Allen & Unwin

van Krieken, R. (1980) 'The capitalist state and the organization of welfare: an introduction' *Australian and New Zealand Journal of Sociology* 16(3): 23–35

——(1985) Children and the State. Social Control and Child Welfare in New South Wales, 1800–1840, PhD thesis, Sydney: University of New South Wales

——(1990) 'The organisation of the soul: Elias and Foucault on discipline and the self', *Archives Europeénes du Sociologie* 31(2): 149–67

van Waters, M. (1926) *Youth in Conflict* New York: Republic

Vandepol, A. (1982) 'Dependent children, child custody, and the Mothers' Pensions: the transformation of state–family relations in the early 20th century' *Social Problems* 29(3): 221–35

Walker, P. (ed.) (1979) *Between Labour and Capital* Hassocks, Sussex: Harvester

Walkowitz, J.K. (1980) 'The politics of prostitution' in C.R. Stimpson and E.S. Person (eds) *Women, Sex and Sexuality* Chicago: University of Chicago Press, pp. 145–57

Weber, M. (1949) *The Methodology of the Social Sciences* New York: Free Press

White, R. (1990) *No Space of Their Own. Young People and Social Control in Australia* Melbourne: Cambridge University Press

Wilkinson, M. (1986) 'Good mothers–bad mothers: state substitute care of children in the 1960s' in H. Marchant and B. Wearing (eds) *Gender Reclaimed. Women in Social Work* Sydney: Hale & Iremonger, pp. 93–103

Wilkinson, P. and Grace, C. (1975) 'Reforms as revolutions' *Sociology* 9(3): 396–418

Williams, R. (1960) *Culture and Society, 1780–1950* London: Chatto & Windus

Williamson, N. (1982) ' "Hymns, songs and blackguard verses": life in the Industrial and Reformatory School for Girls in New South Wales, Pt I, 1867–1887' *JRAHS* 64(4): 375–87

—— (1983) 'Laundry maids or ladies? Life in the Industrial and Reformatory School for Girls in New South Wales, Pt II, 1887–1910' *JRAHS* 68(4): 312–24

Willis, S. (1980) 'Made to be moral—at Parramatta Girls' School, 1898–1923' in J. Roe (ed.) *Twentieth Century Sydney* Sydney: Hale & Iremonger, pp. 178–92

Wilson, E. (1977) *Women and the Welfare State* London: Tavistock

Wimshurst, K. (1981) 'Child labour and school attendance in South Australia, 1890–1915' *Historical Studies* 19: 388–411

Windschuttle, E. (1980a) ' "Feeding the poor and sapping their strength": the public role of ruling class women in eastern Australia, 1788–1850' in E. Windschuttle (ed.) *Women and Class in History: Feminist Perspectives on Australia, 1788–1978* Melbourne: Fontana, pp. 53–80

—— (1980b) 'Discipline, domestic training and social control: the Female School of Industry, Sydney, 1826–1847' *Labour History* 39: pp. 1–14

—— (1982) 'Women and the origins of colonial philanthropy' in R. Kennedy (ed.) *Australian Welfare History. Critical Essays* Melbourne: Macmillan, pp. 10–31

Wines, E.C. (1968) [1880] *The State of Prisons and of Child-Saving Institutions in the Civilized World* Montclair, NJ: Patterson-Smith

Wrong, D.H. (1979) *Power: Its Forms, Bases and Uses* New York: Harper and Row

Zaretsky, E. (1982) 'The place of the family in the origins of the welfare state' in B. Thorne and M. Yalom (eds) *Rethinking the Family: Some Feminist Questions* New York: Longman, pp. 188–224

—— (1986) 'Rethinking the welfare state: dependence, economic individualism and the family' in J. Dickinson and R. Russell (eds) *Family, Economy and State* London: Croom Helm, pp. 85–109

Parliamentary Papers

New South Wales Child Welfare Department (CWD AR)

1921–5 *NSWPP* 1926/27, 1: 660–74
1926–9 *NSWPP* 1930/32, 4:755–93
1930–1 *NSWPP* 1932 2nd Session, 1:525–72
1932–5 *NSWPP* 1935/36, 1:191–231
1936–7 *NSWPP* 1938/40, 1: 965–1035
1938–9 *NSWPP* 1938/40, 1: 1037–1106

New South Wales Parliamentary Debates (NSWPD)

1st Series Session 1880–81, vol. 5 Sydney: Government Printer
2nd Series Session 1902, vol. 7 Sydney: Government Printer
2nd Series Session 1926–27, vol. 111 Sydney: Government Printer
2nd Series Session 1935–36, vol. 145 Sydney: Government Printer

New South Wales State Children Relief Board (SCRB AR)

1882 *VPLA* 1882, 2:1103–34
1883 *VPLA* 1883, 2: 855–907
1884 *VPLA* 1884, 6: 763–801
1885 *VPLA* 1885, 2: 523–61
1886 *VPLA* 1885/86, 2: 741–806
1887 *VPLA* 1887, 2: 729–68
1888 *VPLA* 1887/88 , 4: 753–74
1889 *VPLA* 1889, 2nd Session, 2: 689–711
1890 *VPLA* 1890, 7: 197–215
1891 *VPLA* 1891/92, 7: 385–408
1892 *VPLA* 1892/93, 7: 951–73
1893 *VPLA* 1893, 2: 683–706
1894 *VPLA* 1894/95, 5: 461–82
1895 *VPLA* 1895, 4: 499–520
1896 *VPLA* 1897, 7: 909–27
1897 *VPLA* 1897, 7: 929–54
1898 *VPLA* 1898, 3: 1341–69
1899 *VPLA* 1899, 5: 425–63
1900 *VPLA* 1900, 6: 373–403
1901 *VPLA* 1901, 3: 1293–324
1902 *VPLA* 1902, 3: 1239–62
1903 *VPLA* 1903, 2: 889–922
1904 *NSWPP* 1904, 2nd Session, 2: 1–37
1905 *NSWPP* 1905, 2: 11–50
1906 *NSWPP* 1906, 1: 745–99
1907 *NSWPP* 1907, 2: 131–85
1908 *NSWPP* 1908, 2: 695–752
1909 *NSWPP* 1909, 2: 217–306
1910 *NSWPP* 1910, 2nd Session, 1: 301–83
1911 *NSWPP* 1911/12, 2: 415–94
1912 *NSWPP* 1912, 1: 761–852
1913 *NSWPP* 1914, 1: 701–66
1914 *NSWPP* 1914/15, 2: 802–83
1915 *NSWPP* 1915/16, 1: 851–933
1916 *NSWPP* 1916, 2: 915–1010
1917 *NSWPP* 1917/18, 2: 387–439
1918 *NSWPP* 1918, 3: 59–105
1919 *NSWPP* 1919, 2: 899–940
1920 *NSWPP* 1920, 2nd Session, 2: 885–945

Victorian Child Welfare Department 1924 *VPP* 1925, 2
Inquiry into the Child Welfare Department *NSWPP* 1926/7, 1: 676–682

Inspector of Public Charities *VPLA* 1879/80, 853–81

Orphan Schools at Parramatta *VPLA* 1855, 1: 1007–16

Police Report 1894 *VPLA* 1894/5, 3: 759–68

Prisons Report 1896 *VPLA* 1897, 3: 1317–81

Public Charities Commission *VPLA* 1873/4, 6

Report to the Minister of Labour and Industry on the Working of the Factories and Shops Act; etc. etc. *NSWPP* 1910, 1: 561–614

Report on the General Organisation, Control and Administration, with Special Reference to State Welfare Institutions, (Mr. J.E. McCulloch) *NSWPP* 1934/5, 5th Session, 1: 135–284

Report of the Public Service Board Respecting the State Children Relief Branch (re: boarding-out) *NSWPP* 1917/8, 2: 499–580

Royal Commission on Public Charities, 5th Report *VPLA* 1899, 5: 721–49

Royal Commission of Inquiry into the Hours and General conditions of Employment of Female and Juvenile Labour in Factories and Shops, and the Effects on Such Employees *NSWPP* 1911/2, 2: 1137–1278

Royal Commission into the Public Service of New South Wales, 5th Sectional Report *NSWPP* 1920, 2nd Session, 4: 451–502

Royal Commission (Mr Justice Harvey) into the Administration of the Child Welfare Department *NSWPP* 1927, 2: 773–789

Select Committee on Destitute Children (Progress) *VPLA* 1854, 2: 173–215

Select Committee on the Proposed Nautical School *VPLA* 1854, 2: 135–71

Select Committee on the Condition of the Working Classes of the Metropolis *VPLA* 1859/60, 4: 1263–465

Select Committee on the Unemployed *VPLA* 1866, 5: 619–80

Select Committee on the Randwick Asylum for Destitute Children *VPLA* 1879/80, 2: 893–952

Select Committee on the Whole Administration of the State Children Relief Act (Further Progress), *NSWPP* 1916, 2:1011–65 and 1917/8, 2: 44–97

New South Wales State Archives Material (StaNSW)

3/12486–93	Children's Court Depositions
4/901.1	Colonial Secretary, Special Bundle
5/5229	Colonial Secretary, Special Bundle
5/7750.2	Attorney-General and Justice Department, Special Bundle
7/7584–5	YACS Miscellaneous Correspondence
8/128–37	Notes of Inquiries and Investigations held, Public Service Board, 1920–32
8/809	Widows Pension Branch Investigation, Public Service Board, 1929
8/1740–6	*Vernon* Entrance Books, 1867–97
8/1747–51	*Sobraon* Entrance Books, 1897–1911

8/1753.2	Correspondence and documents relating to *Sobraon* commitals, 1898–1903
8/1754	YACS Miscellaneous Correspondence
8/1755–6	Mittagong Farm Home for Boys, Register of Commitals
8/1758	Industrial School for Girls, Register of Commitals
8/2140	YACS Miscellaneous Correspondence
8/2141.1	Parliamentary questions and answers, annotated, 19 October 1926—27 November 1958
9/6151–3	YACS Miscellaneous Correspondence
9/6156–7	YACS Miscellaneous Correspondence
20/12872	Department of Education Subject Files, Child Welfare Department, 1937–39

Mitchell Library Manuscripts

ML MSS	T.D. Mutch Papers
ML MSS	Frederick William Neitenstein Papers
ML MSS	Minutes of Particular Council Meetings, St Vincent de Paul Society
ML K15498	St Vincent de Paul Society, Miscellaneous Material

Index

abandonment of children, 27, 50
Aboriginal children, 8, 9, 56, 71, 84, 96, 97, 107, 108, 128, 129, 144
Aboriginal families, 132, 133; *see also* Aboriginal children
Aboriginal missions, 71, 108, 129
Aborigines Protection Acts, 8, 84, 129
Aborigines Protection Boards, 8, 9, 129
Act of 1536, 46
agency, 13–15, 20, 21, 32, 33, 39, 40, 134, 138; *see also* coercion
Allard, G. Mason, 114, 115, 120
American Progressivism, 112
Arthur, George, 56
authority, 7, 19, 52, 62, 81, 82, 100, 128, 141, 142, 143, 145; *see also* state

baby health centres, 104, 131
Balmain, William, 53
barbarian hordes, 140
Barnardo, Dr, 16, 70
barracks, critics of, 72, 73, 75, 76, 85, 99, 144, 145; *see also* boarding-out

Benevolent Society, 56, 86; Asylum, 56, 92
Berry, R.J.A., 112
Bethel, Walter, 115
Bigge, Commissioner, 58
birth rate, decline in, 86, 103, 104
boarding-out, 46–9, 51, 52, 73–8, 84–9, 136; allowance for, 47, 106, 111, 116, 131; critics of, 74; *see also* barracks
Boer War, 104
bourgeoisie, 20–9, 46, 47, 59, 74, 100, 105, 135; liberal, 75, 80–2; *see also* respectable working class
Boys' Brigade, 104
Brace, Charles, 16
Brave New World, 142
Bridewells, 47
brothels, 77
bureaucracy 19–22, 110–13, 115–18; *see also* state

Cabbage Tree Hat Mob, 63
capitalism, 13–17, 18, 23, 35; democratic, 36; evil of, 38, 105; maintenance of, 140, 145; rise of, 134, 137

Carpenter, Mary, 72
Carters' Barracks, 56, 57
casual and seasonal labour, 76, 79
child abuse, 70, 72, 77, 91, 108, 144, 145; *see also* girls *and* rape
child guidance clinics, 18, 28, 131, 132
child labour, 51, 70, 80, 89, 102, 103; casual, 90; *see also* street trading
child protection legislation, 104
child psychology, 104
child welfare: asylums, 5, 49, 62, 64, 68, 69, 72, 75–7, 85; church involvement in, 38, 45, 99, 101, 127; and the law, 126; scientific approach to, 10, 111, 112, 123; *see also* orphanages
Child Welfare Department: New South Wales, 111, 115, 117–20, 122, 124–8, 131; Victoria, 117
child-rearing, 18, 36, 126; advice, 143
child-saving 16, 17, 62, 110, 127
childhood, 5, 61–7, 123–6, 131, 143; and modern society, 2, 126; regulation of, 61–4. 97, 102, 123, 126, 138, 145; sociology and history of, 1, 2; *see also* family
children: begging, 46, 49, 95; deserted, 45, 47; destitute and neglected, 24, 48, 49, 51, 55, 56, 60, 64–6, 69, 71; invalid, 87; *see also* Aboriginal children, street children, uncontrollability
Children's Court, 84, 87, 99, 116, 120, 125, 130, 131, 136, 139; *see also* Juvenile Court
church involvement in child welfare, *see* child welfare
Church of England, 54, 55, 99
citizenship, 66, 137
City Arabs, 65
civil society, 3, 7, 9, 10, 31–4, 39, 40, 100, 101, 131, 134
Clarke, Emily, 69

class 18, 20, 23–9, 37–9, 62, 75, 81, 82, 100, 104–7, 134–40; mobility, 104, 134
coercion, 15, 39, 53, 57, 90, 98, 104, 107, 108, 136, 142; internalisation of, 141
Coghlan, Timothy, 81, 115, 116
colonial period 9, 51–6, 58–60, 63, 65, 85
community, 7, 21, 107, 123–6, 135, 142–3; activism, 36; and child welfare, 16, 64, 73, 74, 101; and egalitarianism, 137; and youth work, 10, 68, 131; treatment programs, 141
consciousness, 39; false, 29; formation of, 38; social, 142
consensus, ideological, 29, 35, 81–3, 100, 135, 143
consent, 38, and Aboriginal families, 8, 96, 129; parental, 70, 92, 129; *see also* agency, coercion
consumerism, 123, 126
contraception, 104
control, *see* social control
convicts 45, 58, 60; juvenile, 50–2, 56, 59; ex-convicts, 59
cottage homes, 72, 87, 113; *see also* de Metz, F.
counselling, 131, 139
courts, 5, 27, 70, 71, 88, 93, 98; *see also* Children's Court, Juvenile Court
crime, 63, 67; prevention, 23, 47–9, 73, 90–4; *see also* delinquency
criminal justice, 67, 69
criminal law, 112
criminal offences, 47, 59, 88
culture, 25–8, 37–40, 135, 136; *see also* working-class culture

Danne, Miss, 68
Darling, Eliza, 54, 55
Davidson, Andrew, 120
de Metz, Ferdinand, 72, 73, 75
deinstitutionalisation, 144

delinquency, 64, 90, 93, 102–4, 113, 119–26, 130–2

Department of Public Instruction (New South Wales), 114

dependency, 2, 106

Depression, 1930s, 125, 130, 131

deserted wives, 45, 47, 79, 80, 87, 106, 115, 116, 131, 140

deservedness, 116, 117

destitute children, 50, 65

deviance, 35, 57, 141

discipline, 23–5, 46, 50–2, 57–60, 63, 93–6, 126, 135, 141

disease, 67, 74, 103

disorderliness, 63, 77, 90

doctors, 18–20, 33, 112, 139

domestic service, 50, 54, 55, 57, 78, 80; and rape, 78

domesticity, 19, 29, 62, 71, 93, 106, 126–8, 134, 135; bourgeois, 19; see also family

domination, 32–5, 38–41, 140, 144, 145; see also resistance, social control

Donzelot, Jacques, 19–21, 27, 36, 62, 78, 133, 142

Drummond, David, 119, 125, 126

Dutch Benevolent Society, 51

education, 6, 18, 25, 35, 36, 45–9, 52, 62, 66, 67, 89, 113, 135; see also truancy

egalitarianism, 66, 137, 141

Elias, Norbert, 140, 142

emancipists, see free settlers

embourgeoisement, 107, 133, 138

English Fabianism, 112

equality, 62, 66, 82, 104, 135

eugenics, 104; see also Social Darwinism

evangelicals 54, 55, 57, 60, 67

family: ancient and medieval, 27; and apprenticeship, 46, 59; breakdown, 94, 95, 130, 131, 142, 144, 145; and charity, 68, 70; and Depression (1930s), 126; division of labour, 105; economics, 68, 70, 76, 89, 102, 108, 125, 136; and education, 36, 101; and fostering, 122; history, 4, 134; ideology, 29, 37, 50, 51, 126, 127, 134, 135; and industrialisation, 134; life, 22, 28, 29, 37–9, 48, 79, 105, 106, 123, 127; modern, 126; morality, 28, 39, 52, 96, 105; policing of, 19–21, 62, 78; and probation, 121; regulation of, 27, 126, 131, 139; and social regulation, 142, 143; social work, 28, 68; socialisation, 140; and the state, 3, 6–10, 18–21, 26, 29, 32, 36, 37, 41, 42, 74, 78, 82, 86, 93, 100, 106–8, 111, 117, 124–7, 130, 133, 134, 138, 141–5; violence, 36, 139; women's position in, 139; see also embourgeoisement

family principle, 3, 68, 72, 73, 87, 88, 145

family wage, 79, 105, 135; see also Harvester Judgement

Farm Cove, 50

feeble-mindedness, 87, 104, 112, 114, 115, 120, 128, 131; see also psychological testing, mental defectiveness

Female Factory at Parramatta 56

Female Orphan School, 45, 53, 55, 57, 77

Female School of Industry, 54, 55, 57, 59, 60

feminism, 16, 19, 105, 106, 135, 136

First Australasian Conference on Charity, 86

Fitzjames, see nautical school ships

'fog-horn voice' theory, 124

foster families, 79; and ill-treatment of children, 114; inspection of, 78; payment of, 47; poverty of, 75

fostering, 28, 117, 131, 132; and the barracks, 85; and benevolence, 17; decline in 1930s, 130; early history of,

45, 47; and science, 123, 131, 132

Foucault, Michel, 2, 20, 31–4

free settlers, 50, 60; compared with ex-convicts, 59

friendly and cooperative societies, 26

functionalism, 4, 13–15, 33, 35, 39

girls: apprenticeship, 46; boarded-out, 78, 94; and Children's Court, 88, 94; and Church homes, 99, 101; destitute, 55; as domestic servants, 6, 54, 59, 78; IQ testing, 120; and rape, 93; and reformatories and industrial schools, 69, 71, 73, 76, 77, 86, 93, 94, 114, 125; sexual morality of, 26, 65, 71, 77, 93, 94, 99, 121; stubbornness of, 27; workforce participation of, 103, 129, 136

gold rush, 66

Gramsci, Antonio, 33, 38

Guillaume, George, 86, 87, 106, 107

Hall, G. Stanley, 122

Harvester Judgement, 105; see also family wage

health: analogy with morality, 73, 90, 121, 123–5; and family, 127–8; and institutions, 72; and urban degeneration, 104; and war, 103

hegemony, 29, 38, 81, 100; see also Gramsci, ideology

Hill, Florence and Rosamund, 16, 72, 73

historical sociology, 4, 5, 7, 32, 33, 35

history, 1–5, 14–18, 41, 111–13, 133, 144; 'Whig' view of, 16, 17, 144

Home for Cripples, 114

homelessness, 65

homes, Church-run, 99, 101

housing: and Aboriginal families, 8; cost of, 79; working-class, 64, 65, 104

Hunter, Governor, 49, 50

ideology, 16, 24, 40, 50, 134, 136, 137; of democratic capitalism, 36; family, 29, 37, 50; Gramsci and, 38; of individualism, 21; and law, 35; Marx and, 37

incest, 93

income maintenance, 42

individualism; ideology of, 21

industrial schools, 7, 17, 25, 27, 92, 93, 114, 139; and Aboriginal children, 71; church-run, 86, 99; and Children's Court, 89, 98, 99; closure, 75; establishment of, 61, 68, 84; and family principle, 87; size of, 72, 76, 85, 125; and working-class children, 25, 69, 84; see also reformatories

Industrial Schools Act: Western Australia (1874) 71; New South Wales (1866), 88

Industrial School for Girls, 76, 93, 94, 99, 125

industrialisation, 13, 15, 19, 80, 102, 140; and family life, 134

industriousness, 26, 59, 63, 135

infant mortality, 103

institutional care, 3, 74; alternatives to, 10; and deinstitutionalisation, 144; and family principle, 72, 87, 119; numbers in, 111; and police, 69

institutionalisation of adolescence, 102

intemperance, 58, 63

intolerance of diversity, 137, 141

IQ tests, see psychological testing

Jefferis, Mrs, 16

Jevons, William Stanley, 24

Johnson, Reverend Richard, 49, 52, 53, 74

Joy, Edward, 67; *see also* Ragged
  Schools
juridification, 32
justice; and child welfare, 82,
  142–5
Juvenile Court; American, 17, 18,
  62, 88, 91, 123
juvenile delinquency, 64, 90, 102,
  104, 111, 113, 126, 130–1
juvenile justice, 2, 17–19, 21, 56,
  67, 88–91, 98, 123; American,
  133

kindergartens, 104, 105
King, Anna, 53
King, Phillip Gidley, 45, 49–53
King's Orphan School, 72; *see
  also* orphan schools

labour: market, 6, 42, 46, 57, 59,
  60, 76, 79, 80, 89, 134, 138;
  movement, 25, 29, 42, 60, 81,
  100, 104–6, 141; shortage, 54,
  59; unskilled, 59, 68, 100, 102,
  134
labourism, 100
Lady Visitors, 78; *see also*
  boarding-out
Lasch, Christopher, 18–21, 36,
  66, 133, 137, 139, 142, 143,
  145
law, 5, 7; and ideology, 35; and
  child welfare, 126; and order,
  91
leisure, 23, 29; *see also* youth
  leisure
Lenin, Vladimir, 41
liberal bourgeoisie, 25, 29, 74, 75,
  80–2
living wage, 89, 100, 105; *see also*
  family wage
Locke, John, 52, 67

Mackellar, Charles, 16, 86, 87, 90,
  106, 107, 111, 113, 114; and
  Aborigines, 97; and birth rate,
  103; and feeble-mindedness,
  104, 112, 119, 120; and girls,
  99, 101

Magill Reformatory and Industrial
  School, Adelaide, 72, 85
maintenance of children, 27, 70,
  87
Male Orphan School, *see also*
  orphan asylums
marriage, 50, 123; and Aboriginal
  families, 8, 96; and desertion,
  79; ideal of, 82; *see also* family
Marsden, Samuel, 49, 52, 53, 74
Marx, Karl, 4, 37, 38, 41
marxism, 14, 16, 33, 38
Maxted, Sydney, 96, 120
medicine, 19, 139, 140
mental defectiveness, 86, 112,
  119, 120; *see also* feeble-
  mindedness
Mettray Agricultural Colony, 2,
  72, 73, 119
middle class, 61; aspirations, 41;
  and charity, 55, 62; criticism
  by working class, 24, 39;
  ideology, 6, 24–6, 28, 38, 39,
  83, 103, 105, 107, 135, 136;
  morality, 54; professional, 41,
  16, 18, 20, 83, 104, 137, 145;
  and sobriety, 108; and social
  control, 7, 16, 18, 21, 23, 26,
  62, 80, 138; and the state, 80,
  81
missions: Aboriginal, 71, 108,
  129; Church-run, 129
Mittagong Farm Homes, 86, 93,
  95, 97, 114
modernisation, 2, 32, 84, 85
modernity, 2, 124; critique of, 123
Moore River Settlement, 129; *see
  also* Aboriginal families,
  Aboriginal missions
moral destitution, 28, 48, 54, 57,
  63–6, 73, 77, 87, 90, 96, 97
moral entrepreneurs, 21, 62, 81
moral reform, 19, 20, 25, 26, 39,
  46, 49, 51, 56, 60, 62, 64, 77,
  78, 83, 88, 95, 96, 99, 116,
  126, 132, 135, 138, 141
mothers: Aboriginal, 97; affection
  for children, 70; children
  boarded-out to, 80, 106, 111,

116, 131; convict, 50, 56;
destitute, 95; domestic service,
50, 80; drunken, 94, 116;
health, 103; housing, 65;
responsibility for morality, 121;
single working, 79; and social
workers, 28, 139; unable to
raise children, 37, 71, 92, 93
motherhood, 62, 106, 135
Mutch, Edward, 115–18

National Society for the
Prevention of Cruelty of
Children (UK), 61, 108
Native Administration Act, 129
Native Institution for Aboriginal
Children, 56
nautical school ships; *Fitzjames*,
69; *Proserpine*, 69; *Sir Harry
Smith*, 69; *Sobraon*, 86, 92–5,
87; *Vernon*, 69–71, 76, 79, 85,
86, 97
neglected children, *see* children
neighbourhood justice, 143
neighbours, 97, 143; and child
minding, 65, 95, 135, 136;
cooperation with child welfare,
37, 108; and morality, 98, 107
Neitenstein, Frederick, 71, 86,
88–90
1984, 142
nuclear family, 106, 134

Ormond House, 114
orphan asylums and schools,
orphanages, 5, 14, 17, 45–7,
49, 50–60, 67–70, 72, 74–6,
85; church-run, 99

Parkes, Henry, 16, 25, 26, 59,
63–7, 82, 85, 89, 90
parliamentary reform, 100
Paterson, Elizabeth, 52, 53
pauperisation of women, *see*
women
paupers, 16, 80
Phoenix phenomenon, 31
Platt, Anthony, 16–18, 61, 62

Point Puer, 56; *see also*
reformatories
police, 27, 91, 100, 122, 126, 131;
and children, 5, 67, 70, 90, 92,
95, 108; and Children's Court,
98
Police Citizens Boys Clubs, 121,
131
popular press, 60, 63, 67
population growth, 54, 67, 76, 79,
80, 103, 106
Port Jackson, 51
poverty, 15, 47–50, 58, 75, 81,
96, 97, 100, 125, 134, 135,
141, 142; culture of, 57; and
child welfare, 7, 23, 74, 77,
107, 125, 138; and family
disruption, 130; parental, 65,
71; solutions for, 64
power, 7, 9, 33–7, 39–41, 143,
145; agent of, 20; disciplinary,
32
private justice, 35
probation, 84, 87–9, 96–9, 101,
102, 120–3, 125, 136
professional control, 33, 36, 41,
84, 139, 143
professional experts, 16, 18, 20,
29, 104, 137, 145
professionalisation, 118, 124
professions, 19; helping, 21, 33,
36, 139
progress, 15–18
Proserpine, see nautical school
ships
prostitution, 47, 65, 77, 87, 95,
97
psychiatry, 33, 104, 112, 131
psychological testing, 104, 120,
123
psychologists, 18, 120
Public Charities Royal
Commission, 72
Public Service Board of NSW,
113, 115

Queen's Asylum, 72, 75

radical working men, 24

Ragged Schools, 67, 68
Randwick Destitute Children's
    Asylum, 68, 69, 72, 75, 76, 85
rationalisation, 48, 85; of child
    welfare, 9, 84, 91, 106, 111,
    128; of domestic life, 29; of
    social control, 141
Rauhe Haus, 73, 119
Raymond Terrace Home, 114
reformatories, 45, 49, 76, 77, 89,
    98, 99; closure, 75;
    establishment, 16, 47, 56, 61,
    67, 69, 84, 85; and family
    principle, 87; and social
    control, 22, 23; and working
    class, 27; *see also* girls,
    industrial schools
reformers; child welfare, 16, 73,
    87–9, 106–8, 119; educational,
    19, 47, 48; liberal, 100;
    middle-class, 7, 26, 62, 83,
    105; moral, 62; objectives of,
    22, 62; social, 87, 112
reforms, 18, 97, 128; of Juvenile
    Court, 62; urban, 81; welfare,
    8, 9, 15–17, 22, 23, 36, 82, 86,
    101, 106, 107
regulation, *see* social control
Renwick, Arthur, 16, 76, 77, 86,
    87
resistance, 33, 34, 36, 38, 41, 138
respectable working class, 7, 23–5,
    28, 29, 38, 53, 66, 70, 73–5,
    78, 80–2, 104–8, 134–7, 141
Royal Commission into the Public
    Service (NSW, 1920), 115

St Vincent de Paul Society, 99,
    101
Scouts, 104, 121, 131
Select Committee on the
    Unemployed (NSW, 1860), 68
Select Committee on
    Transportation (1812), 50
self-discipline, 135, 141
sexual delinquency, *see* girls
Shaftesbury Reformatory for Girls,
    85
Simmel, Georg, 39

single mothers, 111; working, 79
slums, 95, 104
Sobraon, see nautical school ships
sobriety, 23; *see also* respectable
    working class
social control, 17–23, 26–42,
    135–8, 140–5
Social Darwinism, 104, 112
social pathologists, 18, 19, 26,
    138, 139; *see also* moral
    entrepreneurs
social policy, 21, 59, 61, 79, 82;
    and science, 113
social regulation, *see* social control
social science, 4, 14, 16, 19, 111,
    119
social workers, 18–21, 28, 33, 36,
    139–41
Society for the Relief of Destitute
    Children, 64; *see also*
    Randwick Destitute Children's
    Asylum
South Australian Education
    Department, 113
South Australian State Children's
    Department, 128
Spence, Catherine, 16, 69, 73, 110
state: bureaucracy 91, 110–18,
    123–31, 133–8, 140–3, 145; as
    father, 106; intervention 5, 6,
    9, 16, 26, 32, 34–7, 40, 41, 68,
    78, 81, 82, 90, 91, 93, 100,
    101, 105–9, 111, 117, 130,
    133, 134, 137, 141–5; *see also*
    family
State Children Relief Board (New
    South Wales), 61, 70, 75,
    77–80, 86, 88, 90, 94–9, 104,
    111–17, 120, 121
State Children's Council (South
    Australia), 75
statism, 101, 106
street children, 79, 90; *see also*
    children
street trading, 85, 91; *see also*
    child labour
structural functionalism, *see*
    functionalism
suburban lifestyle, 105

Surf Life Saving Clubs, 121

teachers, 18, 20, 33, 108, 122
temperance, 19, 59, 63, 64
trade unions, 26
transportation, 60; of children and youth, 48, 49, 56
truancy, 89, 90, 91, 101, 122; inspectors, 25, 113
tutelary complex, *see* Foucault, M.

uncontrollability, 91, 93, 130; girls, 93, 94
unemployment, 64, 66, 79, 80, 125, 126, 130, 131
urban degeneration, 104
urbanisation, 13, 80, 140

vagabondage, 46, 47
Vernon, see nautical school ships
vice, 53, 64, 66, 67, 73, 77, 79, 87, 93, 94; parental, 52, 58, 80, 97, 121
violence, 141, 142; in child welfare institutions, 111, 118, 132; family, 36, 139
Vives, Johannes, 47, 52
vocational guidance, 120, 131

welfare, *see* child welfare, reform, reformers
welfare state, 9, 16, 17, 21, 32–5, 142
Whig view of history, 16, 17, 144
Wichern, Johann, 73–5
widows: income support for, 29, 87, 106, 115–17, 131, 140
Widows' Pensions Act, 115–17

wife desertion, 51
women, 139; and charity, 16, 55; convict, 56; and domestic service, 54, 80; and employment, 138; and labour market, 55, 56, 76, 105; and morality, 71, 77, 95, 97; and poverty, 50, 51, 76, 80, 106, 136, 138; state financial support for, 49, 106, 116, 117, 138
work, *see* labour
work ethic, 21, 28, 47, 82, 93, 135
workforce participation of children and youth, 80, 102, 103, 129, 130
working conditions, 42, 105
working-class, 63, 65, 81–4, 100, 103–8, 133–8; aspirations, 41, 81, 135, 140; militancy, 24; morals, 23; resistance to social reform, 25, 62, 82, 90, 105; sobriety, 7, 66, 108, 136; *see also* respectable working class
working-class culture, 7, 9, 21–8, 37–9, 42, 63, 66, 68, 82, 83, 108, 136, 137
working-class families, 6, 19, 20–4, 27, 28, 35, 41, 62, 73–5, 84, 85, 89, 90, 97, 104, 105–8, 131–8

YMCA/YWCA, 104, 121, 131
youth, 58, 63–5, 93, 102–8, 111, 121–31, 139; colonial, 58; leisure, 111, 125, 126, 129–31, 139; vagrant, 65, 68